Media Composer® Fundamentals I

Avid Technology, Inc.

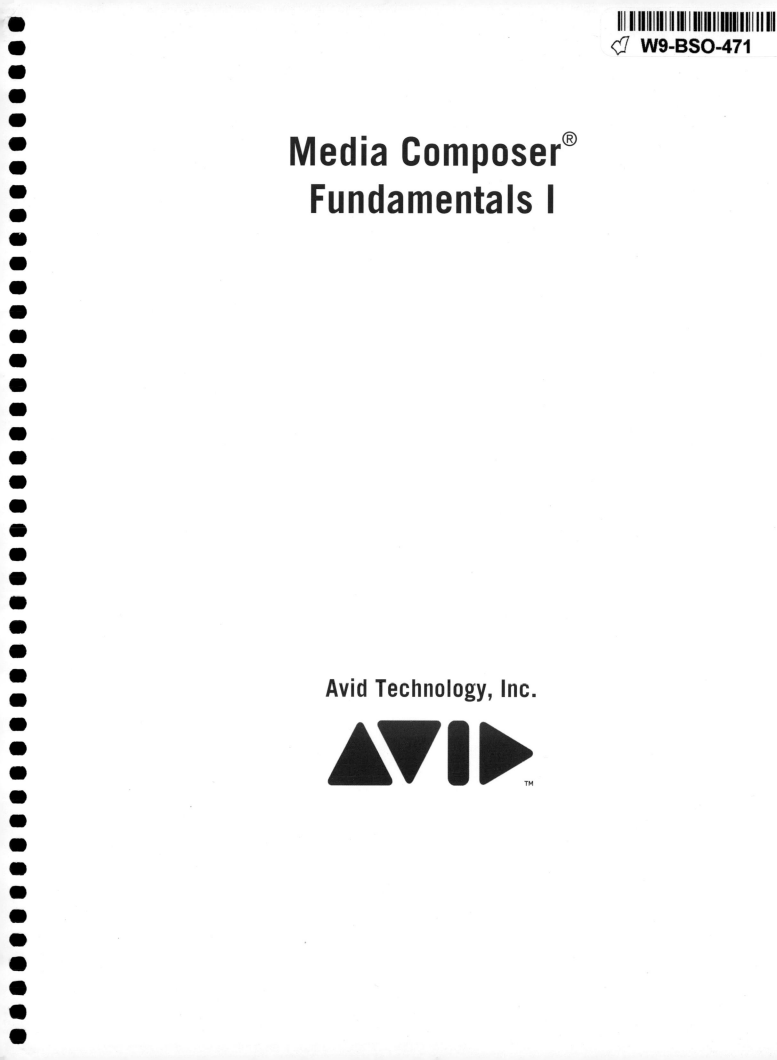

ISBN eBook: 978-1-943446-23-0

ISBN: 978-1-943446-22-3

eBook Part Number: 9511-65980-00

Part Number: 9320-70051-00 - July 2016

This book includes material that was developed in part by the Avid Technical Publications department and the Avid Training department.

Acknowledgments

Avid Education would like to recognize the following contributors for the development of this book:

Bryan Castle, Jr., Trevor Boden, Christine Tilden, Frank Cook, and Karleen McAllester.

We would also like to recognize the immeasurable contributions of the worldwide community of Avid Certified Instructors for their ongoing suggestions and comments, based on their experience in the classroom and their professional expertise, which have resulted in the continued improvement of Avid's curriculum.

About the Media

Avid Education would like to thank our partners for generously proving the media, music and sound effects used in this course.

EditStock

In proud partnership with Avid, EditStock.com provided much of the footage in this course. Schools have the option to upgrade their footage packages, gaining the following features:

- Un-watermarked footage.

- Usage rights for student demo reels.

- Additional footage for every project.

- Lined scripts and music.

- Higher resolutions such as ProRes and RED.

EditStock, footage worth Editing.

PremiumBeat.com

PremiumBeat.com is a curated royalty-free music website that provides high quality tracks and sound effects for use in new and traditional media projects. Our library is sourced from the world's leading producers with exclusive, pre-cleared music. This allows for a smooth licensing experience on popular video sharing sites like YouTube and Vimeo.

With thousands of handpicked tracks in more than 30 styles, PremiumBeat music is ideal for online videos, mobile apps, television, radio, feature films and other professional applications. Be sure to also check out the PremiumBeat blog for the latest news and tutorials on production and post-production.

Table of Contents

Introduction

Welcome to Media Composer Fundamentals I and the Avid Learning Series. Whether you are interested in self-study or would like to pursue formal certification through an Avid Learning Partner, this book provides the first step toward developing your core skills and introduces you to the power of Media Composer software. In addition, Media Composer Fundamentals I is the first course of study for those pursuing Media Composer User certification.

The material in this book covers the basic principles you need to complete a Media Composer project, from initial setup to final mixdown. Media Composer Fundamentals I will teach you what you need to know to be successful with Media Composer.

Using This Book

This book has been designed to familiarize you with the practices and processes you will use to complete a Media Composer project. Lessons and exercises focuses on a phase of the editing process, starting with organizing media, assembling a sequence, refining a sequence, creating titles and effects, and finally outputting your program so others can view it.

Using the Course Material

The MC101 course media can be downloaded from EditStock.com (see "Downloading Media" below). Once the media is downloaded, you will then need to follow the "Installation Instructions" to place the media files in the correct locations on your system.

Downloading Media

The link below will give you instructions on how to create an Editstock.com/Avid account, enter an access code, and ultimately download the media.

Go to http://editstock.com/avidsupport for instructions.

When asked for an access code from EditStock.com:

- If you have purchased the MC101 course through Avid Learning Partner or are using the book in the classroom, you will be given an access code from your instructor.

- If you purchased the MC101 course from the Avid website, and not affiliated with any school, use the access code found in your my.Avid.com account in your order history, to download the media.

Installation Instructions

You will download a zip file. Unzip the file and you should see a folder called Media Composer Fundamentals I Course Materials. There are three sub folders:

- Avid MediaFiles

- Rock Climber QTs

- Running the Sahara

These need to be installed on your system. Please follow the instructions (below) exactly or you may not have access to all the project files and media associated with this course.

1. Make sure Media Composer software is installed and that you have opened the application at least once.

   Opening the application creates important folders that you will use during this installation.

2. Copy the "Running the Sahara" project folder to the following location:

   - **Windows:** Library\Public Documents\Shared Avid Projects\

   - **Mac:** Users\Shared\AvidMediaComposer\Shared Avid Projects\.

3. Navigate to the root (top) level of the hard drive where you want to store the media files. This may be your internal drive, in which case navigate to **C:** (Windows) or **MACINTOSH HD** (Mac). If you have a locally attached external hard drive you want to use a separate partition, navigate to the root level of the external hard drive or that partition. There are two possibilities:

    - At the top level of your hard drive if there is no existing Avid MediaFiles folder: Drag the entire **AVID MEDIAFILES** folder from the download to the top level of your hard drive.

    - If an Avid MediaFiles folder does exist on the top level of your hard drive: Double-click it to reveal the MXF folder and drag the **101** folder from the download (Avid MediaFiles/MXF/101) into the **MXF** folder on your hard drive.

4. Drag the "Rock Climber QTs" folder to the top level of your hard drive.

    This could actually be placed anywhere but we have chosen this location for simplicity.

 Do not rename or move the Avid MediaFiles folder located on the media drive. Media Composer uses the folder names to locate the media files.

Prerequisites

This course is designed for those who are new to professional video editing as well as experienced professional editors who are unfamiliar with Media Composer software. Although this book is not aimed at teaching the theory behind film and television editing, the content of this course does provide some background on the craft of editing, making it appropriate for students or people new to the art. At the same time, its primary focus is on how Media Composer works, making it a perfect introduction to the software for skilled professionals.

System Requirements

This book assumes that you have a system configuration suitable to run Media Composer software. To verify the most recent system requirements, visit www.avid.com/media-composer/specifications.

Becoming Avid Certified

Avid certification is a tangible, industry-recognized credential that can help you advance your career and provide measurable benefits to your employer. When you're Avid certified, you not only help to accelerate and validate your professional development, but you can also improve your productivity and project success. Avid offers programs supporting certification in dedicated focus areas including Media Composer, Sibelius, Pro Tools, Worksurface Operation, and Live Sound. To become certified in Media Composer, you must enroll in a program at an Avid Learning Partner, where you can complete additional Media Composer coursework if needed and take your certification exam. To locate an Avid Learning Partner, visit www.avid.com/education.

Media Composer Certification

Avid offers two levels of Media Composer certification:

- Avid Media Composer User Certification

- Avid Media Composer Professional Certification

User Certification

The Avid Media Composer Certified User Exam is the first of two certification exams that allow you to become Avid certified. The two combined certifications offer an established and recognized goal for both academic users and industry professionals. The Avid Media Composer User Certification requires that you display a firm grasp of the core skills, workflows, and concepts of non-linear editing on the Media Composer system.

Courses/books associated with User certification include the following:

- **Media Composer Fundamentals I (MC101)**

- **Media Composer Fundamentals II (MC110)**

These User courses can be complemented with MC239 Color Grading with Media Composer and Symphony.

Professional Certification

The Avid Media Composer Professional Certification prepares editors to competently operate a Media Composer system in a professional production environment. Professional certification requires a more advanced understanding of Media Composer, including advanced tools and workflows involved in creating professional programs.

Courses/books associated with Professional certification include the following:

- **Media Composer Professional Editing I (MC201)**
- **Media Composer Professional Editing II (MC210)**

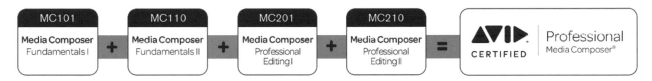

These Professional courses can be complemented with MC239 Color Grading with Media Composer and Symphony.

For more information about Avid's certification programs, please visit www.avid.com/en/education/certification.

Avid Certified. Real skills, proven.

Avid Certification helps professionals attain and demonstrate the skills and credentials they need to increase their value, competency, and efficiency in the highly competitive media industry.

Avid certification programs cover the broad range of Avid products, as well as other professional roles, including Avid Certified Instructor, Avid Certified Support Representative, and Avid Certified Administrator.

If you want to learn more about Avid training, please check out our official online resource by going to www.avid.com/education. There you will find information about our training partners, specifics on the various certification options available, and detailed course descriptions for each course offered through our programs.

Introduction to Media Composer

"The journey of a thousand miles begins with a single step."

—Chinese proverb

How far you want to go in learning the craft of editing for TV or film or in learning to use Media Composer is up to you.

Media: Running the Sahara

Duration: 60 minutes

GOALS

- Launch Media Composer
- Identify the primary windows of Media Composer and understand their basic functions
- Recognize project assets in the bins
- Organize the clips into bins
- Create User Profiles
- Use workspaces
- Map user-selectable buttons
- Save the project

Launching Media Composer

Launching Media Composer is like launching any other application on your computer. The Media Composer icon appears in Figure 1.1. Go ahead and launch it now if you know how. If you have never launched an application before, then read on.

Figure 1.1 The Media Composer application icon looks identical on Windows and Mac OS.

To launch Media Composer in Windows:

- Double-click the **MEDIA COMPOSER** icon on the desktop. Or, select **START > ALL PROGRAMS > AVID > AVID MEDIA COMPOSER**.

To launch Media Composer in Mac OS X:

- Click the **MEDIA COMPOSER** icon in the Dock to launch the application. Or, double-click the **MEDIA COMPOSER** icon found in **APPLICATIONS > AVID > AVID MEDIA COMPOSER**.

   Once launched, the Media Composer splash screen appears and your computer begins to load the application. (See Figure 1.2.)

Figure 1.2 The Media Composer splash screen.

 The splash screen does more than just build your excitement. It shows you the specific version of Media Composer you are running and indicates the various components being loaded. If you ever encounter a problem, this information will be helpful to the Avid Customer Support representative helping you.

Understanding the Select Project Window

Once Media Composer loads, you will see the Select Project dialog box, shown in Figure 1.3.

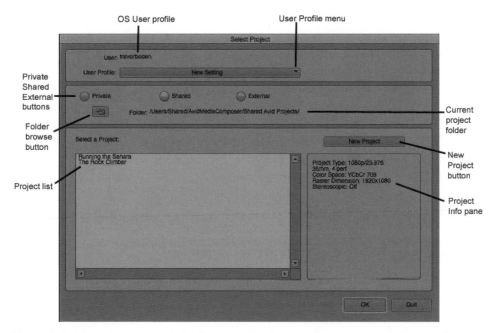

Figure 1.3 The Select Project dialog box is used to locate and open existing projects and to create new ones.

Take a moment to identify each of the following features using the callouts in Figure 1.3:

- User

  - **OS user profile**: The name you used to log in to the computer appears here.

  - **User Profile menu**: Use the menu options to select, import, or create a Media Composer User Profile. In Media Composer, you use User Profiles to customize the application.

- Project Location

  - **Current project folder**: Where Media Composer is currently looking for projects.

  - **Private/Shared/External buttons**: Click to select the location of your project.

  - **Folder browse button**: Use this button to point Media Composer to any location you have placed your project.

- Projects

  - **Project list**: These are the projects in the Current Project Folder directory.

  - **Project Info Pane**: Displays the format info for the selected project.

  - **New Project button:**Click this button to generate a new project.

 Exercise Break: Exercise 1.1
Pause here to practice what you've learned.

Learning the Interface

Before you can do anything else, you need to learn your way around. Let's start with the nickel tour, as they say. As we do, pay special attention to the names of windows and buttons. The more quickly you recognize them, the less confusing things will seem and the faster you will get up and running.

The Media Composer Interface

When the project opens, you will see the primary windows of the Media Composer interface. These are as follows (see Figure 1.4):

- The Composer window

- The Timeline

- The Project window

- The Bin window

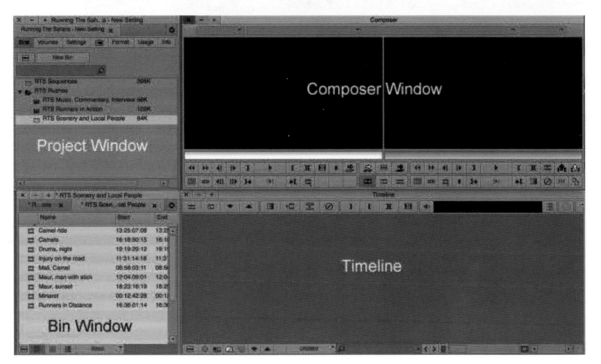

Figure 1.4 The Media Composer interface.

Let's begin with an overview, starting with the big monitors in the upper-right.

The Composer Window

If you have worked in any professional non-linear editing application (NLE), this two-up monitor display is instantly familiar. By default, the Composer window displays two monitors (windows). The left one, called the Source monitor, is used to play source media that you will edit into the program sequence. The right one, the Record monitor, displays the sequence material in the Timeline.

The Composer window, shown in Figure 1.5, is actually a multifunction media viewer. During the edit process, the Composer window will change to show you different images—two, three, four, or six at a time—depending on what you need to see while performing a particular editing operation (e.g. trimming or customizing visual). In fact, during multi-camera editing, you can see up to nine images on one side! You will learn about these specialized displays as you go through this course.

Figure 1.5 The Composer window.

Across the top of the Composer window are informational displays that show you the name and timecode of your clips and sequences. (Each info window actually contains a menu with additional info or options. More on this later.) All buttons and tools are across the bottom, arranged in two rows. You will notice redundant buttons on both sides, because each set corresponds to its respective monitor—i.e., the Play button under the Source monitor plays the source clip, while the same button under the Record monitor will play the sequence (a sequence is what we call what you are creating).

The Timeline

The Timeline, shown in Figure 1.6, displays a graphical representation of your program sequence, organized into tracks. In Figure 1.6, a fairly basic sequence is displayed in the Timeline. Initially, your Timeline is empty because no sequence is loaded.

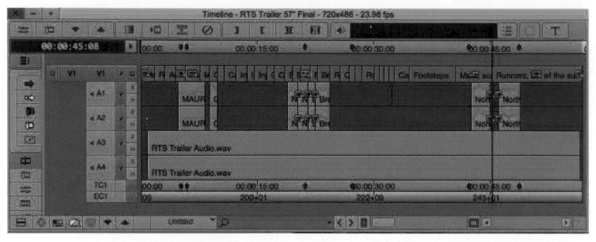

Figure 1.6 This Timeline displays a fairly basic sequence.

 A sequence is a series of video and audio segments that comprise your film or your program. It is the thing you're creating. The Timeline is the window you build it in.

In the Timeline, the sequence is played from left to right. The blue position indicator marks the current frame of video and audio being shown in the Record monitor. (Many editors refer to the blue position indicator as the "playhead.") The sequence in Figure 1.6 contains two video tracks and six audio tracks. You can have up to 64 tracks of audio and 24 tracks of video in a Media Composer sequence.

The Track Panel, shown in Figure 1.7, displays a track button for each track of source material and every sequence track. You will use the track buttons extensively while editing in Media Composer. There are two columns of "Track Selectors." The left column (in the image V1, A1, and A2) refers to the tracks which are part of what is loaded in the Source monitor. The right column (in the image V2, V1, A1 through A7) refers to the tracks available in your sequence. Since the sequence is displayed in the Record monitor, we call these the "Record Track Buttons."

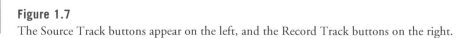

Figure 1.7
The Source Track buttons appear on the left, and the Record Track buttons on the right.

The Record Track buttons enable you to select tracks for locking, resizing, deleting, and editing. Source Track buttons are used for selecting which tracks of source material you want to use when making an edit.

If you click the red button marked with an × in the upper-right (Windows) or upper-left (Mac) corner of the Timeline, you will close the Timeline window. Closing the Timeline window does not close the sequence or cause you to lose work. Just reopen the Timeline, and you will see your sequence again, intact. To reopen the Timeline window, do one of the following:

- Choose Tools > Timeline.

- Choose Windows > Workspaces > Source/Record Editing.

The Project Window

The Project window is the central hub of Media Composer. The buttons across the top change what is visible in the display pane and gives you access to the project bins, format, settings, effects, and more. (See Figure 1.8.)

Figure 1.8 The Project window is the central hub of your project.

You will learn about each of these panes as you need them. You will spend most of your time using the Bins pane, which is discussed in more detail later in this lesson. One important thing to learn right now is this: If you close the Project window, you will close the project. Actually, that's important enough for a note.

ℹ️   **If you close the Project window, you will exit the project.**

Thankfully, Media Composer will save all your work when you exit the project, but you want to be careful to not do it by accident. It breaks your creative flow and makes you look like a newbie in front of the producer. ("Yeah, I meant to do that...")

The Bin Window

Named after the physical container used to hang celluloid film in an editing room, a Media Composer bin is a container file that holds the assets in your project. No assets can be placed simply within the Project window. All project assets are stored in a bin, including audio and video master clips, subclips, sequences, titles, effects, graphics...everything!

Every project is created with one default bin, named after the project. In most projects, you will use multiple bins to organize your project assets. Plus, you can put bins into folders to further organize the project.

Working with Bins

Since everything in the project must go into a bin, you will be using bins almost constantly as you edit. Let's go through some of the basic features and controls to get you comfortable with them.

Changing Bin Layouts

The bin is far more than just a container. It also functions as a database, a light table, and a log sheet. There is a special layout that goes with each of these functions, and three quick-access buttons at the bottom of the bin to change between these layouts, as shown in Figure 1.10.

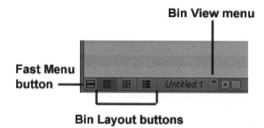

Figure 1.10 The Bin Layout buttons and Bin View menu.

Text View

Text view displays the contents of the bin in a list. Think of it as the "database" mode. This is the default view. In Text view, you can choose to display additional columns for tracking metadata information associated with each item. The advantages of Text view is that it shows you a lot of information in a small amount of space, with quick access to all the info associated with your project assets.

Media Composer automatically tracks basic statistical info about clips and sequences, like the duration, timecode, source, etc. Camera-written metadata is preserved and tracked in columns you can display. Plus, you can add any custom columns and metadata you need to your assets here.

 Get in-depth training on creating custom fields and managing metadata in larger projects in the course, MC110: Media Composer Fundamentals II.

Frame View

Frame view shows you a representative frame for each item in the bin, as shown in Figure 1.11. It's a bit like looking at your shots on a virtual light table. Because most editors are visually oriented, this can be a nice way to work. What we see below is a bit of a mess. In just a moment, we will show you how to quickly clean things up.

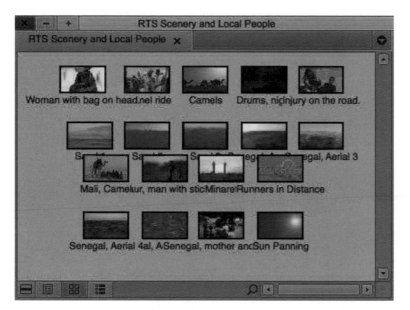

Figure 1.11 Frame view is like a light table, letting you see an image for each asset rather than just a name. (Obviously, this needs to be cleaned up a bit!)

Frame view enables you to easily rearrange your shots just by clicking and dragging them to a new location. Do this to group similar shots together, plan out the edit as a virtual storyboard, etc. You are free to arrange them however you like. To make working in Frame view easier, there are several functions to be aware of.

Changing Frame Size

You can make the frames smaller or larger using menu commands or keyboard shortcuts. (My recommendation, of course, is to use the keyboard shortcuts.)

To make the frames bigger, select the bin, then:

- Choose **EDIT > ENLARGE FRAME**.

- Press Ctrl+L (Windows) or Command+L (Mac).

To make the frames smaller:

- Choose **EDIT > REDUCE FRAME**.

- Press Ctrl+K (Windows) or Command+K (Mac).

 These are universal keyboard shortcuts in Avid. Depending on which window is active, they also affect the size of the tracks in the Timeline or the zoom level in the Composer window. To remember them, think "L for larger" and "K for ka-smaller" (or just remember that the K key is next to the L key).

Tidying Up the Frame View Display

After resizing headframes, you will most likely want to tidy up the arrangement. Often, the clips end up outside the visible section of the bin.

To tidy up the Frame view of your bin:

- CHOOSE BIN > FILL WINDOW to arrange the clips to a grid pattern as wide as your current window. If they don't all fit, you can scroll vertically to see the others, either using the scroll wheel on your mouse or the scroll bar on the right side of the window.

- CHOOSE BIN > FILL SORTED, this is the same as choosing Fill Window, except clips are arranged in the order they are found in Text view.

- CHOOSE BIN > ALIGN TO GRID if you have been rearranging the clips in the bin yourself, such as grouping together shots that are visually similar. You can clean them up by having those shots aligned to the same invisible grid, without reordering or significantly changing location. (See Figure 1.12.)

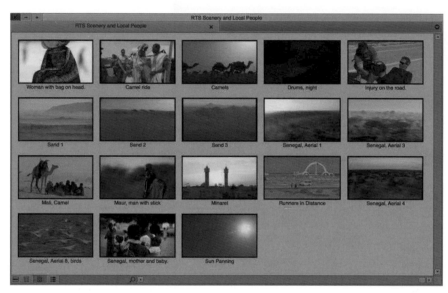

Figure 1.12 The same bin as in Figure 1.11 with larger headframes, aligned to grid.

Changing the Representative Frame

By default, the first frame of a clip or sequence is displayed when in Frame view. In a television environment, this first frame may be color bars or video black. On a feature film, it is often the slate. In these cases, you may want to change the first frame to be more representative of the material within the clip.

To change the representative frame:

1. Select the **CLIP** or **SEQUENCE** by clicking one time on the clip frame.

2. Do any of the following:

   - Step through the clip using the Step Forward and Backward keys on the keyboard. These are by default on the 1, 2, 3, and 4 keys. As a shortcut, press the 1 key to move 10 frames back, the 2 key to move 10 frames forward, the 3 key to move one frame back, or the 4 key to move one frame forward.

   - Play through the clip by pressing the space bar or the 5 (play) key. Press 5 again or the space bar to stop.

   - Press the Home (first frame) key on the keyboard to see the first frame in the clip or sequence or press the End (last frame) key to see the last frame.

   - Use the arrow keys to move from frame to frame.

3. Optionally, press **CTRL+S** (Windows) or **COMMAND+S** (Mac) to save the bin.

Script View

Script view is like a combination of Text view and Frame view with an added comments field. (See Figure 1.13.) You can type anything you like in the Comments field, but it is typically used for logging notes and keywords.

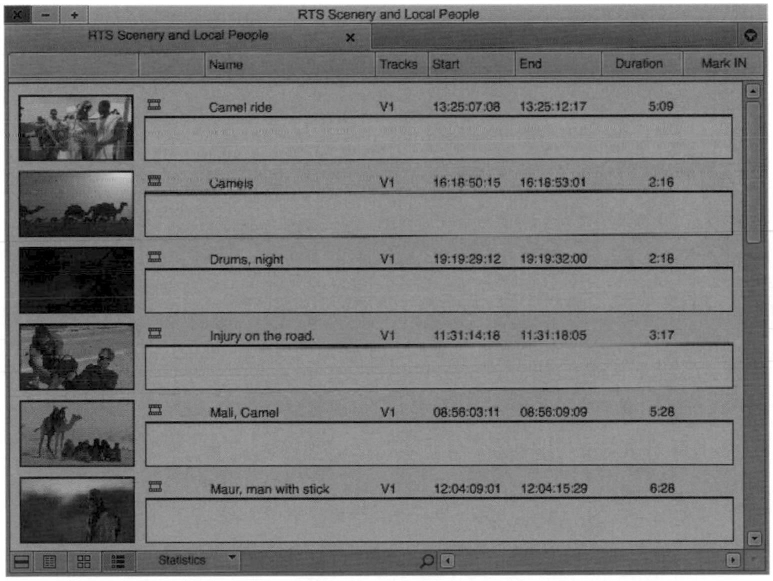

Figure 1.13   Script view combines the visual thumbnail of Frame view and the statistical info of Text view with a handy Comments window.

The comments you create here automatically appear in Text view, in the Comments column. The arrangement of columns in the last "Bin view" you chose to display prior to switching to Script view determines the columns shown. As in Frame view, you can use the same methods to change the size of the frame.

Creating a New User Profile and Changing User Profiles

The user settings covered in this section are stored as part of your Avid user profile. The first step to customizing your user settings is to create a user profile. The default user is named after your system login, but you can choose another existing user profile or create a new one.

In the Settings tab of the Project window the User Profile Selection menu displays the active user profile. If you click on this, a menu appears which allows you to create a new profile, as shown in Figure 1.14.

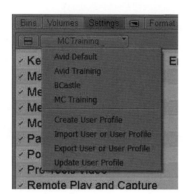

Figure 1.14 The User Profile menu in the Settings tab.

To create a new user setting:

1. Click the **SETTINGS** button in the Project window to display the Settings pane.

2. Click the **USER PROFILE** pop-up menu and choose **CREATE USER PROFILE**.

3. Type a name for the new profile in the **CREATE USER PROFILE** dialog box and click **OK**.

    The new user profile appears in the User Profile pop-up menu.

4. Modify the **USER** settings as you like.

5. To save your changes, activate the **PROJECT** window; then press **CTRL+S** (Windows) or **COMMAND+S** (Mac).

    Saving with the Project window active will save all open bins **and** update the settings of the current user profile.

  To save their work, many Avid editors have developed a good habit of using a combination of shortcuts: Ctrl+9 (Windows) or Command+9 (Mac) to activate the Project window, followed by Ctrl+S (Windows) or Command+S (Mac) to save. This way, any work—and any settings changes—are always saved.

To change the active profile:

1. Click the **SETTINGS** button in the Project window to display the Settings pane.

2. Click the **USER PROFILE** pop-up menu and choose the desired **USER PROFILE**.

  Exercise Break: Exercise 1.2
Pause here to practice what you've learned.

Personalizing the Application

Great, so you have a shiny new user, now what?

Media Composer lets you change many aspects of its appearance and functionality. This includes the arrangement of windows and tools, the placement of many of the visible buttons, the keyboard shortcuts associated with those functions, and more. All of these preferences are saved as part of your User profile, and all these controls are conveniently located all in one place – the Settings tab of the Project Window.

Using Workspaces

The first and perhaps the most obvious way to start customizing Media Composer is simply to rearrange the windows. Depending on your preferences, screen size, and even the task at hand, you may prefer to have the windows sized and placed differently than the system defaults.

Media Composer includes a number of predesigned work environments, called workspaces, which are designed to provide a window arrangement and useful set of tools for different stages of the editing process. These preconfigured workspaces are found under the Windows menu, as shown in Figure 1.15.

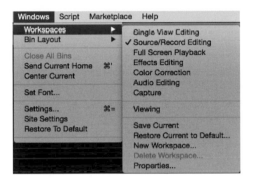

Figure 1.15 Choose a workspace from the menu to activate it.

To activate a workspace:

■ Choose **WINDOWS > WORKSPACES > DESIRED WORKSPACE**.

Customizing a Workspace

Each workspace can be customized to your own, personal liking. The changes that are saved include the size and placement of the Project, Composer, and Timeline windows, as well as the presence and location of any tools. The bins are not included in the workspace.

To customize a workspace:

1. Choose the **WORKSPACE** you want to customize from the **WORKSPACE** menu.

2. Arrange, add, and remove **WINDOWS** on the desktop.

3. Choose **WINDOWS > WORKSPACES > SAVE CURRENT**.

   Any time you return to this workspace this arrangement appears.

To reset a workspace:

■ Choose **TOOLS > RESTORE CURRENT TO DEFAULT**.

Combining Windows into Tabs

Media Composer uses tabbed windows to save space. You can combine bins with bins, and tools with tools. A workspace will even save tools in your tabbed configuration, if you like. Media Composer automatically remembers the last location of a bin. For example, Figure 1.16 shows a window that contains several bins. This is especially convenient when working with a single computer monitor.

		Name	Tracks	Start	End	Duration	Mark IN	Mark OUT
		Camel ride	V1	13:25:07:08	13:25:12:17	5:09		
		Camels	V1	16:18:50:15	16:18:53:01	2:16		
		Drums, night	V1	19:19:29:12	19:19:32:00	2:18		
		Injury on the road.	V1	11:31:14:18	11:31:18:05	3:17		
		Mali, Camel	V1	08:56:03:11	08:56:09:09	5:28		
		Maur, man with stick	V1	12:04:09:01	12:04:15:29	6:28		
		Minaret	V1	00:12:42:28	00:12:48:25	5:27		
		Runners in Distance	V1	16:36:01:14	16:36:04:24	3:10		
		Sand 1	V1	15:03:37:18	15:03:45:02	7:14		
		Sand 2	V1	07:16:17:08	07:16:25:06	7:28		
		Sand 3	V1	01:00:03:09	01:00:10:24	7:15		
		Senegal, Aerial 1	V1	00:30:15:28	00:30:22:27	6:29		
		Senegal, Aerial 3	V1	00:30:43:24	00:30:49:07	5:13		
		Senegal, Aerial 4	V1	00:45:14:09	00:45:20:07	5:28		
		Senegal, Aerial 8, birds	V1	00:59:15:06	00:59:19:26	4:20		
		Senegal, mother and baby.	V1	17:07:32:10	17:07:36:26	4:16		
		Sun Panning	V1	13:19:10:00	13:19:19:01	9:01		
		Woman with bag on head.	V1	15:19:57:26	15:20:02:22	4:26		

Figure 1.16 Combine multiple bins into a single window to save space.

To combine windows together into tabs:

1. Click the **TAB** at the top of the tool window and drag it on top of the window with which you want to combine it.

2. Release the **MOUSE** button.

   The tab will appear with the other(s) in the window.

3. Optionally, drag the **TAB** left or right to rearrange the order in which it appears.

To separate tabbed windows:

1. Click the **TAB** of the bin or tool you wish to separate from the window and drag it outside the boundaries of the current window.

2. Release the **MOUSE** button.

   The tab will appear by itself in a new window.

To close a tabbed bin:

■ Clicking the small "×" on the tab itself will close just that particular bin.

■ Clicking the red "×" in the corner of the tabbed set will close all the bins that are tabbed together.

When working with multiple tabs in a single window, the system will automatically resize the tabs. As the number of tabs increases, it may reach the point that the tab is too short to display the entire name, and the name will be abbreviated—sometimes to the point of being indecipherable. This is more common with bins than tools. To select the tab you want when you can't read the name, use the drop-down menu instead, as shown in Figure 1.17.

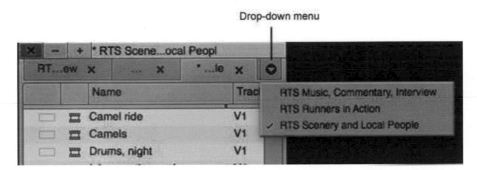

Figure 1.17 Use the drop-down menu to select the desired tab, particularly when the names are abbreviated.

 Trouble reading the interface? Make the text more legible by changing the font and/or size. To do so, select Windows > Set Font, select the font from the drop-down menu that appears, and type the point size you wish to use. The display font is set on a per-window basis, so consider mapping the Set Font command to a key on the keyboard.

Changing Interface Colors

By default, Media Composer's color scheme is a medium gray with blue highlights. You can change the overall brightness of the interface, and the color of the highlight.

To change the interface colors:

1. Click the **SETTINGS PANE** in the Project Window.

2. Scroll through the list to find the **INTERFACE SETTING**, and then double-click it to open it.

 The Interface Setting window opens, as shown in Figure 1.18.

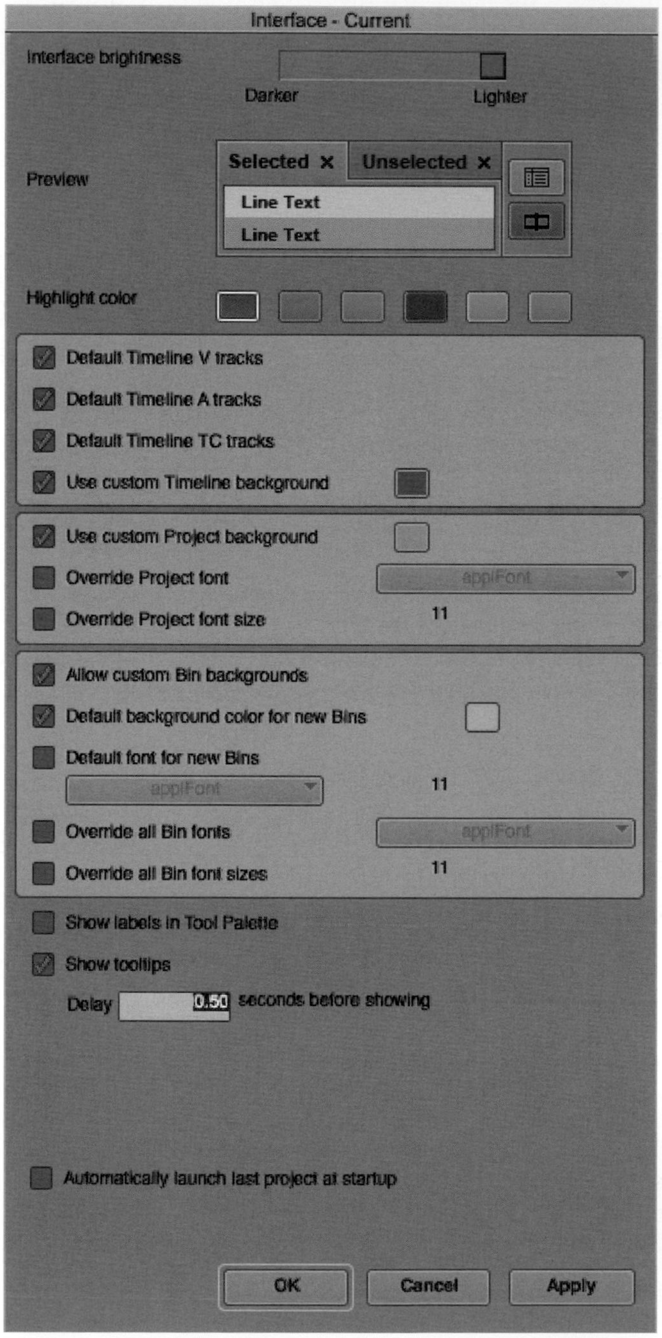

Figure 1.18 Use the Interface Setting to change the look and feel of Media Composer.

3. Drag the **BRIGHTNESS SLIDER** to your preferred shade of gray.

4. Select the desired highlight color by clicking on the color tile.

5. Click the red × to close the window and save your settings.

Mapping User-Selectable Buttons

Media Composer allows you to change the arrangement of virtually all of the buttons on the interface and on the keyboard. Most editing professionals have highly-customized settings, and in time, you may find that you want to start making changes to the default arrangement on the interface or keyboard too.

For now, it is useful to at least learn the mechanics of how to assign a function to the keyboard and/or a button on the interface. There are some very useful functions, including ones covered in this course, that do not appear by default on the keyboard or interface, which you may find you want to add.

To make any changes to the buttons you need to open the Command Palette.

To change the keyboard mapping, you also need to open the Keyboard setting.

Understanding the Command Palette

The Command Palette, shown in Figure 1.19, is opened from the Tools menu and is the one place to find all user-selectable buttons. It presents them in groups by category: Move, Play, Edit, Trim, FX, 3D, CC (Color Correction), MCam (Multicam), Tracks, Smart Tools, Other, More, and Workspaces.

Command Palette
Move	Play	Edit	Trim	FX	3D	CC	MCam	Tracks	Smart Tools	Other	More	Workspaces

Step Forward 1 Frame	▶		Go to IN	⊺◆	Go to Previous Edit	⊩◆	Step Forward One Field	⫶▶
Step Backward 1 Frame	◀		Go to OUT	◆⊺	Go to Next Edit	◆⊩	Step Backward One Field	◀⫶
Step Forward 8 Frames	‖▶	Go to Audio Mark IN	⫶◆	Rewind	◀◀	Go to Previous Marker	⦙◀
Step Backward 8 Frames	◀‖	Go to Audio Mark OUT	◆⫶	Fast Forward	▶▶	Go to Next Marker	▶⦙
		Go to Start	⊺ʟ				
		Go to End	⅃⊺				

○ 'Button to Button' Reassignment   ○ Active Palette   ○ 'Menu to Button' Reassignment

Figure 1.19 The Command Palette enables you to remap buttons on the interface and keyboard.

The radio buttons across the bottom determine the mode of the Command Palette:

- **Button to Button Reassignment:** This allows you to remap buttons by dragging them from the Command Palette to the interface or to the open keyboard setting. When active, you can also drag the buttons in any of the toolbars of the interface to rearrange them.

- **Active Palette:** This enables the Command Palette to function as an editing tool. When set to Active Palette, clicking a button in the Command Palette will perform the function.

- **Menu to Button Reassignment:** This allows you to map menu commands for which there is no preset button for the keyboard or interface—for example, Export.

When Button to Button Reassignment is active, none of the buttons on the interface will work. It is similar to when you rearrange the apps on an iPhone or iPad: if the apps are jiggling, you can rearrange them, but not open them. Media Composer icons don't jiggle, but the principle is the same.

The Keyboard Setting

The Keyboard setting, shown in Figure 1.20, shows you a map of the functions assigned to the physical buttons of the keyboard. Keyboard mappings in Media Composer have two layers. Holding the Shift key on the keyboard displays the second layer.

Figure 1.20 The Keyboard Setting shows you a map of the buttons on the keyboard.

Remapping Buttons

Remapping buttons is the most common way to customize the interface and keyboard.

To remap buttons or keys using the Command Palette:

1.   If you want to map a button to the keyboard, open the **KEYBOARD** settings from the Settings pane.

2.   Choose **TOOLS > COMMAND PALETTE**.

      The Command Palette opens.

3.   Click the **BUTTON TO BUTTON REASSIGNMENT** button if it's not selected.

4.   Click the **TAB** for the category that contains your user-selectable button.

5.   Click and drag the **BUTTON** from the Command Palette to the Keyboard Palette or to a location on a row of buttons—for example, under a monitor or in the Tool Palette.

      If you press the Shift key down as you drag the button to the Keyboard Palette, you can map to Shift+[key].

6.   Close the Command Palette when you are finished.

Adjusting Auto-Save Settings

Another setting worth looking at now is the Auto-Save settings.

The Auto-Save settings, found within the Bin setting, does just what the name implies. They control the frequency with which Media Composer automatically saves a copy of your bin(s) – that is, your work. Media Composer is generally a very stable application with few crashes, but even the best computers and apps crash sometimes. If you have your Auto-Save settings dialed in to the "right" values, it can save you loads of stress should your system ever crash.

Let's look at the default settings, as shown in Figure 1.21, to better understand how these work. There are three duration values:

- AutoSave: 15 minutes

- Inactivity Period: 15 seconds

- Force Auto-Save: 17 minutes

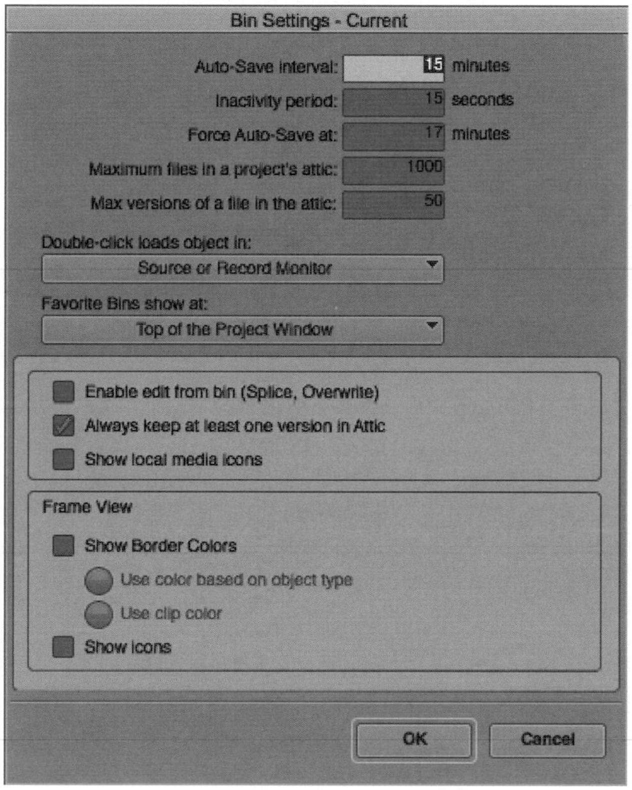

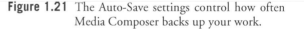

Figure 1.21 The Auto-Save settings control how often Media Composer backs up your work.

With these settings, Media Composer will wait 15 minutes before it *tries* to save. It will only save after you pause for at least 15 seconds. If after 17 minutes you have not paused for at least 15 seconds, being such an editing-machine that you are, Media Composer will interrupt you and force an auto-save.

What's the "right" setting for you? There is no real answer to that question, since it is strictly a personal preference, but there are a couple of things to consider that can help you figure it out for yourself.

Questions to ask yourself:

■ How fast do I edit?

The faster you edit the more work you accomplish in a given amount of time.

■ How much work can I afford to lose if the system crashes – 2 minutes? 5 minutes? 20 minutes?

If the system crashes when you are nearing the next auto-save point, you would have to recreate any recent changes from memory.

■ How often am I willing to be interrupted?

There is a momentary interruption when Media Composer performs the save, so that is a consideration for some editors.

Ultimately there is no right or wrong answer here. Many editors choose to work with the defaults. Dial in whatever values you think might be best for you, and try them out. The best thing to remember is that you can change them at any time. As your skills and confidence increase, the "right" values will also change.

To change your AutoSave setting:

1. Select the **SETTINGS** pane in the Project Window.

2. Scroll through the list to find the **BIN** setting, and then double-click it to open it.

The Bin setting opens, as shown in Figure 1.19. The Auto-Save settings are at the top of the window.

3. Type the number you prefer for each of the following settings:

• **Auto-Save Interval:** The number of minutes until Media Composer *tries* to save another copy of the bin. It will only save if you stop editing for more than X seconds, as defined in the Inactivity Period.

• **Inactivity Period:** The number of seconds you want Media Composer to wait before it recognizes that you've stopped editing.

• **Force Auto-Save:** The number of minutes after which Media Composer will interrupt you to save if it hasn't been able to yet.

When you save Media Composer, not only does it update the bins in your Project Folder but creates a backup copy in a folder called the Attic. We will look at this folder and how to restore from it at the end of this course. The last two options deal with the way the files in the Attic folder are managed.

 Exercise Break: Exercise 1.3
Pause here to practice what you've learned.

Review/Discussion Questions

1. Where does Media Composer store the project files for private projects?

    a. On the desktop

    b. In the logged on users' Documents folder

    c. In the Shared Documents folder

    d. On an external hard drive

2. Which button in the Select Project dialog box (refer to Figure 1.3) is used to navigate to the location of an external project?

    a. The Private button

    b. The Shared button

    c. The External button

    d. The Folder Browse button

3. Name the four principal windows of the Avid interface.

4. Which window serves as the central hub of your project?

5. What is a bin?

6. How do you combine one open bin with another open bin?

7. What are the two ways you create your own User Profile?

8. How do you save changes to a Workspace?

9. Which setting allows you to change the look of your interface?

10. What is saved during an Autosave?

Lesson 1 Keyboard Shortcuts

Key	Shortcut
Ctrl+9 (Windows)/Command+9 (Mac)	Activate the Project window
1	Step backward eight frames/ten frames
2	Step forward eight frames/ten frames
3, left arrow	Step backward one frame
4, right arrow	Step forward one frame
5, space bar	Play forward
Home	Jump to first frame
End	Jump to last frame
Ctrl+L (Windows)/Command+L (Mac)	Enlarges height of Timeline tracks, changes the size of clip frames in a bin, and changes the zoom factor of the Source, Record, or Effects monitor.
Ctrl+K (Windows)/Command+K (Mac)	Reduces height of Timeline tracks
Ctrl+S (Windows)/Command+S (Mac)	Save
Ctrl+Q (Windows)/Command+Q (Mac)	Quit the application

Setting Up

In this exercise we will launch the Avid Media Composer software, examine its interface and view some material.

Media Used: Running the Sahara

Duration: 20 minutes

GOALS

- Launch Media Composer
- Create a User Profile
- Examine the main elements of the interface
- Save the project

Exercise 1.1: Opening a Project and Creating a New User Profile

You will launch Media Composer, examine how projects and bins are organized, load clips and sequences into the Composer window to view them and save the project. All of this is done using an existing project. In the next exercise you will learn how to create a new project and bring some material into that project.

To launch Media Composer:

1. Launch Media Composer, and wait for the Select Project screen to appear.

2. Click on the **USER PROFILE MENU**, and then select **CREATE USER PROFILE**.

    The Create User Profile window appears. (See Figure 1.22.)

Figure 1.22 The Create User Profile window.

3. Enter your name, and click **OK** to create your own user profile.

    Any changes to the Avid Media Composer interface that you make during this course will be saved and can be taken to another system.

4. Back in the Select Project window; click the radio button next to Shared, to use the Shared Projects folder.

    If you followed the directions in the Introduction for setting up your system, you should see the Running the Sahara project listed in the Shared Projects list. If you don't see the Running the Sahara project, quit the application and check the instructions before continuing.

5. Click the name "Running the Sahara" to select the project.

6. Click **OK** to open it.

Exercise 1.2: Organizing the Project

To see how a project is organized:

1. Click the disclosure triangle to the left of the "RTS Rushes" folder to open the folder. Notice that the "RTS Rushes" folder contains three bins.

   Let's make two new bins and use one of them for the titles you will create in this project.

2. To begin, click twice on the **NEW BIN** button in the Project window's Bins pane.

   Two new bins appear at the root level of the Bins pane. In addition, two windows open, representing the two new bins. By default, Media Composer names all new bins after the project.

   We actually need only one new bin at the moment, so let's rename one of them, and throw the other in the Trash.

3. To rename a bin, first click once on its name (not the icon) in the Bins pane, in this example, "Running the Sahara Bin," to highlight it.

4. Type "Titles," and press **ENTER** (Windows) or **RETURN** (Mac).

   The name on the bin and in the title bar of the bin's window changes to "Titles."

5. Next, delete the remaining new bin. To begin, click the icon (not the name) for the other new bin, Running the Sahara Bin1.

6. Press the **DELETE** or **BACKSPACE KEY** to delete the bin. Alternatively, right-click the bin and choose **DELETE SELECTED BINS** from the menu that appears.

   A red Trash bin appears at the bottom of the Project window, with your deleted bin inside. (See Figure 1.23.)

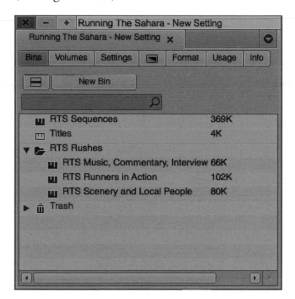

Figure 1.23 The Trash folder appears when we delete a bin.

7. In Fast Menu of the Project window (all windows have Fast Menus), select **EMPTY TRASH**.

   The bin is deleted permanently (no **UNDO** is possible) and the red Trash bin disappears.

To see how a bin is organized:

Bins can open in separate windows as we have seen already. They can also be tabbed in the same window.

- If two or more bin windows are already open, you can combine them by dragging the tab from one window into another.

- To open a bin as a tab in an existing bin window, drag the closed bin (solid "black" icon) to the open bin window.

- You can also open a number of bins at once into a tabbed window.

To open several bins in one tabbed window:

1. Select all the bins in the RTS Rushes folder – "RTS Music, Commentary and Interview," "RTS Scenery and Local People," and "RTS Runners in Action."

2. Right-click on the selected bins and select **OPEN SELECTED BINS IN ONE WINDOW** or click on the Fast Menu and select Open Selected Bins in One Window.

   They open tabbed in the one bin window and in the project Bin tab they display a transparent "white" icon. By default the bin items in the bin are displayed in Text view showing columns of information about the clips.

3. Move the tabbed bin window to below the Project window by dragging its header (where it says "RTS Scenery and Local People" – the current tab), then drag the lower-right corner of the bin window down to make the bin fill the available space to the left of the timeline. (I'm assuming you are working with one screen here, if you have two then you can probably nearly fill the screen with the bin window, just make sure to leave the project visible).

   Now is a good time to identify the different clip icons, located in the Icon column on the far left side of the bin window. Three different types of clips can be seen currently in this project, each with their own icons: master clips including video, master clips with audio only, and sequences. (There are also master clips which use linked media rather than Avid native media, but we will see these in the next lesson). We will work our way through these.

4. The master clip icon looks like a single frame of film. Double click on the "Sand 1" Master Clip icon (not the name).

   It loads into the Source monitor in the Composer window and you can play and pause it using the space bar (We will look at other ways of playing through our clips and sequences later).

5. Now, select the "Music, Commentary and Interview" tab. If you cannot read the tab names there is a little icon (circle with triangle in it) at the right of the tab bar, which will allow you to select from a list. Drag MATT VO2 into the source monitor (just for a change).

6. The Source monitor looks empty. However, the clip name and the center duration indicate something has been loaded. There just is no picture, because it is audio only. Play and pause it using the space bar and you will hear Matt Damon's narration for "Running the Sahara."

7. Now drag the closed RTS Sequences bin (solid "black" icon) down to the bin window with the other tabbed bins. It opens up as an additional tab.

   This contains four versions of the Running the Sahara Promo. The sequence icon looks like a filmstrip, or a series of clips side by side.

8. Double click on the "RTS Promo 57 Final" sequence icon (not the name).

   It loads into the Record monitor in the Composer window and you can play and pause it using the space bar. Notice that the entire sequence is visible in the Timeline window. Much more on that later.

9. To help us understand the relationship between the Avid native media files in the Avid MediaFiles folder and master clips and sequences in the bin, highlight each in turn and press the **DELETE** key (DON'T CLICK OK). You get two different Delete windows with different options. (See Figures 1.24 and 1.25.)

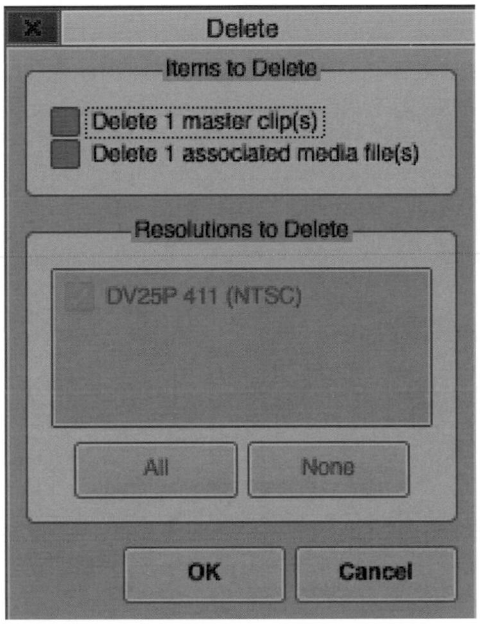

Figure 1.24 Deleting a Master Clip.

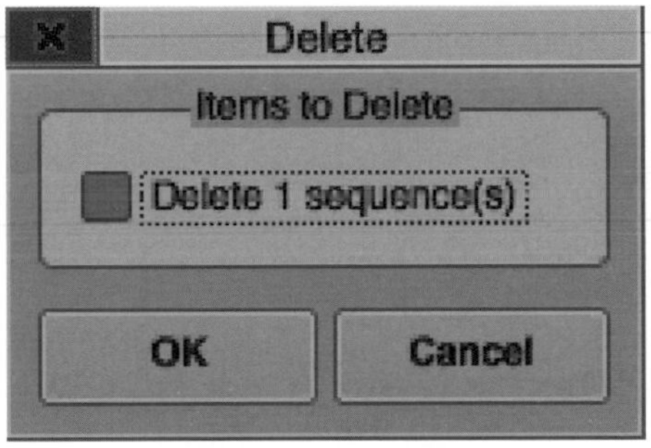

Figure 1.25 Deleting a Sequence.

These differences indicate that master clips are linked to MediaFiles while sequences are not. Sequences are actually linked to Master Clips and use the media linked to those clips. Much more on this later.

Exercise 1.3: Adjusting Settings

We have looked at the main components of the Interface which are: the Project, Composer, and Timeline windows. As we have seen, the arrangement of these is called a "Workspace." There are a number of default workspaces. We can choose between these workspaces, alter or restore the defaults, and create new workspaces. Let's try a very simple change.

Adjusting the Workspace:

1. Select **WINDOWS > WORKSPACES > SOURCE/RECORD EDITING**.

    It is very important that you check what workspace you are in before you start. The checkmark next to the name indicates the currently selected workspace. It is annoying to make a lot of changes and find you are in the wrong workspace.

2. Make any changes you want to make.

    I'm working on a Mac and I like my Dock to be fixed at the bottom of the screen. That means when I click at the bottom of the Timeline window, I find myself mistakenly launching Applications. So I adjust my Timeline window to sit above the Dock.

3. Select **WINDOWS > WORKSPACES > SAVE CURRENT**, so that Media Composer locks-in, and remembers your change.

4. Then, as a test, switch to another Workspace. Now, return to the Source/Record Editing Workspace. It should return with the changes you have made. If at any time you want to restore back to the default workspace, select Windows > Workspaces > Restore Current to Default.

Adjusting the Interface:

It is also possible to change the appearance of the interface, all the colors and the typefaces. Let's again take a simple example of making the interface darker.

1. In the Project window select the **SETTINGS** tab.

    By typing the first two letters of the word "Interface" you will jump directly to that setting, saving you the work of scrolling to locate it.

2. With the Settings displayed, you can now type "in."

    The Interface setting is selected.

3. Double-click on it.

    The "Interface – Current" dialog window opens.

4. At the top is a slider. Move it to the left to darken the interface and click **APPLY**.

    You will not be surprised to see that the interface has become much darker.

Adjusting the Auto-Save Settings:

Media Composer saves your bins automatically. The frequency of this can be adjusted in the Bin setting and I recommend that you adjust the default settings, which do not take full advantage of the Auto-Save capability.

1. In the Project window select the **SETTINGS** tab and type "b" to jump you to the Bin Settings in the list.

    The Bin setting is selected.

2. Double click on it.

    The "Bin Settings – Current" dialog opens.

3. There are five boxes we can fill in. The first asks us how often we want the system to Auto-Save. The default is 15 minutes, which is very conservative given the next adjustment. Change it to 2 minutes.

4. An Auto-Save can, of course, interrupt your flow of work but Media Composer has a system which only performs an Auto-Save after an inactivity period that you can determine. The default is 15 seconds. Leave this for now or shorten it, if you like.

5. Finally, the Force Auto-Save does not wait for the inactivity period. It is a safety net, which you are hardly ever likely to use. I set mine to 30 minutes.

    When you save Media Composer, not only does it update the bins in your Project Folder but creates a backup copy in a folder called the Attic. We will look at this folder and how to restore from it at the end of this course. The last two options deal with the way the files in the Attic folder are managed.

Getting Started

Whether you want to become a professional TV or film editor, or just want to learn to edit videos as a basic skill, how far you go is up to you. Thankfully, you don't need to decide now; you just need to take the first step to get started—which is exactly what you'll do in this lesson.

Media: Rock Climber

Duration: 60 minutes

GOALS

- Create a New Project
- Use the Source Browser to locate camera files
- Link to camera files
- Import music files
- Rename master clips
- Organize the project media into bins
- Add notes and keywords to master clips
- Adjust the volume of video and audio clips

Creating a New Project

Now that you can find your way around the application, it's time to create your own project and get started on your own work.

The first thing to do when starting a new project is to decide where you want to save it. You can move the files later if you choose. Most facilities have a standardized save location, so you may need to ask the post supervisor or media manager. If you are working by yourself, you may simply choose to save all your projects in the Private folder.

Set the Save Location

The buttons along the top of the Select Project dialog box designate the location where the project will be saved (see Figure 2.1). They are as follows:

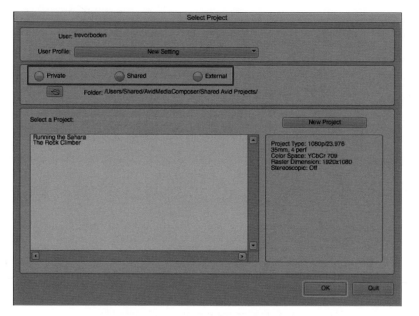

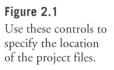

Figure 2.1
Use these controls to
specify the location
of the project files.

- **Private:** Private projects are saved in the Documents folder of the current OS user. Someone logging onto the computer using a different OS user will not be able to access these.

- **Shared:** Shared projects are saved in the Shared folder, in a folder called Shared Avid Projects.

- **External:** External projects are saved in any location you choose except the two default locations above. It does not need to be external to your computer.

The locations for Private and Shared projects are hard-coded and cannot be changed, but External projects can be saved in any location you choose. Because External projects can be saved anywhere, you need to tell the system where you want to save them.

 The file path for the current project directory is always displayed next to the Browse Folder button.

To set the location for external projects:

1. Click the **BROWSE FOLDER** button in the top section of the Select Project dialog box.

    A standard OS browse window will open.

2. Navigate to the **FOLDER** where you want to save your project files.

3. Click **OK**. The directory path in the Folder field is updated.

Create the Project

With the save directory set, you are ready to create the project.

To create a new project:

1. Click the **NEW PROJECT** button in the Select Project dialog box.

    A New Project dialog box opens with the Project Name field highlighted, as shown in Figure 2.2.

2. Name the **PROJECT**.

3. Click the **FORMAT** menu and select the desired format from the list that appears. There are many choices which depend on a number of factors. For this project, you will select **1080P/23.976**.

    This designates the project format to be the HD frame size of 1920 x 1080, the video type to be "Interlaced" (the letter "I"), and the frame rate to be 29.97 "Frames" per second (which is 59.94 "Fields" per second).

4. If necessary, change the **ASPECT RATIO**, **COLOR SPACE**, and **RASTER DIMENSION** settings. (This is uncommon and we will not change it here.)

5. Click **OK**.

    The project files are created and the new project appears in the project list, highlighted and ready to be opened.

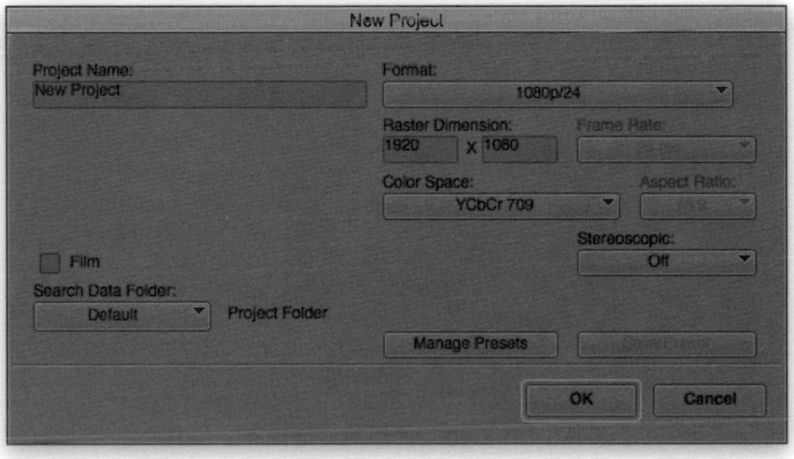

Figure 2.2 Create a new project using the settings shown.

It is recommended that you name the project carefully. There is no option in Media Composer to rename a project. Do not name the project with a version number. Rather, simply name it what it is. For example "Move of the Century," "Episode 52," etc. You will keep track of the different versions within the project itself.

At the OS level, each Media Composer project is actually a folder, not just a single file. This is quite different than what you may be accustomed to. A new project folder is created with three files inside: a project file, project settings files, and a bin file. (See Figure 2.3.) All additional bin files are also saved into this folder. The project folder does not contain any media; rather, it contains all the information about your clips and sequences—in other words, your work! To move (or archive) the project, you would need to move the entire project folder, not just the project file alone.

Name	Kind	Size
▼ 📁 Demo Project	Folder	--
▶ 📁 Statistics	Folder	--
📄 Demo Project.avp	Avid Project File	842 bytes
📄 Demo Project Settings.xml	XML File	144 KB
📄 Demo Project Settings.avs	Avid Preferences File	15 KB

Figure 2.3 The project folder and initial files for a project named Demo Project. (Mac OS shown.)

Open the Project

After you create the project, you still need to open it. With Avid Media Composer, we do not open a project by clicking on a project file of any kind. Instead, we launch the application and make our selections in the Project Selection dialog box.

To open a project:

1.   Select the **PROJECT NAME**.

2.   Click **OK** or press **ENTER**.

Understanding the Project's Format Setting

In Media Composer, a project's format is a combination of frame size and frame rate. If the chosen format supports both 4×3 and 16×9 aspect ratios, the Aspect Ratio menu will be available to set. Likewise, if the format supports more than one raster (frame size), these will be available in the Raster Dimension drop-down menu.

The Format setting controls how Media Composer processes media, including which codecs are available to you for capture, render, and transcode. The easy rule of thumb here is to set the Format and Raster settings to whatever most of your media for a project will be. Refer to the list of supported formats in the lower half of the dialog box if you are unsure.

The Format settings can also be changed after a project is created. The only thing you cannot change later is the family of formats, which is based on the frame rate chosen here. For example, you can change a project from 1080i/50 to 25i PAL because they are both based on 25 fps.

 Exercise Break: Exercise 2.1
Pause here to practice what you've learned.

Setting Up Your Project

Projects grow and evolve over time, and keeping them organized requires deliberate effort.

The best way to set yourself up for success is to create some structure to your project from the start. This gives you a place to put everything so that the minute you need it, it's already there waiting. In this section, you will learn to create and name the bins required for a typical small project.

Working with Bins

The Bins pane of the Project window, shown in Figure 2.4, lists all the bins in the project, either as a flat list or organized into folders you create. In most of your projects, you will use multiple bins to organize your material. A news editor may use one bin per story. A small project may have five to ten bins. Feature films may have hundreds.

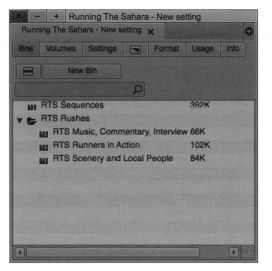

Figure 2.4 The Bins pane of the Project window shows the bins and folders in a project.

Creating New Bins

Creating new bins is a simple process, and like most things in Media Composer, there are several ways to do it.

To create a new bin:

- Click the New Bin button at the top of the pane.

- Right-click in the empty gray space of the Bins pane and choose New Bin.

- Choose File > New > New Bin.

 When starting a project, you might find that it is easiest to create a batch of bins. Rename them and delete any extras.

Media Composer automatically opens any new bins when create and names each with a default name: the name of the project + "Bin" and a number. It's very important to name the bins with a meaningful name instead of using the default name. For example, it would be very common to have a bin to store only your sequences, another bin for your titles, and another for your music, and so on for sound effects, graphics, etc.

To rename a bin:

1. In the Bins pane of the Project window, click once on the **BIN NAME**.

    The bin name becomes highlighted, ready to be renamed.

2. Type the new **NAME**.

3. Press **ENTER**.

 There's a subtle difference between pressing Enter and Return on a Mac. Pressing Enter (on the numeric keypad) simply renames the bin and exits the name field. Pressing Return accepts the name and exits the field, but also moves the highlight down to the next bin name in the list, making it useful for renaming multiple bins.

Opening and closing bins is as easy as you might imagine.

To open or close a single bin:

■   To open a single bin, double-click the bin icon. (Remember, clicking the name will allow you to rename the bin.)

■   To close an open bin, simply click the red × in the upper-right (Windows) or upper-left (Mac) corner.

To open or close multiple bins:

1. Select the **BINS** you want to open or close.

    •   If the bins are in a contiguous group, Shift-click the bin icon of the first and last bin in the group.

    •   If the bins are not in a contiguous group, Ctrl-click (Windows) or Command-click (Mac) the bin icon of each bin.

2. Click and drag a **LASSO** through the names of the bins to select them.

3. Right-click on one of the selected **BINS**. From the context menu that appears, choose **OPEN SELECTED BINS** or **CLOSE SELECTED BINS** as desired. (See Figure 2.5.)

Figure 2.5
Right-click on a selected group of bins to open, close, or delete them as a group.

Deleting unwanted bins is just as easy.

To delete a bin:

1. Click on the **BIN** icon in the Project window to select it.

2. Press the **DELETE** or **BACKSPACE** key on your keyboard.

   The bin is sent to Media Composer's recycle bin, called Trash, shown in Figure 2.6.

3. To permanently delete the bin file (forever, with no "Undo" possible), click the **FAST** menu in the Project window and choose **EMPTY TRASH**, or right-click in the gray, open area of the Project window and select from the menu.

   You can pull bin files out of the Trash for reuse. To do so, drag the bin icon from the Trash folder and release it among the other bins. It will be restored to the bin list and appear in its alphabetical location.

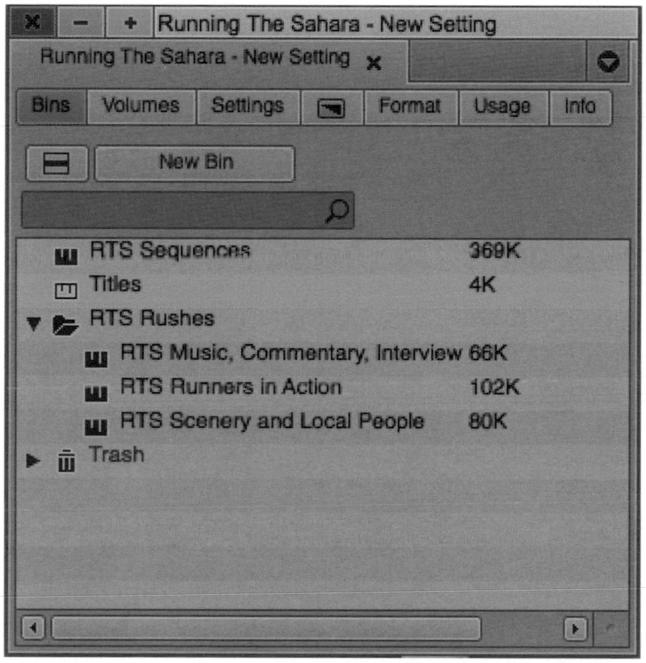

Figure 2.6 The Trash icon appears after a bin or folder is deleted.

Bin files are small, taking up very little space on the drive. Some professionals prefer to never empty the Trash folder until they complete and deliver the project.

Combining Bins in One Window

Media Composer features a tabbed interface that allows you to combine similar windows to save space. This is especially useful when working on a single monitor, such as a laptop. (See Figure 2.7.)

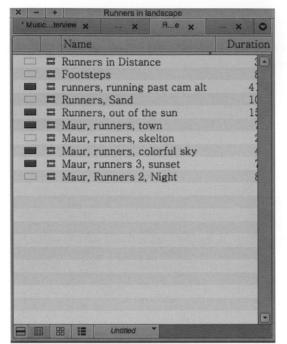

Figure 2.7
You can select tabbed bins by clicking the tab or drop-down menu.

To combine bins in one window:

■   With both bins open, drag the tab with the name of the first window and release it on the second.

■   With one bin open, drag the icon of the closed bin(s) from the Project window to the open bin window. The bins will open in the target window.

■   With no bins open, select the bins in the Project window, right-click, and choose Open Bins in One Window.

To activate a tabbed bin:

■   Click the tab with the bin name.

■   Click the drop-down menu to select the bin name from the list.

Identifying Objects in Your Bins

All project assets will be stored in your bins, including audio and video clips, titles, effect templates, and more. As you start adding items to the bin, it will be easier if you can identify them from the start. Each asset type is identified as an object in the bin with its own unique icon. Table 2.1 lists the most common asset types.

Table 2.1: Common Asset Types

Icon	Object Type	Description
	Master clip	A clip that references audio and video media files formed from captured footage or imported files
	Master clip on shared storage	A master clip that references media files located on a shared storage system
	Subclip	A clip that references a selected portion of a master clip
	Subclip on shared storage	A subclip that references media files on a shared storage system
	Audio clip	A clip that references audio media files formed from captured audio or imported files
	Audio clip on shared storage	An audio clip that references media files located on a shared storage system
	Sequence	A clip that represents an edited program, partial or complete, that you create from other clips
	Effect	A clip that references an unrendered effect that you create
	Motion effects	A file in the bin that references effect media files generated when you create motion effects
	Group clip	Clips containing two or more grouped clips, combined according to common timecodes or manual sync points. These are used for MultiCamera editing, such as sitcoms.

How to Input Video and Audio Clips

Before you can start editing, you have to get your video and audio clips onto the computer and then into Media Composer. In post-production terms, this process is sometimes referred to generically as *ingest*. Media Composer uses the term *input*.

Getting the files onto the computer can be as simple as mounting the SD card from the camera, or the portable hard drive on which the camera files have been copied.

Remember to always back up original camera files to another hard drive for safe-keeping:

 Remember to always back up original camera files to another hard drive for safe-keeping.

There are several ways to get media into your Media Composer project (or multiple drives):

- **Tape Capture:** This allows you to input video and audio through cabled connections from a video tape deck, satellite, or live camera feed. Today, tape use is becoming less and less common.

- **Import:** Importing ingests a media file by copying the media to a predefined location and converts it to Avid native media at the same time. It's important to take note that in Media Composer, the term "import" means to create a brand new file which is a separate copy of the original.

- **Link:** Linking connects a media file to the project in Media Composer. It does not move or copy the media file. Media Composer will read the file from its current location and in its current format.

 This course assumes that you are working with all file-based media. To learn more about using Tape Capture, refer to the Media Composer Help.

Using the Source Browser

Media Composer v8.6 introduced a new input tool called the Source Browser, shown in Figure 2.8, which combines the controls for linking and importing into a single window.

To open the Source Browser, do one of the following:

- Select File > Input > Source Browser.

- Right-click in an open bin, and then select Input > Source Browser.

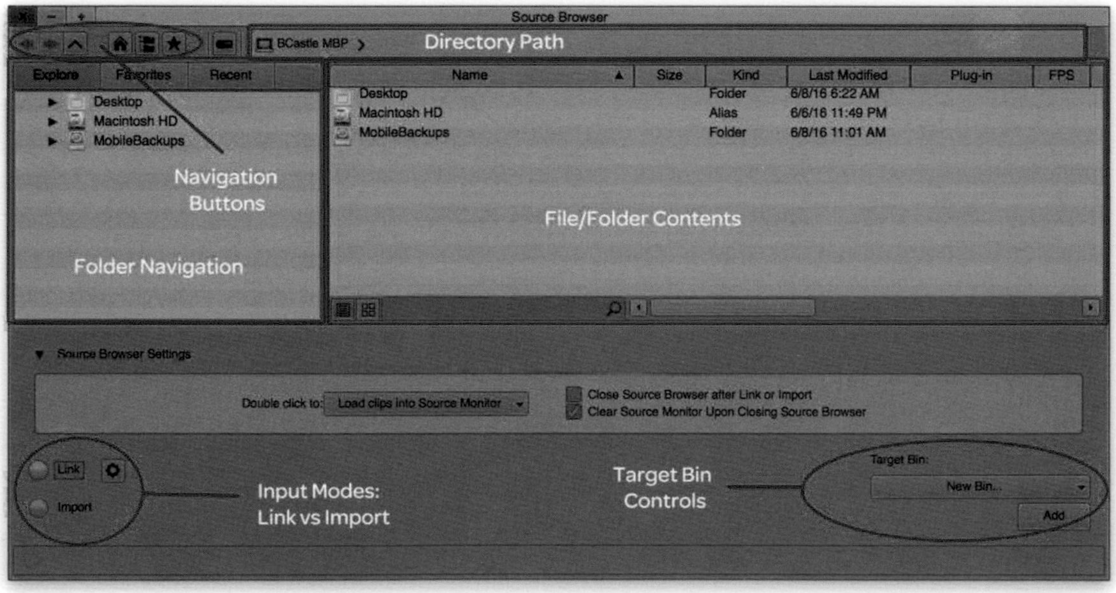

Figure 2.8 Use the Source Browser to link and import clips to your project.

The Source Browser is set up like a standard OS window, so it is intuitive and easy to use.

The window pane on the left displays your computer's folders, and the large pane to the right lists the files inside each folder. Across the top there are navigation buttons – Back, Forward, and Go to Parent Folder – and the current directory path. Along the bottom is a collapsible settings pane. You can resize the panes by dragging the divider lines between them.

The folder tree has three tabs:

- **Explore**: Shows all your system folders.

- **Favorites**: Lists shortcuts to the folders you've tagged as favorite.

- **Recent**: Lists the folders you've used in previous sessions.

Marking a Favorite Folder

If you have folders that you use on a regular basis, for example a folder full of stock music or the folder containing all the clips for this course, you can save time by marking it as a favorite.

To mark a folder as a Favorite:

1. Navigate to the folder, and select it in the directory tree.

2. Click the **STAR** button at the top of the Source Browser.

    A star appears to the left of the folder in the directory tree, indicating that it is marked as a favorite. (See Figure 2.9) The folder also appears in the Favorites pane, making it an easy find the next time.

3. Click the Star next to the Folder icon to deselect a Favorite.

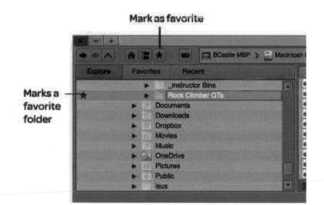

Figure 2.9 Use the Star button to mark a folder as a favorite.

Browsing Your Media Files

Seeing your files in a list is fine, but it is more meaningful to be able to watch the video clips. Most cameras, for example, name files with a meaningless code. The code ensures that each file name is unique, but doesn't tell you which is a close-up, or a wide shot, nor which take was a blooper vs a good take.

The Source Browser lets you play the media files before deciding if you want to add them to the project. You can view and play them as thumbnail images, or load them into the Source monitor for more careful viewing.

To view clips in Frame View:

1.   Click the **SWITCH TO FRAME VIEW** button, shown in Figure 2.10.

2.   (Optional) Drag the slider to adjust the size of the thumbnails.

3.   Click on the file to select it, and do one of the following:

     •   Move the mouse over the selected thumbnail to scrub through the video frames.

     •   Press the Spacebar to play the clip.

To load a file into the Source monitor:

■   Double-click the file. (With default settings.)

■   Drag the file to the Source monitor.

Figure 2.10 Set the Source Browser to Frame View to view your video clips.

Adding Linked Clips to Your Project

Once you decide which clips to use, add them to your project so they appear in a bin.

Placing the clips in a bin saves them as part of the project, so that if you close out of Media Composer (or the project) and come back to it later, the clips will be there waiting for you.

You can do this either as a group – for example, all the files in a folder, or on a camera card – or one-by-one. You can even choose to do this through the process of editing them into your sequence. Media Composer offers the flexibility to input them however it works best for you at the moment.

To add a group of clips to a bin:

1. Select the clip(s) in the Source Browser. To select a group, do one of the following:

    •   Click the first clip, then Shift+click the last one you want to select. All clips in between are selected.

    •   Ctrl+click (Windows) or Command+click (Mac) each file you want.

    •   Ctrl+A (Windows) or Command+A (Mac) to select all clips.

2. Drag the selected clips to an open bin.

    The clips will appear in the bin with the linked master clip icon, as seen in Figure 2.11.

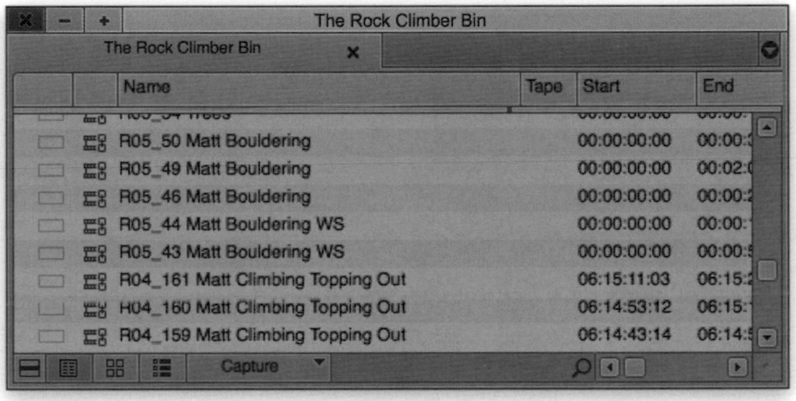

Figure 2.11 Linked master clips in the bin are saved with the project.

Understanding Media Linking

When you input media files into your project, a link (a connection) is created between the *master clip* in the bin and the *media file,* which contains the actual images and sounds that you see and hear in the clip. A master clip is a tiny bit of metadata – that is, textual information like timecode, clip name, etc. about the media – including the information the system needs to identify and link to the media file(s). The master clip information is stored in the bin file; meanwhile the media file is stored on the hard drive or memory card. If Media Composer ever cannot find the media file, the master clip will appear as "Media Offline". (You will learn more about how to solve "Media Offline" problems in Lesson 12, Basic Troubleshooting.)

Broadly speaking, Media Composer uses two types of media files: *Camera Native* and *Avid Native.*

Camera Native means that the original audio and video files created by the camera. You can input, play and edit most camera native file types in Media Composer using plug-ins, called *AMA (Avid Media Access) plug-ins.* When you input camera native clips, Media Composer creates a link to the original file in its current location and reads it from there using the plug-in to decompress and playback the file. You manage camera native files yourself through the Mac Finder, or Windows Explorer, by copying, moving or deleting the files directly. If you move, rename or delete the files in the OS, you will need to relink them inside Media Composer. You will learn more on relinking in Lesson 12.

If you are working with a camera that's new on the market, or just new to you, it may be necessary to download an additional AMA plugin before Media Composer will be able to read the camera files.

To download additional AMA plug-ins, click the Marketplace menu > AMA Plug-ins.

> *Avid Native* media is the media created by Media Composer when you Import, Consolidate (copy only), or Transcode (copy and convert codecs at the same time) camera native files. Avid Native media is always created in the MXF format and is stored in a very specific location (the Avid MediaFiles folder). Media Composer generally performs better and faster when you use Avid Native media. It also saves you the hassle of needing to keep track of all your own media files in the OS. You will learn more about how to manage Avid Native media in Lesson 12.

Importing Media Files

Importing is a great way to ingest your media when you are getting started.

Importing is more time consuming than linking because it copies the media to Avid's standard media storage location (the Avid MediaFiles folders), instead of just linking to the existing media files.

There are two big advantages to importing your footage:

■ All your media files will be safely in Avid's managed media directory

■ Overall system performance is better with Avid native media

Since you will be creating new media files, and investing some time in the process, it is best to double-check your Import settings before you perform the Import.

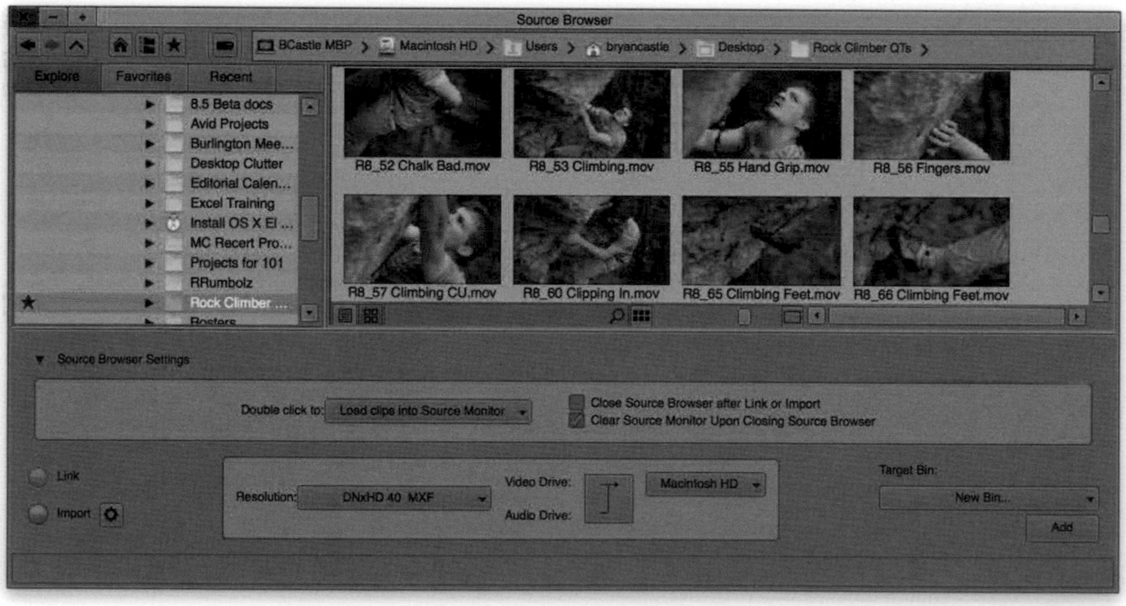

Figure 2.12 Set the Source Browser to Import Mode and set the format for the new media files using the Media Creation controls that appear.

To prepare for Import:

1. Click the **IMPORT** button in the bottom left corner of the Source Browser, Settings pane.

    The Source Browser changes to Import mode and a new group of Media Creation controls appear in the Settings pane, as shown in Figure. 2.12.

2. Click the gear icon next to the Import button.

    The Import Settings dialog box opens, as shown in Figure 2.13.

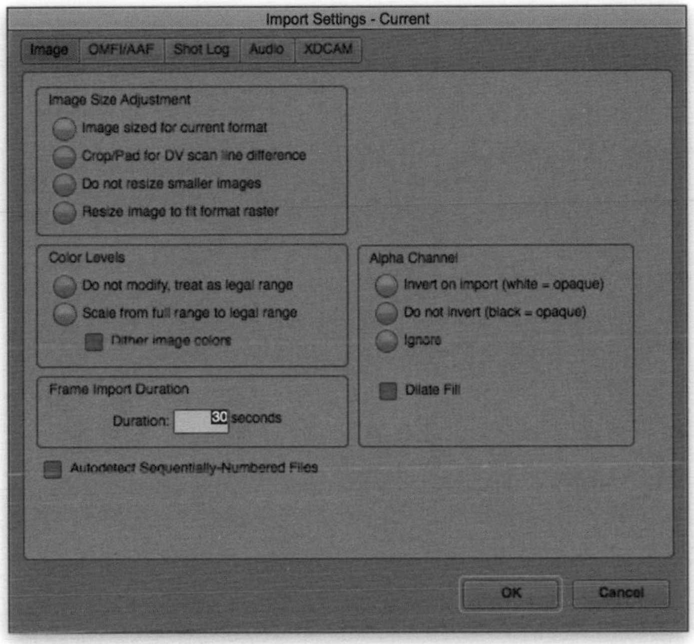

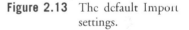

Figure 2.13   The default Import settings.

The default settings work well for video and audio files of the same format as the project. If importing still images, you may wish to modify the settings.

3. To import still images or graphic files, select **RESIZE IMAGE TO FIT FORMAT RASTER** in the Image Size Adjustment section. This keeps your images from being distorted on import.

4. If importing graphics with any transparency information, such as a TV station logo, select **INVERT ON IMPORT** in the Alpha Channel section.

    This is the default setting, and you'll rarely need to change it.

    Color and brightness for broadcast television is different than on a computer. When receiving files from a graphic artist it's most common to scale their file to legal (broadcast) level. From cameras, they will need to consult the camera crew as to how the files were shot, in order to determine whether scaling is required or not.

5. Click **OK** to close the Import Settings dialog box.

6. Click the **RESOLUTION** drop-down menu and select the desired video resolution. For this example, choose either **DNxHD 36 OR ProRes MXF**.

7. Select the DRIVE on which to save the new media files.

8. Click OK.

You are now ready to import. Using the Source Browser to import is the same as using it for linking – simply drag the clips you want from the Source Browser to the bin.

 Looking for a shortcut? You can skip the Source Browser and drag files directly from the desktop to a bin. Media Composer will import them based on the current Import and Media Creation settings, so be sure these are configured as needed before drag-and-drop importing.

To learn more about working with graphic images and animations, take the MC110: Media Composer Fundamentals II class from your nearest Avid Learning Partner.

Input Clips with Drag-and-Drop

You can input clips to your project by dragging them directly from an OS window to a bin. The default behavior is to import them, but you can use a modifier key to link the clips instead.

To import clips:

-   Drag the clips from the OS window to an open bin.

To link to clips:

-   Hold the Alt key (Windows) or Option key (Mac) and then drag the clips from the OS window to an open bin

If you plan to import clips using drag-and-drop, it is best to check your Input settings first, since the clips will be imported using the current settings.

Deleting Unwanted Clips

As you're busy inputting the media for your project, you may find that you accidentally include a clip you don't want in the project. No problem. You can just delete the clip from the bin.

To delete a clip:

1. Select the unwanted clip(s) in the bin.

2. Press the Delete key on the keyboard.

   A window pops up, asking you what you want to delete, as shown in Figure 2.14. If working with linked clips, the only option is to delete the clip.

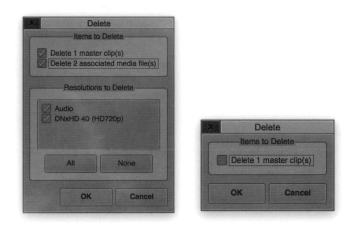

Figure 2.14   The Delete window differs for Avid native master clips vs linked master clips.

3. Click the **CHECKBOXES** to select the items to delete, and then click **OK**.

   If you selected media files to be deleted, a confirmation box will appear.

4. Click **OK** to continue.

> ⚠️ **Warning: Media deletion is permanent. You cannot undo a media deletion. Anytime you are deleting media, it is best to double-check your selections.**

 Exercise Break: Exercise 2.2
Pause here to practice what you've learned.

Preparing to Edit

The first step in the editing process happens well before you make your first cut. It is to review your footage and organize your shots into bins. We will start with a simple process that works for the starter project you are editing here. In a large, feature-length project, this is a more complex and formal process, requiring one or more full-time assistant editors.

There are several things to do before you get started:

1.   Watch the footage.

2.   Name (or rename) the master clips and organize them into bins.

3.   Set edit marks around selected sections.

4.   Add comments or keywords.

Watching the Footage

The first step of organizing the footage is to simply watch it. At the most basic level, you need to be able to identify clips (and possibly rename them). More importantly, you are watching the footage with a critical eye to really see what you have to work with.

Most editors are not on set during production, so this may be the first opportunity you have to see the material. (Some editors even steer clear of going on set to avoid having it bias their perspective of the footage.) On the other hand, you may have been on set or even running the camera yourself. Even if this is the case, it is important to watch the footage critically. You may notice things in the dailies that you missed on set. Maybe something in the background is distracting; maybe there are focus or exposure problems, maybe what you remember to be a really emotional moment on set plays really flat on camera, or maybe you discover a gem that you didn't know was there.

 As you watch the footage, also look for those happy accidents—a focus adjustment between takes when the talent is looking pensive, a great reaction (regardless of the thing they are reacting to), etc. These are hidden gems that you can use to make the piece shine!

As an editor, this is your only chance to get a first impression of the footage. Savor it! Pay attention to the experience. The thoughts and impressions you have the first time you watch the footage are invaluable!

What you look for in the footage and how you critique the performances of the talent will vary depending on the genre of the piece, but the questions are always similar. Ask yourself:

■   Which performances are best? Which are the weakest?

■   Which performances convey the best emotion? Which moments are most believable?

■   When do you find yourself getting absorbed in the story?

■   Which images are the most visually striking or best convey the mood of the scene?

■   How extensive is the coverage? Do you have options for cutting around weak performances?

■   Which sounds define the scene? Are they present where/when you need them to be?

■   Is it hard to hear or understand the dialogue?

Watch and listen! Remember, you can manipulate audio and video elements separately. Take note of natural sounds that you can use, especially in b-roll.

Above all, enjoy this moment. Here at the beginning of your project, the pressure is at its lowest and the possibilities at their greatest.

Loading and Playing a Master Clip

There are several different ways to play a master clip in Media Composer. Let's go through a couple, and then you can use the one that's most intuitive for you. You can play a clip in the Composer's Source monitor, in the bin.

To load a master clip into the Source monitor:

- Double-click the icon in the bin (in Text view).

- Double-click the thumbnail image (in Frame or Script view).

- Drag one or more clips from the bin.

To play a master clip in the Source monitor:

- Click the Play button below the Source monitor.

- Press the space bar.

Playing a clip at normal speed is all you need to do to watch the footage the first time. However, you will be doing a lot more than that. You will be working to precisely edit this material, cutting both picture and sound, and for that, you need more advanced controls—namely, J-K-L.

Playing a Clip using J-K-L

The J-K-L keys (see Figure 2.15) are used to *shuttle* through footage—that is, to play forward and backward at varying speeds. The J-K-L functions, pioneered by Avid, are nearly universal with NLEs today. If you learned to use them in another app, they work pretty much the same here. If not, now is a great time to learn to use them. Learning to use J-K-L now will save your sanity and make you much more efficient as an editor.

Figure 2.15 The J-K-L keys offer refined multispeed playback.

The J-K-L keys work as follows:

- To play forward at normal speed, press the L key once. Normal speed is typically 24, 25, or 30 fps (whatever is the frame rate of your project).

- To stop, press the K key.

- To play backward at normal speed, press the J key once.

- To play forward faster than normal, press the L key repeatedly. Every time you press the L key, the system will play faster, at 1×, 2×, 3×, 5×, and 8× normal speed, respectively.

- To play backward faster than normal, press the J key repeatedly. The system plays in reverse by the same increments: 1×, 2×, 3×, 5×, and 8× normal speed.

- To play backward at 1/4 speed, press and hold the K+J keys.

- To play forward at 1/4 speed, press and hold the K+L keys.

- Hold down the "K" key, and then quickly tap either J or L to move just one frame at a time.

During slow-shuttle, not only does the playhead move through the footage at a slow six to eight frames per second, but you also hear slow-speed, analog-style audio. This is perfect for setting the position indicator precisely at the beginning of a sentence or word. The J-K-L features also work when trimming, which we'll discuss later. Because the J-K-L features work when selecting portions of shots, as well as when trimming, they are incredibly useful. Many would say indispensable. For cutting dialogue, it is just brilliant.

 You can use the same techniques described here to play a clip in the bin in Frame or Script view. This can be a great way to quickly review a clip to make sure it's the one you want before loading it.

Adjusting Audio Levels of Source Clips

As you watch the raw footage, you may come across clips that are too loud or too quiet. It is best to adjust these as you encounter them. Any adjustments you make to the master clip will persist to the segments you put into the sequence. This not only saves time – one adjustment to the master clip vs adjusting each segment in the sequence – but produces a more consistent result, right from the start.

To adjust the audio levels of source clips, you will use the Audio Mixer, shown in Figure 2.16. The number of faders displayed in the Audio Mixer is based on the number of audio tracks in the master clip, so don't be surprised if yours appears slightly different.

Figure 2.16: Use the slider in the Audio Mixer to adjust the audio level of a master clip that plays too quietly or too loudly.

To adjust the audio level:

1.   Select **TOOLS > AUDIO MIXER**.

2.   With the master clip loaded in the Source monitor, **PLAY** the clip.

     Look at the level meter in the Audio Mixer as the clip plays. A good level for most sounds you want to hear is between -20 dB and -8 dB. The level you set here is not permanent, and can be adjusted in the sequence at any time in the future.

3.   Drag the slider up to raise the level, drag down to lower the level.

Organizing Clips in Bins

It is best to start organizing your material right from the start so it's easier to find what you want, when you want it. For now, that will simply mean moving the master clips to another bin, grouping similar types of clips, and renaming the clips to make it easier to identify them. The process for each of these tasks is easy and intuitive.

 Media Composer tracks master clips to their corresponding media files using other bits of data besides the name, so renaming a clip does not cause any problems in Media Composer. However, if you are collaborating with editors on non-Avid systems or going to a non-Avid system for finishing, it may be useful to keep the camera-created name intact.

To move a master clip from one bin to another:

1.   Open the destination **BIN**.

2.   Drag the clip's **ICON**, or the **HEADFRAME**, from the source bin to the destination bin.

To rename a master clip:

1.   In the bin, click on the master clip's **NAME**.

     The name becomes highlighted, ready for you to type a new name.

2.   Type a new **NAME**.

3.   Press **ENTER**.

     Just like with renaming bins, pressing Return on a Mac will select the next name down; while pressing Enter (on the numeric keypad) will simply accept the name you entered.

Marking Clips

In addition to organizing your master clips, the other thing to do while watching the footage is to mark the parts of each clip that interest you. This is done using edit marks. *Edit marks*, specifically IN marks and OUT marks, indicate the beginning and end of a region of media with which you want to do something. Every editing application has some form of edit marks, so you may already be familiar with them in concept.

At this point, you will use edit marks to denote a region of interest—some piece of the clip that you think you may want to use later. Media Composer will remember the marks you apply. The next time you open that master clip, the marks will still be there. Marking the footage at this stage is a great way to speed up the editing process and keeps you from having to remember later what you liked from each shot.

You can have only one set of marks per master clip. Markers and subclips are two other tools that you can use to mark multiple areas of interest in a master clip. You will learn more about these later in the course.

Identify the Mark IN and Mark OUT Icons

The tools for making edit marks are found on either side of the Play button in each monitor (see Figure 2.17) and in the Timeline toolbar. You can also use shortcut keys on the keyboard.

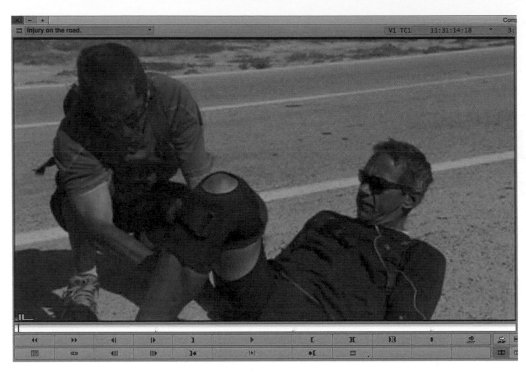

Figure 2.17 Buttons for marking clips are found under each monitor.

The marking button icons, their functions, and their keyboard shortcuts are listed in Table 2.2.

Table 2.2: Buttons for Marking Clips

Button	Function	Keyboard Shortcut(s)
]	Mark IN	E, I
[	Mark OUT	R, O
][	Mark Clip	T
▐]	Clear IN	D
[▌	Clear OUT	F
][	Clear Marks	G
]◄	Go to IN	Q
►[	Go to OUT	W
|►|	Play IN-OUT	6

You can reposition an IN or OUT mark by placing the position indicator where you want the mark to be and then clicking the Mark IN or Mark OUT button. (You don't need to clear the previous mark first.)

Note that you can mark a clip on the fly, as you play it. If this is done from the keyboard, the clip continues to play. If this is done with the mouse, the clip will stop playing.

Adding Comments and Keywords

As you learned in Lesson 1, a bin's Script View is ideal for adding production notes, comments and keywords to help you remember things about each clip and to locate clips with Media Composer's robust "Find" feature. (Figure 2.18) Don't rely on your memory. As your projects get bigger and more complex, it will be harder and harder to remember every detail.

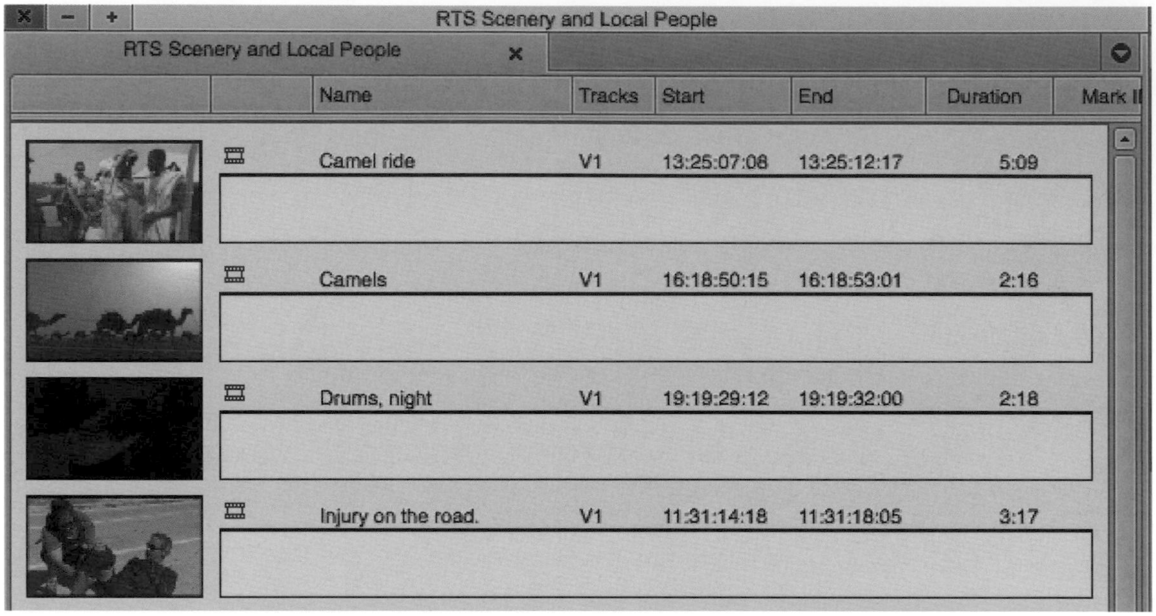

		Name	Tracks	Start	End	Duration	Mark I
		Camel ride	V1	13:25:07:08	13:25:12:17	5:09	
		Camels	V1	16:18:50:15	16:18:53:01	2:16	
		Drums, night	V1	19:19:29:12	19:19:32:00	2:18	
		Injury on the road.	V1	11:31:14:18	11:31:18:05	3:17	

Figure 2.18 Use the Script View to make notes about the footage when you watch it.

To add comments and keywords to clips:

1. Click the **SCRIPT VIEW** button in the bin.

2. Load and play a clip to decide what info needs to be added.

3. Click in the **COMMENTS** field next to the clip in the bin, and type the keywords, phrases, or comments.

 Exercise Break: Exercise 2.3 and 2.4
Pause here to practice what you've learned.

Saving Your Work

It is important to save and back up your work. Although the Avid system automatically saves for you at regular intervals, you should get into the habit of manually saving your bins to protect your work in case of power outages or other mishaps.

Manual Saves

You can save a project yourself, manually, any time you want. An asterisk in the title bar of your bin indicates that a change has been made which has not been saved yet. This change may be as simple as renaming a clip in your bin or even adding marks to a clip. When you manually save a bin, your original bin file is updated and a backup copy is placed in the Attic.

You can save an individual bin or all bins in the project at once. Because everything needs to be in a bin, saving all open bins means that all work is saved.

To save a single bin:

1. Click the **BIN** you want to save to select it.

2. Press **CTRL+S** (Windows) or **COMMAND+S** (Mac). Alternatively, choose **FILE > SAVE BIN**.

To save all bins in a project:

1. Click the **PROJECT WINDOW** to activate it, or press the shortcut keys **CTRL+9** (Windows) or **COMMAND+9** (Mac).

2. Press **CTRL+S** (Windows) or **COMMAND+S** (Mac). Alternatively, choose **FILE > SAVE ALL**.

 Exercise Break: Exercise 2.5
Pause here to practice what you've learned.

Review/Discussion Questions

1.   What is the difference between linking and importing media?

2.   True or false: When linking media, you can remove the original source drive or camera card containing the media and your media will remain online.

3.   Where can you get additional AMA plug-ins?

4.   What modifier must you use when dragging clips to a bin to link rather than import?

5.   Name two ways to load a clip in the Source monitor.

6.   What function is associated with the space bar by default?

7.   What is the value of using the J-K-L keys to control playback?

8.   Name the default keys for marking IN and OUT marks.

9.   How can you save your work?

Lesson 2 Keyboard Shortcuts

Key	Shortcut
Ctrl+N (Windows)/Command+N (Mac)	Create a new bin
J-K-L keys	Shuttle
Ctrl+S (Windows)/Command+S (Mac)	Save
Ctrl+9 (Windows)/Command+9 (Mac)	Activate the Project window
Ctrl+A (windows)/Command+A (Mac)	Select all (clips)
Ctrl+L (Windows)/Command+L (Mac)	Enlarges height of Timeline tracks, enlarges clip frames, and enlarges image in a selected monitor

Ingest

In this exercise, we will create a New Project and Ingest some audio and video media to the project. Then, you will begin the process of reviewing the clips and preparing them for editing.

Media Used: Rock Climber

Duration: 30 minutes

GOALS

- Create a new project
- Use the Source Browser to input media files
- Review raw footage
- Add keywords and comments to the master clips
- Adjust Clip Gain to make the interview more audible
- Save the project

Exercise 2.1: Create and Setup a New Project

In this exercise, you will start by creating a new project.

To create a New Project and Bins:

1. In the Select Project window, click the **NEW PROJECT** button.

    A dialog window opens, as shown in Figure 2.19.

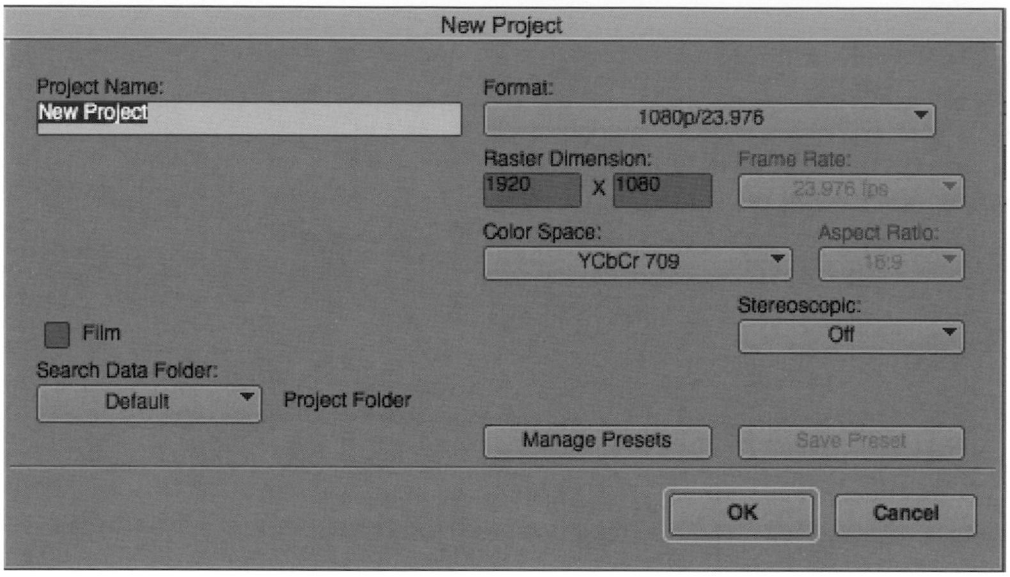

Figure 2.19 The New Project dialog.

The Project Name field is already highlighted, ready for you to type the name.

2. Type the name, **THE ROCK CLIMBER**.

3. Set the project format to **1080P/23.976**; leave all other settings at their default values.

4. Click **OK**, and the new project will appear in the Select Project window.

5. Click the name "The Rock Climber," to select the project. Click **OK** to open it.

6. Rename the default bin to be "RC Sequences."

7. Click the **NEW BIN** button several times to create additional bins.

8. Rename two bins as "RC Music" and "RC Raw Footage" respectively.

9. Delete any extra bins.

Exercise 2.2: Input

We will link to material that we will work with in the following three exercises before returning to Running the Sahara to later learn about adding some effects.

In the lesson you learned about the difference between importing media into Avid Media Composer (which creates new Avid native MXF media files) and linking to the camera native media using AMA (Avid Media Access) plug-ins provided by the camera manufacturers. It is the linking method we'll be using here. When we were looking at Running the Sahara, we were looking at Avid native media.

To input media:

1. Select **FILE > INPUT > SOURCE BROWSER**.

    The Source Browser window opens.

2. In the Explore window on the left of the Source browser, browse to your Media Drive and in the main window in the Source Browser find the **ROCK CLIMBER QTS** folder and select it.

3. Double-click on the folder.

    The clips should populate the main window in the Source Browser.

4. Click in the main window in the Source Browser and select all the clips. Press **CTRL+A** (Windows) or **COMMAND+A** (Mac).

5. In the lower part of the Source Browser make sure that **LINK** is selected (a radio button), and that the Target Bin is set to The RC Raw Footage bin.

6. Click **LINK**.

    The bin will fill with the clips. Notice they all have the link icon.

7. Close the Source Browser.

8. Drag the clip **179_SHORT_WE ARE YOUNG WE ARE FREE_0037** from the RC Raw Footage bin to the RC Music bin.

 If you are taking this course at an Avid Learning Partner school, and do not have the folder 'Rock Climber' on the Media Drive, your instructor can direct you where to find it.

Exercise 2.3: Setting up to View Your Shots

Now that you have some video clips in a bin, you can use the different bin views to determine which will work best for previewing and organizing this project's clips.

In the lower-left corner of the bin window, next to the Fast menu, are three buttons controlling how we view the bin. We are currently on the left-most of these, "Text."

To set a bin view:

1. Click on the middle button, **FRAME**.

    The items in your bin now appear as images displaying the first frame of each clip. This is not only a handy way to visually identify the content of each clip, but it also makes it very apparent which clips are video and which are audio only.

    It may be that the default first frame is not a good indicator of the clips content. We can change that by changing the "representative frame."

2. Move the bin window to the top left of your screen by dragging its header and then drag the lower-right corner of the bin window down to the make the bin fill the screen.

    I'm assuming you are working with one screen, if you have two then you should already have a sufficiently large bin.

3. Press **CTRL+L** (Windows) or **COMMAND+L** (Mac) to enlarge the frames.

    Now you should be able to see the selected clip better.

4. When you have done this, use the **ALIGN AND FILL > FILL WINDOW** command in the bin's Fast menu to make sure all the clips are on the screen.

    There is also the Fill Sorted command as these shots are numbered sequentially; this displays them in their shooting order.

5. Select **R8_36 CLIMBING HANGING**.

    This clip's representative frame shows an overhanging outcrop of rock. There is no sign of Matt, but the shot does eventually pan over to him.

6. Press the **SPACE BAR** to play the clip frames. When you see Matt, press the **SPACE BAR** again to stop.

    Next time you glance at this clip in Frame view, you will know exactly what the contents are.

7. Now click on the rightmost button, **SCRIPT**.

    Script view is like the best of both worlds. You get a frame to identify the clip visually, plus some columns of information. The columns in Script view are based on the current Text view columns.

    There is also a large Comment text field, where you can write comments for clips as needed. Any comments you type will also appear in the Comments column in Text view.

Exercise 2.4: Viewing Your Clips

The Source monitor is where you can play and mark your clips before editing them into a sequence. Let's take a quick tour of the Source monitor to help you understand the different tools. The top of the Source monitor includes two menus that display information about the current clip: the Clip Name menu on the left and the Tracking Information menu on the right. You can use the Tracking Information menu to view a clip's timecode and a variety of other related information.

To play clips in the Source monitor:

1. Load **R8_112 SLOW FINGERS WALL** into the Source monitor.

    We can see in the Timeline Track panel that this clip has a video track and an audio track.

    Below the image in the Source monitor is the position bar. The blue position indicator shows which frame you are viewing as it moves along the position bar. Try out all the different ways of playing the clip.

2. Drag the **POSITION INDICATOR** right or left in the position bar to scrub through your clip.

3. Click anywhere on the position bar to move the position indicator to that frame.

4. Press the **HOME** key to go to the beginning (head) of the clip or the **END** key to go to the end (tail) of the clip.

5. Press the **SPACE BAR** or click the **PLAY** button in the Source monitor's toolbar to play the clip.

    When the clip finishes playing, it stops on the last full frame of the clip.

6. On the keyboard, press the **RIGHT ARROW** and **LEFT ARROW** keys to step one frame back or forward.

    The functions called Step Forward/Step Backward are also on the 1, 2, 3, and 4 keys. 1 and 2 step ten frames (8 frames in a 24 fps project), while 3 and 4 step 1. 5 plays and stops play while 6 plays between IN and OUT, which currently is from the Position Indicator to the end of the shot.

7. Finally, try the exceptionally useful J-K-L shuttling. Place three middle fingers over the J, K, and L keys.

8. Press **L** once to play forward at normal speed.

9. Pause by pressing **K**.

10. Pressing multiple times increases shuttle speed 2×, 3×, 5×, and 8×.

11. J does the same playing in reverse.

12. Holding K in combination with either J or L plays the footage in slow motion (at about one-quarter speed).

13. Holding K while tapping either J or L shuttles the footage one frame at a time, either forward or backward.

14. You like this clip and would like to use it in the opening sequence (You will actually) and you want to make a note to that effect.

15. At the bottom of the bin, click on the rightmost of the three Bin View buttons, **SCRIPT**.

16. In the large Comment text field, write a comment such as "use for opening sequence."

17. At the bottom of the bin, click on the leftmost button, **TEXT**.

    You will find that a text column, called Comments, has your comment associated with the clip when the "Basic" Bin view is displayed. (You may have to scroll to it depending on the Bin view you are in.)

18. Double-click the master clip **R02_02(b) INTERVIEW** to load it into the Source monitor, or drag it in using the icon (not the name). Play it. The audio level is very low. We should adjust this now.

19. Select **TOOLS > AUDIO MIXER**.

20. The Audio Mixer opens with one channel, as this is a mono clip.

21. Drag the slider up to +12 (dB) to raise the level as far as we can in this tool.

22. Listen to the clip and confirm that this is a level you can work with.

Exercise 2.5: Saving Your Work

Despite the excellent Auto-Save feature, a manual save of all open Bins is an excellent thing to do when you have a moment. You can save bins on an individual basis, but the best way is to save them all at once.

To save your work manually:

1. Press **CTRL+9** (Windows) or **COMMAND+9** (Mac) to select the Project window.

2. Press **CTRL+S** (Windows) or **COMMAND+S** (Mac) to save all bins and settings.

3. (Optional) If ending your edit session now, close the application by pressing Ctrl+Q (Windows) or Command+Q (Mac). Confirm application shutdown by clicking **LEAVE** in the dialog box.

Building Your Sequence

With some media in your project, you are ready to start editing!

Paul Cézanne, the famous French painter, said, "It is so fine and yet so terrible to stand in front of a blank canvas." Indeed! Getting started in any creative work can be a difficult thing. It is both exciting and oddly intimidating. Where do you start? How will you know if it's the right edit?

The key is to just plunge in, knowing full well you can (and will) change it later. The beauty of non-linear editing is that your "first step" doesn't have to be at the beginning of the project—which is often the most difficult place to begin.

Duration: 60 minutes

Media Used: Rock Climber

GOALS

- **Create a new sequence**
- **Locate audio cues in source material using audio waveforms**
- **Build your sequence using splice and overwrite using three-point editing techniques**
- **Remove material from the sequence using Lift and Overwrite**
- **Learn the default keyboard mappings for common edit functions**
- **Manage tracks to maintain sync**

Overview

Now that you have done all the prep work, it's time to start editing. The first step in any editing process is to create a *rough cut*. A rough cut is a full assembly of the scene or video that focuses on story structure, with an understanding that there are many details yet to be polished.

In this lesson, you will create a documentary scene. It uses a common and versatile sequence structure, being fundamentally the same as how you would build a news package, a magazine segment, a commercial spot or promotional video for a company website, and more.

This sequence will be a combination of *talking heads* – people being interviewed or talking to the camera – and a montage of images over that narration, with some music and sound effects underneath. So what does that look like in the Timeline? Take a look at a finished sequence, shown in Figure 3.1.

Figure 3.1 A rough cut sequence of a documentary scene.

Here's how the sequence is laid out:

- **V1:** Picture
- **A1:** Natural Sound
- **A2:** VO (Voice Over)
- **A3:** Music (Left Channel)
- **A 4:** Music (Right Channel)

 If you want to make it easier to remember how you're using the tracks, you can rename tracks in the Timeline. To do so, in the Track Selector Panel, right-click on a track number, select Rename Track, and type a new name for the track. It is highly suggested to include the actual track name within your name. For example: "A2 - Voice Over."

How an editor chooses to approach the rough cut can vary, depending on personal creative impulses, the genre, and the size of a project. Many new editors want to immediately start cutting the video. Instead, I'm going to teach you another strategy.

To build this piece efficiently, we will be following these general steps:

1. Create the **SEQUENCE** and add **TRACKS**.
2. Add the **INTERVIEW SEGMENTS** to structure the narrative.
3. Cut a montage of **ACTION SHOTS** to visually support the story.
4. Refine and tighten the **EDIT**.
5. Add **SFX**, **VIDEO EFFECTS**, and **TITLES**.

A Deliberate Approach

Many young editors today want to immediately start editing using drag-and-drop. You can certainly work that way in Media Composer, and you will learn how to do so in the next lesson. But, we are intentionally starting with a more deliberate approach.

In this lesson, we begin by teaching you the core editing functions – Splice-In, Overwrite, Extract, and Lift – and do so using the buttons on the interface and the keys on the keyboard. This may seem a little slower to start, but be patient. A bit like playing the scales when learning a musical instrument, this approach allows you to focus your attention on the mechanics of editing and start building the muscle memory that will actually let you edit much faster, and more accurately in the long run than you could using drag-and-drop. Plus, once you deeply understand how editing in Media Composer works, you can easily work with the mouse or the keyboard, however the mood strikes you.

Creating a New Sequence

Creating a new sequence is a bit like clicking the New Message button in any messaging app, which creates a blank message ready for you to start typing. When you create a new, blank sequence, the system gets everything ready for you to start editing – it places the sequence in the bin, gives it a generic name, and loads it into the Timeline and Record monitor.

One way to create a sequence is to just edit something into an empty Timeline. Media Composer will automatically create a sequence to record the edit. You can also create and save a sequence ahead of time prior to making any edits.

To create a new sequence:

- Right-click in the Timeline and choose **New > Sequence**.

- Select **Timeline > New > Sequence**.

    If several bins are open but none highlighted (also referred to as, *active*), the Select dialog box will open, asking you which bin you wish to create your new sequence in (see Figure 3.2). Select a target bin, and click **OK**.

    The new sequence appears with the generic title "Untitled Sequence n." Each new sequence is numbered incrementally until you rename it. You should immediately rename the new sequence by typing a new name while the Name field is still active in the bin. For example, "My Movie Name version 1." Adding a version number will be very helpful in keeping track of revisions.

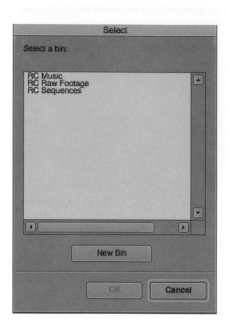

Figure 3.2 Choose the bin in which to save the new sequence.

 The keyboard shortcut to create a new sequence is shown in each menu: Ctrl+Shift+N (Windows) or Command+Shift+N (Mac). Learn to use keyboard shortcuts to keep your edit sessions moving quickly.

Working with Tracks

Like most NLEs today, Media Composer is a track-based editor. Tracks are used to organize the clips of video and audio in the sequence. What's more, the activation and deactivation of tracks (using the Track Selector buttons) is how you control where edits are made, where effects and markers are added, where volume is adjusted, and more.

In other words, tracks matter!

You can edit up to 64 audio tracks (including multichannel audio tracks) and up to 24 video tracks in the Timeline. By default, each new sequence provides V1, A1, and A2. As you have already seen, you will eventually need more tracks than that.

In addition, because you are not dragging clips to the location you want, you will need to connect—that is, *patch*—source video or audio tracks to different record tracks if you want to edit it to an alternate track in the sequence (e.g. putting music onto A5 and A6). It sounds more complicated than it is, and we'll show you how it's done in a moment.

Adding Tracks

To add the next mono audio track:

- With a sequence in the Timeline, choose TIMELINE > NEW > AUDIO TRACK > MONO.

- Right-click in the Timeline, and choose NEW > AUDIO TRACK > MONO.

- Press CTRL+U (Windows) or COMMAND+U (Mac).

Media Composer supports multichannel tracks, including stereo and surround sound tracks. You will learn more about working with multichannel tracks in later books in the Avid Learning Series.

Manually Patching Tracks

Patching tracks enables you to edit a source track onto any track in the sequence.

To patch a track from a source clip to a different track in the sequence:

■ Click the Source Track Selector button (V1 in the picture below) and drag the arrow to the target record track on which you want to make the edit (see Figure 3.3). The source track you selected jumps next to the record track and becomes highlighted.

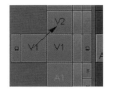

Figure 3.3
Drag from the source track to the target record track to patch the track.

■ Click and hold the left mouse button with the pointer on the source track and the system will offer you the available Record tracks you can patch to (see Figure 3.4). This is useful when the source clip's audio is on track A1, but you'd like to place it on track A5 in your sequence.

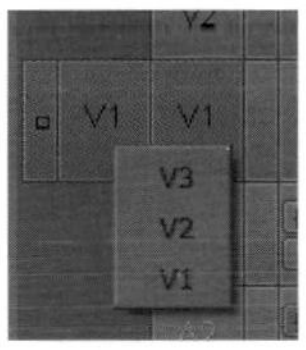

Figure 3.4
You can also patch tracks through the pop-up menu. To access it, click and hold on the source track.

Auto-Patching

Auto-Patching is a setting that allows you to automatically patch tracks based on track activation. If you use keyboard shortcuts to change the activation of your tracks, you can patch tracks without reaching for the mouse.

To patch tracks using Auto-Patching:

1. Disable the **TRACKS** in the Record column of the Track Selector Panel to which source tracks are currently patched.

2. Now, enable the desired **TRACKS**, by clicking on the Record Track Selectors.

   The source tracks will jump to the new enabled Record tracks, indicating the patch has occurred.

Locating Audio Cues

Many edit decisions are motivated by sound. It may be a word, a pause, a gasp, the slamming of a door, or a musical cue. That cue may tell you where to mark or where to cut. Being able to find it quickly will keep you moving rather than slowing you down. Media Composer provides several tools to help you locate these audio cues.

The Track Control panel, shown in Figure 3.5, is a collapsible panel with numerous per-track audio controls.

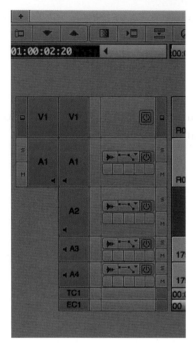

Figure 3.5 The Track Control panel contains useful per-track audio controls. To open and close the Track Control Panel, click the small disclosure triangle next to the green Timecode display.

Displaying Audio Waveforms (Per Track)

Audio waveforms display a sample plot of the entire amplitude of the track and can help you visually locate points in an audio track for editing or trimming. You can display waveforms for all audio tracks in the Timeline or you can select individual tracks for waveform display.

To display audio waveforms for selected tracks:

1.   Open the **TRACK CONTROL PANEL** by clicking the small triangle next to the green timecode display.

2.   Click the **WAVEFORM** button in the Track Control panel for the tracks for which you want to display audio waveforms. The waveform button looks like this. (See Figure 3.6.)

Figure 3.6 The waveform appears in the selected tracks.

 Hold the Alt key (Windows) or Option key (Mac) to activate waveforms on all tracks simultaneously.

Improving the Visibility of the Waveform

Depending on the recorded volume of the audio, the waveform plot may be quite small or quite large. Music clips, for instance, often display with solid black waveforms because they are so loud. In Media Composer, you adjust the size of the waveforms independent of the volume or clip gain. This means the display of the waveforms change without changing the audio's loudness level.

■ To enlarge the size of the waveform display without enlarging its track, select the track(s) to adjust (using the Track Selectors) and then press Ctrl+Alt+L (Windows) or Command+Option+L (Mac).

■ To reduce the size of the waveform display without reducing its track, select the track(s) to adjust (using the Track Selectors) and then press Ctrl+Alt+K (Windows) or Command+Option+K (Mac).

Toggling Source/Record in the Timeline

You can display the waveform graphs for source material in the same way that you display waveforms for sequence material. Waveforms can be a helpful visual guide when editing audio in the Timeline. It also helps when setting marks on master clips with dialogue, as you will be doing in the exercise.

The key to seeing source waveforms is to display your source material in the Timeline first.

To display waveforms for source audio:

1. Load a **MASTER CLIP** with audio into the Source monitor.

2. In the bottom-left corner of the Timeline, click the **TOGGLE SOURCE/RECORD IN TIMELINE** button. (See Figure 3.7.)

Figure 3.7 The Toggle Source/Record in Timeline button.

When active, the button glows bright green, and the position indicator changes to the same bright green, indicating that you are looking at the Source material. (See Figure 3.8.)

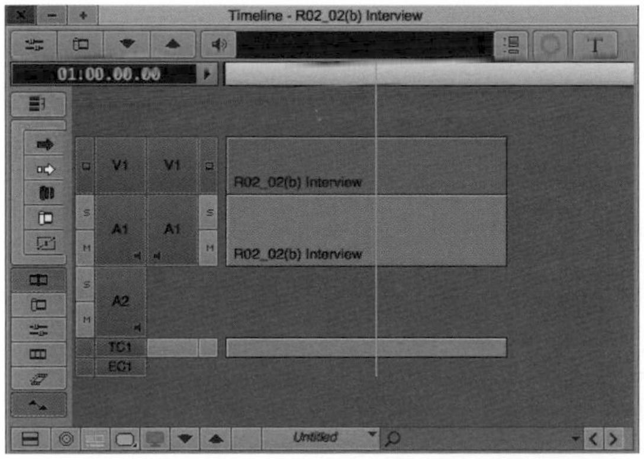

Figure 3.8 The bright green position indicator alerts you to the fact that you are looking at the source material.

The Timeline now displays the Source tracks. This is especially evident in the Track panel. The two Source-side track selectors now appear on the right, and the three Record-side track selectors now appear on the left..

At this point, you enable waveforms on the source tracks in exactly the same way that you did previously on the record tracks.

3.   In the Timeline, click the small **DISCLOSURE TRIANGLE** next to the Timecode window to open the Track Control panel.

4.   While pressing the **ALT** (Windows) or **OPTION** (Mac) key, click the **WAVEFORM** button on one of the audio tracks.

The waveforms on all audio tracks are enabled.

Building Your Sequence with Splice-In

The two most common ways to add shots to the sequence is using *Splice-In* or *Overwrite*. Splice-In adds more material to the sequence. Overwrite replaces material that is already there.

Splicing Video Clips

"Splice" is a term that Avid borrowed from film editing. To add a new shot to a reel of film, the editor would splice it in by cutting the existing film at the point the new shot was supposed to start and then taping the shot, or segment, at each end. With the new piece added, the film was longer. The Splice-In function works in much the same way. It adds the new shot into the sequence by creating a cut point and inserting the segment between the existing frames. The new shot makes the track longer—which also, frequently, makes the sequence longer.

 Other NLEs often call this type of edit an insert edit or a ripple edit. If you are familiar with insert editing in Final Cut Pro or Premiere Pro, you already understand how the Splice-In function works.

Splice-In is often used to build the scene. If you are adding segments in order, though, you don't see the real behavior of Splice-In. Splicing a shot between existing segments shows its real value. Splice-In pushes all subsequent, or downstream, material further down the Timeline (to the right). As shown in Figure 3.9, when adding a new shot between others, shot Y (and every other shot after it, like shot "Z") is pushed along and now plays over a slightly later portion.

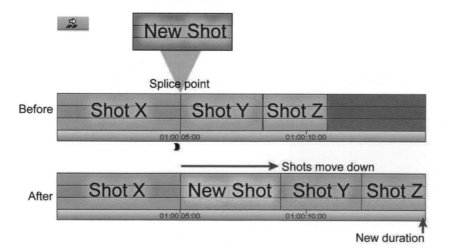

Figure 3.9 Splicing a segment between others moves all subsequent segments down the Timeline to the right.

The yellow Splice-In button is found between the Composer monitors (see Figure 3.10). Better yet, its keyboard equivalent: the V key.

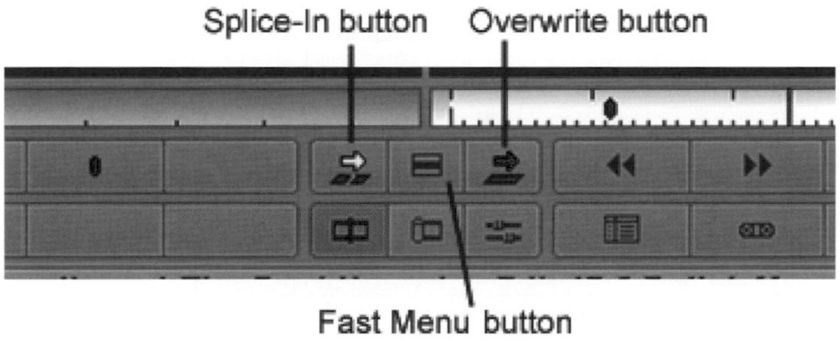

Figure 3.10 The Splice-In button between the Source and Record monitor.

To splice a shot into your sequence using the Splice-In:

1. View and mark IN and OUT within the **SOURCE CLIP**.

2. In the Timeline, place the **POSITION INDICATOR** where you want to splice the shot into the sequence. Optionally, mark an **IN** point.

   If you mark an IN point, the splice will happen at the IN point. If don't, the system will splice at the location of the position indicator.

3. Select the **SOURCE TRACK** and **RECORD TRACK** buttons for the tracks you want to use for the edit and ensure other tracks are deselected.

   In this example, source material on tracks V1 and A1 will be edited onto Record tracks V1 and A1 between existing segments because the blue position indicator is placed there (and because there is not an IN or OUT mark in the sequence). (See Figure 3.11.)

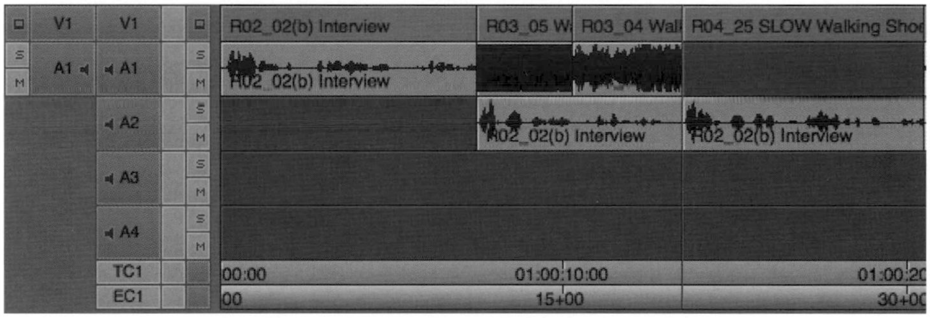

Figure 3.11 This patch has source V1 and A1 going to the same record tracks.

4. Press the **V** key on the keyboard or click the yellow **SPLICE-IN** button.

The clip is spliced into the sequence. (See Figure 3.12.)

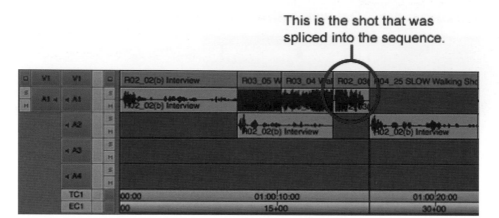

Figure 3.12 The audio and video segments are spliced between existing ones.

Maintaining Sync

Sync is the term that is used to describe when elements line-up as they should. One good example of this is the fact that the video from a shot of an actor speaking needs to line-up (i.e. "be in sync") with the audio that goes with it. If they do not line-up (i.e. are "out of sync") then the actors lips will move and the audio will be heard at a different time, making it look as if we're watch watching a poorly dubbed foreign film!

Maintaining the sync relationship between picture and sound is a very important component of editing – or at least, you should only break it intentionally, never by accident. Like any "yellow" function, Splice-In ripples (pushes) downstream material in the sequence and therefore can break sync. To maintain sync between picture and sound, you must edit tracks that are supposed to stay in sync equally. In other words, to stay in sync, be sure to add, or remove, the same amount (duration) from all tracks that have to stay in sync.

Figures 3.11 and 3.12 illustrate a fairly common scenario. You want to splice-in a shot that has only one or two audio tracks, but there is sync sound on other tracks further down the Timeline. How can you make the edit without breaking sync?

Simple: Enable all the tracks on which you need to maintain sync– e.g. A1-A4.

Because you've enabled A1–A4, your edits will affect those tracks equally. Because there is no source audio to put into A2-A4, Media Composer simply fills the space with filler, as shown in Figure 3.12.

 Tracks matter! Always glance at your track selection in the Track Selector panel before you perform an edit.

Concept: Understanding Filler

Filler refers to the empty space in the Timeline. The term is derived from the blank celluloid film used to keep picture and sound tracks in sync whenever there was a temporary gap in one or the other during the edit process. If you've used other editing applications you may be familiar with the term "slug." Filler and slug serve the same purpose. Thinking of it as filler rather than empty space is more accurate. In Media Composer, you can manipulate filler in the same ways you edit video or audio segments. You can add edits to it, trim it, apply effects to it, and more. This is different from any other NLE on the market, and provides some real advantages, specifically with trimming and in working with effects.

Exercise Break: Exercise 3.1
Pause here to practice what you've learned.

Editing with Overwrite

While Splice-In adds new material to the sequence; Overwrite replaces material already there. (Technically, you can use Overwrite to add a shot to the end of the sequence, but that's the rare exception to the rule.)

Overwrite is the perfect tool for adding *b-roll* or *cutaway* shots – action shots which visually support the interview.

To edit a clip using Overwrite:

1. Load your **CLIP** into the Source monitor.

2. Mark a combination of three **POINTS** in total between the source clip and the sequence by doing one of the following:

    *   Mark an IN point and an OUT point in the Timeline and mark an IN point or OUT point in the source clip. Alternatively, in the clip, simply place the position indicator where you want the overwrite to begin. The system figures out how many frames to overwrite in the segment to replace the exact number of frames marked in the Timeline. If the clip does not contain sufficient footage, the screen displays the message, "Insufficient source material to make this edit."

    *   Mark an IN point and an OUT point in your clip and mark an IN point or an OUT point in the sequence. Alternatively, in the sequence, simply place the position indicator where you want the overwrite to begin. The marked clip will be added into the sequence at the IN or OUT point you marked.

3. Click the **SOURCE TRACK** and **RECORD TRACK** buttons for the tracks you want to use for the edit.

4. Click the **OVERWRITE** button or press the **B** key on the keyboard.

    The marked section in the sequence is overwritten by the material you selected in the clip. The total length of the sequence does not change unless the new shot extends beyond the end of the sequence.

Exercise Break: Exercise 3.2
Pause here to practice what you've learned.

Removing Material from a Sequence

The rough cut is not an endless march forward, only adding material and making the sequence longer and longer. There are plenty of times when you will want to remove material from the sequence—because you want to change the shot, because you want to remove a portion of it for better timing, or for creative purposes.

You can remove footage from your sequence and either close or retain the gap that results. You'll be marking the portion you want to remove by placing IN and OUT marks in the sequence.

Lift

Lift removes material from the Timeline, leaving filler in its place. It is represented by a red up arrow (see Figure 3.13).

 Figure 3.13 The Lift button.

Lift is used if you want to maintain the rhythm of a sequence or the synchronization of the picture and audio tracks. This action is the inverse of overwriting; both lifting and overwriting maintain the integrity and duration of the sequence.

To lift material from the Timeline:

1. Mark an **IN** point and an **OUT** point at the start and end of the material to be removed.

2. Select the desired record **TRACKS** by enabling just the desired Track Selector buttons.

3. Press **Z** on the keyboard or click the **LIFT** button in the Timeline.

 You can use the Mark Clip button (or press the T key) to quickly select a whole clip for removal. Based on the record tracks you have selected and the location of the blue position indicator, the Mark Clip function automatically finds the IN and OUT of a clip in the sequence.

Extract

Extracting removes material from the Timeline and closes the gap left by its removal. This action is the inverse of splicing; both extracting and splicing affect the length of a track and/or the sequence. It is represented by a yellow arrow pointing upward (see Figure 3.14). In some other applications, they refer to what Avid calls "Extract" as a "Ripple Delete."

 Figure 3.14 The Extract button.

To extract material from the Timeline:

1. In the sequence, mark an **IN** point and an **OUT** point at the start and end of the material to be removed.

2. Select the desired record **TRACKS** by enabling their Track Selector buttons.

3. Press **X** on the keyboard or click the **EXTRACT** button in the Timeline.

Exercise Break: Exercise 3.3
Pause here to practice what you've learned.

Essential Tools

There are a number of tools that are essential to efficiently building a rough cut.

Timecode Displays and Center Duration

Timecode is used in numerous ways in production and post. Timecode on video assigns a unique number—an address, as it were—to every frame of video. This allows you to find any specific frame when needed. Timecode is expressed in the form of hours, minutes, seconds, and frames (HH:MM:SS:FF).

Information displays, above the Source monitor and the Record monitor, in the Composer window can be set to display a variety of timecode information. There is also a quick reference display, called Center Duration, which always displays the currently marked duration. See Figure 3.15.

The value displayed depends on the arrangement of marks in the monitor:

- If two marks are present, Center Duration shows the duration between the marks.
- If one mark is present, it shows the duration between the mark and the position indicator.
- If no marks are present, it displays the duration between the position indicator and the end of the clip.

Center Duration responds to which side of the Composer window is active. Press the Esc key a couple times to toggle the active side, and you will see these numbers change. The format of the duration shown is MM:SS:FF. The value of 1:15:29, for example, would be read as 1 minute, 15 seconds, 29 frames.

Source Monitor Tracking
Information menu

Record Monitor Tracking
Information menu

Composer

| V1 TC1 | 11:49:36:02 | ▼ | 2:02 | Mas 25PD | 01:00:00:18 | ▼ |

Center Duration

Figure 3.15 This field at the top of the Composer window shows your marked duration.

Clicking on Center Duration will toggle the value between Timecode, Frame Count, and Footage (Feet + Frames). If you see a value that is confusing or just unwanted, simply toggle through the values until you see the measurement you want.

Fast Forward and Rewind

Fast Forward and Rewind are essential navigation tools. They are found in the toolbar of each Composer window and have common-looking icons, as shown in Figure 3.16.

 Rewind

 Fast Forward   **Figure 3.16** The Rewind and Fast Forward buttons.

Fast Forward and Rewind functions a bit differently in Media Composer. Rather than playing at high speed, like J-K-L, these buttons jump the position indicator through the edit points. By default, they respond to the active tracks, stopping only at common edit points on the tracks that are enabled. When working with a large complex sequence, this default behavior gives you precise control over where the position indicator will stop. When you're just getting started, you may find it more useful to simply have the playhead stop at every edit point, regardless of what Track Selectors are enabled.

To set FF/RW to stop at every edit point:

1. Right-click on the **COMPOSER** window and choose **COMPOSER SETTINGS**.

    The Composer Settings–Current dialog box opens. (See Figure 3.17.)

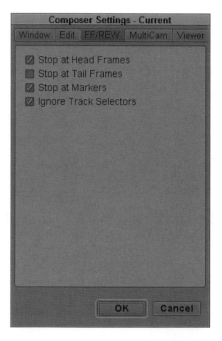

Figure 3.17 The Composer Settings—Current dialog box.

2. Click the **FF/REW** tab.

3. Click the **IGNORE TRACK SELECTORS** check box to select it.

4. Click **OK**.

 The Fast Forward and Rewind buttons are not mapped to the default Media Composer keyboard. If you want to have them on the keyboard you will have to map them to a function key or a shifted key. Many editors map them to A and S.

Snapping to Edit Points

Just as Fast Forward and Rewind make the position indicator jump from edit to edit, you can also jump, or "snap," the position indicator to edit points by clicking or dragging/scrubbing.

As you work in the sequence, there will be times when it is useful to snap the position indicator to the location of the edit points. This can be helpful for marking specific clips.

To snap the position indicator to the head frame (the first frame) at the edit points:

■ Press and hold the **CTRL** key (Windows) or the **COMMAND** key (Mac).

To snap the position indicator to the tail frame (the last frame) at the edit point:

■ Press and hold the **CTRL+ALT** keys (Windows) or the **COMMAND+OPTION** keys (Mac).

While using either of the keyboard commands above, click your mouse cursor to different locations in the sequence, and you'll see that the position indicator "snaps" to the transition. As you scrub/drag the position indicator through the sequence, it will also snap.

How do you know you've snapped to the Head or Tail of a Segment? Look in the bottom left or bottom right of the Record monitor. When your position indicator is on the Head frame, you'll see this symbol (Figure 3.18) in the lower-left corner. When your position indicator is on the Tail frame, you'll see this symbol (figure 3.19) in the lower-right corner.

Figure 3.18 Head frame symbol.   **Figure 3.19** Tail frame symbol.

Snapping is a lifesaver when doing drag-and-drop editing, which you will learn in the next lesson. These same shortcuts allow you to precisely snap the *head* or the *tail* – the first and last frame, respectively – of the segment you are moving to the edit point. This is critical to avoiding unwanted flash frames.

 Flash frames are caused by making an edit that cuts off a frame or two. Use snapping to keep your edits clean.

 Exercise Break: Exercise 3.4
Pause here to practice what you've learned.

Review/Discussion Questions

1. What is the principal goal of the rough cut?

2. How can you view the audio waveforms of your source material?

3. What is AutoPatching? How does it work?

4. The following figure shows the waveforms for a music track but they are of little use because there is almost no definition in the waveforms. How can you make them more useful?

5. With which editing function(s) are you more likely to break sync—Splice-In, Overwrite, Lift, or Extract? Why?

6. What are two ways you've learned about to ensure that you maintain sync when editing segments into the sequence?

7. What do FF and RW do?

8. Describe the process of backtiming an edit.

9. What is the difference between Lift and Extract? When might you use one or the other?

10. What is filler?

Lesson 3 Keyboard Shortcuts

Key	Shortcut
Ctrl+U (Windows)/Command+U (Mac)	Adds a new mono track
Ctrl+Shift+U (Windows)/Command+Shift+U (Mac)	Adds a new stereo audio track
Ctrl+L (Windows)/Command+L (Mac)	Enlarges height of Timeline tracks that are enabled
Ctrl+K (Windows)/Command+K (Mac)	Reduces height of Timeline tracks that are enabled
Ctrl+Alt+L (Windows)/Command+Option+L (Mac)	Enlarges the waveform display
Ctrl+Alt+K (Windows)/Command+Option+K (Mac)	Reduces the waveform display
Alt-click the waveform button (Windows)/ Option-click the waveform button (Mac)	Enables/disables all waveform displays
Z	Lift
X	Extract
V	Splice-In
B	Overwrite
Home	Go to Start of clip in the Source monitor/Sequence in the Record monitor/Timeline
End	Go to End of clip in Source monitor/Sequence in the Record monitor/Timeline.
Fast Forward	Jumps to Next Edit Point
Rewind	Jumps to Previous Edit Point
Caps Lock	Toggles Digital Audio Scrub
Shift	Temporarily enables Digital Audio Scrub

Rough Cut Your Scene

In this exercise, you will start building up your program sequence, a documentary called "Rock Climber." You will use Avid Media Composer's basic editing functions to lay down some interview material as narration and edit action shots over it to illustrate what is being mentioned.

Media Used: Rock Climber

Duration: 60 minutes

GOALS

- Create a new sequence
- Add audio and video tracks needed to build your sequence
- Edit Interview, Narration and Images into the sequence
- Manage tracks to maintain sync

Exercise 3.1: Laying the Foundation of Your Sequence

In this exercise, you will first create a new sequence and add the interview clips listed below. Next, you will add additional shots to match the narration. These tasks will be done using Media Composer's core functions: Splice, Overwrite, Lift, and Extract.

When finished, the narration in the sequence should say the following:

- "The approach to the route is one of the bigger things that captured me into rock climbing."

- "It gives me a chance to meditate um to think about what I'm about to do ... as I get to the rock."

- "There is something about approaching the rock and touching the rock that brings me closer with nature. I get the opportunity to look up and see what I'm about to conquer. Sometimes it gives you like chills. It's pretty cool."

Create a new sequence:

1. Create a new sequence using one of these methods:

    - Press **CTRL+SHIFT+N** (Windows) or **COMMAND+SHIFT+N** (Mac)

    - Select **TIMELINE > NEW > SEQUENCE**.

    If you have not selected a bin, and have more than one bin open, the Select dialog will allow you to choose the bin in which you will place the sequence (See Figure 3.20.)

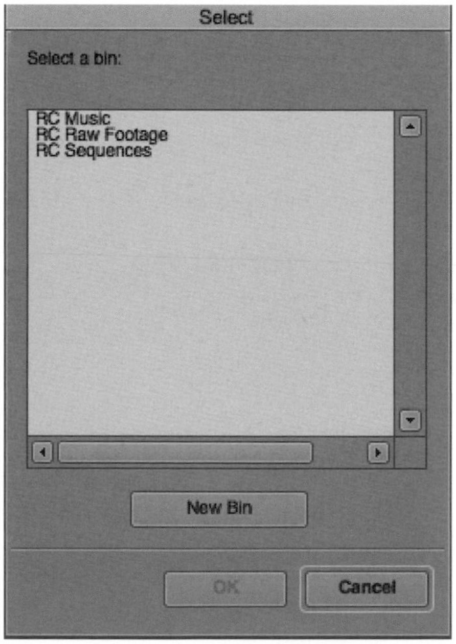

Figure 3.20 The Select dialog.

    If you have selected a bin, or have only one bin open the new sequence is placed in that bin.

    The new sequence is given the default name "Untitled Sequence." This name is also visible in the Timeline and the Record monitor. The new sequence has 1 video track and 2 mono audio tracks.

2. Click on the name (not the icon) and call the sequence **ROCK CLIMBER_OPENING**.

3. Let's add the narration. Double click the master clip **R02_02(B) INTERVIEW** to load it into the Source monitor, or drag it in using the icon (not the name).

    We are going to find the useful sections of this and edit them into our sequence.

    Before we do this we are going to enable waveforms to make our selection easier.

4. To see this interview clip in the Timeline, click the **TOGGLE SOURCE/RECORD IN TIMELINE** button located in the lower-left corner of the Timeline window.

    Both the button and the position indicator turn bright green to indicate that the material in the Source monitor is showing in the Timeline. In this case the R02_02(b) Interview master clip is visible in the Timeline window.

5. In the Timeline, click the **DISCLOSURE TRIANGLE** next to the green timecode display to open the **TRACK CONTROL PANEL**.

6. Click the button with the **WAVEFORM ICON**.

    The waveform on the audio track is displayed.

7. You might want to make the audio track larger to see the waveform in more detail. To do this, With only the track you want to enlarge active, choose **EDIT > ENLARGE TRACK** or press **CTRL-CLICK+L** (Windows) or **COMMAND-CLICK+L** (Mac). Do this a couple of times if you want.

8. Find the sentence, "The approach to the route is one of the bigger things that captured me into rock climbing."

9. Click the **MARK IN** button in the Toolbar under the Source monitor or press the I or E key on the keyboard to mark an IN point at the beginning of the statement.

10. Click the **MARK OUT** button in the Toolbar under the Source monitor or press the O or R key on the keyboard to mark an OUT point after the statement.

    The highlighted section in the Timeline between the IN and OUT points shows the marked section. (See Figure 3.21.)

Figure 3.21 Highlighting indicates the chosen section of the clip.

11. Click the **PLAY IN TO OUT** button in the Toolbar under the Source monitor or press 6 on the keyboard to listen to the section.

12. Click the **TOGGLE SOURCE/RECORD IN TIMELINE** button to return to viewing the sequence in the Timeline.

 It is possible to make the edit while looking at the Source material. The result would be the same.

When you use these interview sections as narration with action shots over them you need to leave room for the audio from those action shots, so you will edit this interview audio onto track A2.

13. Patch A1 to A2. Although you are going to edit over the video there is no reason not to cut it in at this stage.

14. Click the **SPLICE-IN** button or press V on the keyboard.

The clip becomes the first segment in your sequence.

Notice that the position indicator jumps to the first frame after the shot that has just been edited into the sequence. That means it is set up for the next edit. Now you want to mark up the second section in the interview.

15. Click on the Source monitor. Find the sentence "It gives me a chance to meditate um to think about what I'm about to do ... as I get to the rock."

Using the timecode display above the Source monitor will help you here. The beginning of the sentence is at approximately 00:09:03:00.

16. Click the **MARK IN** button in the Toolbar under the Source monitor or press the I or E key on the keyboard to mark an IN point at the beginning of the statement.

17. Click the **MARK OUT** button in the Toolbar under the Source monitor or press the O or R key on the keyboard to mark an OUT point after the statement.

18. Click the **PLAY IN TO OUT** button in the Toolbar under the Source monitor or press 6 on the keyboard to listen to the section. If it is correct, then move on to the next step. If not, then make the necessary adjustments.

19. Click the **SPLICE-IN** button or press V on the keyboard.

20. Click on the Source monitor. Find the statement "There is something about approaching the rock and touching the rock that brings me closer with nature. I get the opportunity to look up and see what I'm about to conquer. Sometimes it gives you like chills. It's pretty cool." You'll find it near timecode 00:10:15:00.

21. Click the **MARK IN** button in the Toolbar under the Source monitor or press the I or E key on the keyboard to mark an IN point at the beginning of the statement.

22. Click the **MARK OUT** button in the Toolbar under the Source monitor or press the O or R key on the keyboard to mark an OUT point after the statement.

23. Click the **PLAY IN TO OUT** button in the Toolbar under the Source monitor or press 6 on the keyboard to listen to the section. If it is correct, then move on to the next step. If not, then make the necessary adjustments.

24. Click the **SPLICE-IN** button or press V on the keyboard.

25. Click the Tracking Information menu above the Record monitor, and select **DURATION**.

    You'll see that you now have about 30 seconds of interview, which you are going to illustrate with some of the other shots soon. (See Figure 3.22.)

Figure 3.22 First 3 interview segments cut in as narration.

Exercise 3.2: Add Action Shots

Now it's time to edit in video clips that supports the interview statements. The audio of these shots will go on to track A1.

1. Patch the A1 Source Track Selector to the A1 Record Track Selector.

2. Press **HOME** to bring the position indicator to the beginning of the sequence or simply drag it there in the Timeline or the position bar.

3. Load **R03_05 WALKING**. Set **IN AND OUT MARKS** around approximately 3 seconds from the middle of the shot where he walks by the large puddle.

    Remember that you can refer to the Center Duration display to see the duration of your selection.

4. Click **OVERWRITE** or press B on the keyboard.

5. Load **R03_04 WALKING**. Select 3 seconds from early in the shot.

6. Click **OVERWRITE** or press B on the keyboard.

7. Load **R04_25 SLOW WALKING SHOES**.

    This time you are going to edit this shot to the length of the sentence "It gives me a chance to mediate."

8. Click **MARK IN** in the Timeline before " ...It gives me."

9. Place the position indicator after the word "mediate."

10. Click **MARK OUT** in the Timeline.

    The selection is now highlighted.

11. In the Source monitor, place the position indicator anywhere a few seconds into the clip.

    The frame you park on will be the first frame of the shot in the sequence.

    The position indicator will act as an IN point so you do not need to Mark IN.

12. Click **OVERWRITE** or press B on the keyboard.

13. Load **R8_112 SLOW FINGERS WALL**. Select 3 seconds of him dragging his fingers along the rock, which is toward the end of the clip.

14. Click **OVERWRITE** or press B on the keyboard.

15. Load **R8_114 SLOW WALL FINGERS**. Select 3 seconds of him drawing his hand away from the rock, which is towards the end of the clip.

16. Click **OVERWRITE** or press B on the keyboard.

17. Mark an IN after the last shot you edited into the Timeline.

18. Load **R8_117 SLOW WALL FINGERS REVERSE**. Select 4 seconds where he approaches the crag looking up. You should **MARK OUT** where he stops (the camera keeps moving).

19. Click **OVERWRITE** or press B on the keyboard.

20. Load **R8_105 SLOW WALL STARE**. Select 3 seconds of him looking up. The camera doesn't stabilize until halfway through the shot.

21. Click **OVERWRITE** or press B on the keyboard.

22. Load **R9_01 BOULDER PLANNING**. Select the long tilt up the crag from when the figures leave the shot to when the camera movement settles. This should be about 10 seconds.

23. Click **OVERWRITE** or press B on the keyboard.

    This series of shots extends beyond the last segment from the R02_02(b) Interview. That is OK. We can survey the route in awed silence.

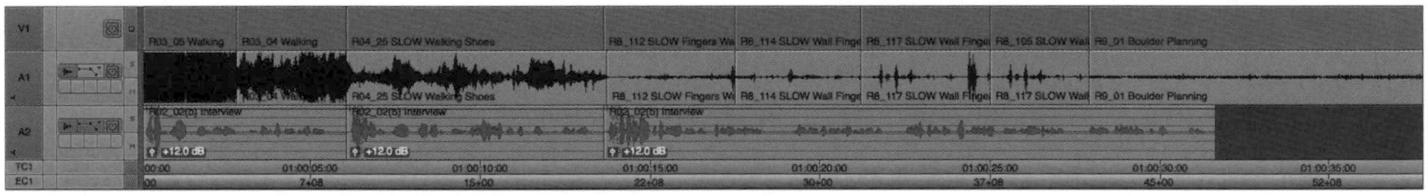

Figure 3.23 Action shots cut in over the narration.

Exercise 3.3: Add the Talking Head

The director would like us to see Matt in sync before we use him as narration. He would like to lead with another section from the R02_02(b) Interview.

1. Load **R02_02(B)** into the Source monitor. Find the sentence "There is something about climbing that continues to draw me in. It's just addicting," and mark it. The sentence begins near timecode 00:12:16:15.

2. Click the **PLAY IN TO OUT** button in the Toolbar under the Source monitor or press 6 on the keyboard to listen to the section. Make sure you leave out the little glance to the director for approval when he finishes speaking.

3. Select the Timeline or Record monitor and then press the **HOME** key or click at the beginning of the Timeline to get the position indicator to the head of the sequence.

4. Patch the Source V1 Track Selector to the Record V1 Track Selector. Then patch the Source A1 Track Selector to the Record A2 Track Selector.

    Now is the time to see the difference between Splice-in and Overwrite.

5. First click **OVERWRITE** or press B.

    We lose part of our opening shots.

6. Press **CTRL+Z** (Windows) or **COMMAND+Z** (Mac).

    We are back with the opening shots in place.

7. This time we'll Splice it in. But, before we do, it's very important to also enable the Record A1 Track Selector as well as A2.

8. Now click **SPLICE-IN** or press V.

   The new segment is inserted before R03_05 Walking and our sequence is now 45 seconds long. (See Figure 3.24.)

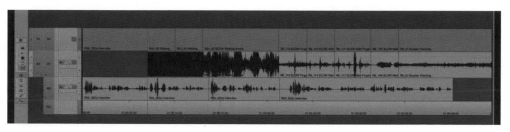

Figure 3.24 Sequence with the sync segment in place.

9. Just for purposes of learning, let's see what would happen if you did not enable track A1 before making the Splice In edit. To do this: Undo the last edit with Ctrl/Command+Z. Next, deselect the A1 track. Now perform the Splice-in edit. Uh-oh! We got our tracks out of sync! No worries, just Ctrl/Command+Z to undo that edit and repeat the Splice-in with A1 selected.

Exercise 3.4: Remove Unwanted Material

Play through the sequence so far. There is a lot of wind noise in the walking shot which will have to be reduced by the Sound Designer/Mixer at the end of the editing process, but on R04_25 SLOW Walking Shoes, there is a strange sound that is a voice distorted by the camera speed. We won't be using any of this anytime soon so let's just remove it.

1. Make sure only **RECORD A1 TRACK SELECTOR** is selected and the blue position indicator is parked on the segment. Click the **MARK CLIP** button or press T.

   The segment is marked.

   Now is the time to see the difference between Extract and Lift, which are the opposites of Splice-in and Overwrite.

2. First click **EXTRACT** or press X.

   All segments that came after the audio you removed have moved up (to the left) move up, and further down the sequence we see white numbers called "Sync Break Indicators," which show how many frames the picture and sound have gone out of sync.

3. Choose **FILE>UNDO EXTRACT** or simply press **CTRL+Z** (Windows) or **COMMAND+Z** (Mac).

4. Now we'll perform the edit again, this time using Lift. Click **LIFT** or press Z.

5. Press the **G** key on the keyboard to "Clear Both Marks" in the Timeline.

   Now we can see that the segment is removed but dark gray filler fills its place. Downstream everything stays in sync.

6. Review your completed sequence.

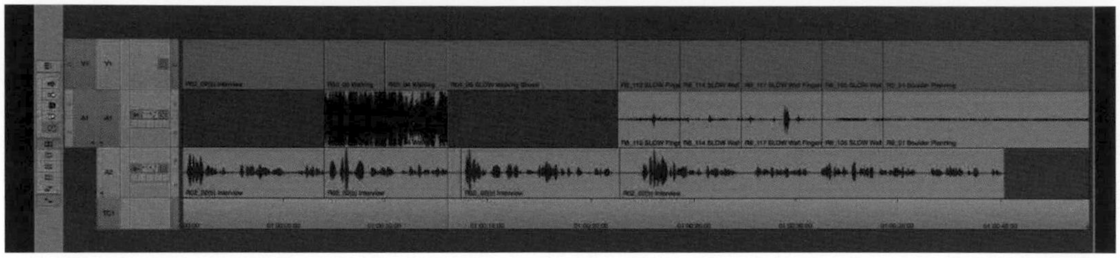

Figure 3.25 The finished sequence.

Drag-and-Drop Editing in Segment Mode

For any of you who have been dying to just drag your clips into the Timeline, your moment has come. Media Composer offers the flexibility to edit any way you want. But rather than forget everything you've learned in the previous lessons, we will build on to it.

In this lesson, you will learn to edit a rough cut sequence using drag-and-drop editing. In the next lesson, you will refine it.

Media Used: Rock Climber

Duration: 45 minutes

GOALS

- Use the Smart Tool
- Build a sequence using Drag-and-Drop
- Adjust the pacing of narration with Overwrite
- Adjust the audio level of segments in the sequence

Understanding the Smart Tool

The Smart Tool is a collection of tools for editing directly in the Timeline using the mouse. Because you will be working with these tools extensively in this lesson, take a few minutes to familiarize yourself with them before going further. First, identify the tools, which are shown in Figure 4.1.

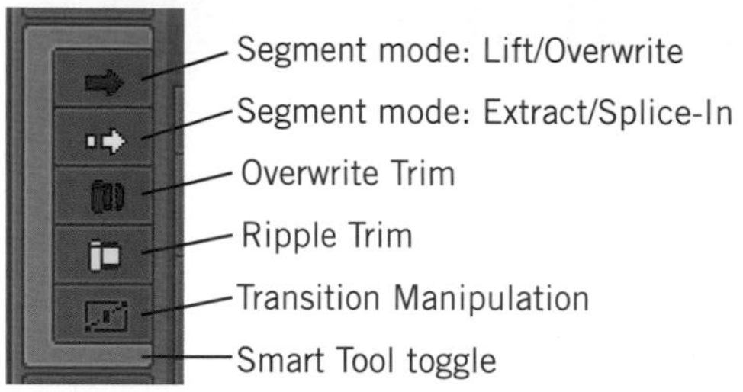

— Segment mode: Lift/Overwrite
— Segment mode: Extract/Splice-In
— Overwrite Trim
— Ripple Trim
— Transition Manipulation
— Smart Tool toggle

Figure 4.1 The Smart Tool is really five tools in one.

Each tool within the Smart Tool can be activated and deactivated by clicking on its individual icon. In Figure 4.1, all tools are active and show the blue highlight color. (The highlight color is a user preference. Yours may be different.) You can toggle the Smart Tool itself on and off by clicking the border button on the left side of the tool, which is called the Smart Tool toggle. If you have only certain tools activated when you toggle the Smart Tool off, those same tools will be the only ones to reactivate when you toggle the Smart Tool back on.

 The keyboard default to enable/disable the Smart Tool is Shift+Tab on both Windows and Mac.

How the Smart Tool Works

The Smart Tool is called "smart" because it automatically switches to the appropriate tool based on the location of the mouse pointer within the Timeline tracks. Once you learn to use it, you can work very quickly in the Timeline because the "right" tool will always be available when you need it.

Media Composer is fundamentally modal. There is the Source/Record editing mode, Segment mode, Trim mode, Effects mode, etc. The tools in the Smart Tool are tied to different modes, but by automatically switching tools, the Smart Tool allows you to move in and out of the various modes seamlessly.

Here's how it works (see Figure 4.2):

- Place your mouse pointer in the middle of a clip, and the pointer will change to a Segment mode arrow. Segment modes are used to move Timeline segments—for example, to reposition an audio segment or relocate a video shot.

- Move the mouse pointer near an edit point (the transition between two segments of video or audio), and the pointer will change to a trim roller. Trim rollers change the length of segments and/or the location of the edit point.

- The top half of the track will activate the red functions (Segment mode or trim roller). The bottom half of the track will activate the yellow function.

- When the pointer is over a transition effect, such as a dissolve, the pointer changes to the Transition Manipulation tool, which, you may have guessed, is used for manipulating transition effects.

Figure 4.2
The active tool changes based on the position of the mouse in the track.

Moving the Position Indicator

When the Smart Tool is active, you can make changes to the sequence by clicking directly in the Timeline. To move the position indicator when the Smart Tool is active, you need to click on the timecode ruler at the top of the Timeline or on the timecode track. When the Smart Tool is disabled, you can click anywhere in the Timeline to move the position indicator. Many experienced Avid editors prefer to work this way to avoid inadvertently changing the sequence.

By default, the keyboard shortcut for the Smart Tool toggle is Shift+Tab. Use this to quickly activate and deactivate the Smart Tool to enjoy frustration-free use of this little wonder tool.

Concept: Color-Coded Tools

You may have noticed that there is a red and a yellow version of both the segment mode arrows and the trim roller. This reflects a simple design theme: color code the tools to indicate the ones with similar behaviors. Once you understand the theme, it makes learning the other tools easier.

Red = Stop

- These tools affect only the segment(s) or track(s) you are manipulating.

- Like a four-way traffic stop, all other elements in the Timeline stay locked in place while you move, trim, or edit the one you clicked.

Yellow = Caution, Moving Objects

- These tools affect the segment you are manipulating **plus** its downstream neighbors, opening or closing gaps as needed.

- You have multiple things moving so pay extra attention—hence the color yellow. If you don't, you might break sync by inadvertently moving only the audio or video material, without moving its audio or video mate. Later, you'll learn about Link Selection Toggle and Sync Locks which help you to keep your video and audio in sync, described shortly, can help with this.

Building a Montage with Drag-and-Drop

The fundamental process and workflow of editing a basic video package is the same regardless of whether you are using professional three-point editing techniques, or using drag-and-drop methods.

In this lesson, and the corresponding exercises, you will build another basic video package, with a montage of video clips, underscored by music and narration. As we learn different tools, we will also explore a different approach to the edit. After learning the different tools and methods, you can decide which you prefer to use at any given moment. Each has its advantages, and as you grow more familiar with Media Composer, you will likely find yourself switching between tools and techniques depending on the situation at hand.

Emptying the Timeline and Creating a Sequence

Media Composer will automatically create a new sequence if you edit a clip to an empty Timeline. Of course, if your Timeline already has a sequence loaded, you need to empty it. The trick is in recognizing that the sequence is viewed in the Record monitor. If you empty the monitor, you empty the Timeline.

To empty the Record monitor and Timeline:

■   Right-click the Record monitor and select **CLEAR MONITOR**.

With the Timeline empty, you can just drag your first clip to the Timeline, to begin creating a sequence. As before, if multiple bins are open, Media Composer will ask you to select the bin to put the new sequence in, and create a new, untitled sequence there. Just remember to name it!

And, if the sequence appears in the incorrect bin, be sure to move it to the one you created for Sequences. Proper labeling and being organized will save you much confusion and many headaches.

Choosing the Source

As usual, we start editing by loading a clip into the Source monitor. Then, you must decide from which source-tracks you want to use material. The source-side track selectors in the Track Selector panel determine which source material will be added to the Timeline when you perform the edit.

You might be thinking, "Didn't we just do this? I already know how to patch tracks and make an edit." But, there is a subtle difference here. The focus now is on the *source side only*. Because you will manually drag the segment(s) to the tracks you want, the record-side selectors are irrelevant.

If all source tracks are selected, the edit will include both audio and video. To create a video-only segment (also called a MOS shot) from a master clip containing audio, you would simply deselect the audio tracks as shown in Figure 4.3.

Figure 4.3 Deselect the A1/A2 source tracks to use only the video from the source clip.

To create an audio-only edit from a master clip containing both audio and video, simply deselect the V1 track, as shown in Figure 4.4.

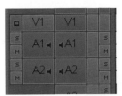

Figure 4.4 Deselect the V1 source track to use only the audio from the source clip.

Adding Clips with Drag-and-Drop Splice-In

Once the source clip is marked and your source tracks selected, you can click anywhere on the image in the Source monitor and drag it to the Timeline. The default mode for drag-and-drop editing is Splice-In mode. As you remember, Splice-In inserts material into the Timeline, which is perfect for assembling a montage.

To splice a clip into a sequence:

1. Load the **CLIP** into the Source monitor.

2. Set **IN** and **OUT** marks around the segment you want to add to the sequence.

3. Click in the **SOURCE MONITOR** and drag the **MOUSE POINTER** to the gray space in the Timeline.

    The arrow changes to the yellow Splice-In arrow and a small, ghosted box appears next to it.

4. Release the **MOUSE POINTER** where you want to make the edit.

    For the first clip you add to the sequence, you can release anywhere in the Timeline. The result is the same.

 Remember, hold the Ctrl key (Windows) or the Command key (Mac) to snap to existing edit points, or the position indicator. This shortcut is a lifesaver with drag-and-drop editing.

As you drag additional shots to the Timeline, you will see that Media Composer dynamically updates the Timeline, giving you a real-time preview of what the sequence would look like if you released the clip at any given moment. Since the default mode is Splice-in, each segment you drag will appear to split the others already in the sequence as you pass over them.

If you don't like these "live updates," you can disable the feature and see a wire-frame version of the segment you're adding instead.

To disable live updates in the Timeline:

1. Right-click in the Timeline and select **TIMELINE SETTINGS**.

2. On the Display tab, select the checkbox for **WIREFRAME DRAGGING**.

3. Click **OK** to close the Settings window.

    Media Composer not only allows you to drag the segments left and right, earlier or later in the sequence, but you can also move the segments between tracks vertically, placing new segments above or below existing ones. We'll explore this more in a minute. For now, be careful to continue placing the audio and video clips onto the same tracks to avoid breaking sync between picture and sound.

Concept: Recognizing Broken Sync

It is important to know how to recognize if you have broken sync. Media Composer will indicate if audio and video segments that come from the same source are out of sync by overlaying little white numbers onto the segments, as shown in Figure 4.5. The value indicates the number of frames they are out of sync.

Figure 4.5 The small white numbers indicate the amount these segments are out of sync.

For now, if you accidentally break sync, simply use the Undo function, repeatedly pressing Ctrl+Z (Windows) or Command+Z (Mac) until sync is restored.

Understanding the Four-Frame Display

When dragging clips to the Timeline, the Composer window also changes to show you a four-frame display. As shown in Figure 4.6, the four frames, from left to right, are:

- The last frame before the edit point

- The first frame of the shot you are adding

- The last frame of the shot you are adding

- The first frame of the shot afterward

Figure 4.6 The Composer window's four-frame display when splicing **between** existing segments.

If you drag the new shot into the middle of an existing segment, the four-frame display will show you what appears to be the same frame in the first and last box, as shown in Figure 4.7. This is because these frames are adjacent to each other in the original footage and represent a difference in time of only 1/24 to 1/60 of a second, depending on the frame rate.

Figure 4.7 The Composer window's four-frame display when splicing **into** an existing segment.

Adding Tracks by Dragging

You have already learned how to add tracks using the menus and keyboard shortcuts. You can also add tracks automatically as you drag clips to the Timeline. Simply drag the segment to a track above or below the existing ones, and Media Composer will create the next track to accommodate the edit. Figure 4.8 illustrates this in a very simple configuration.

Figure 4.8 Drag clips to the next audio or video track, and Media Composer will automatically create it for you.

 Media Composer will only add the next track. If you want to add multiple tracks, it is still necessary to use the keyboard shortcut or menu command.

It is worth noting that although the video segment moved up to V2, the audio segment remained in its default location of A1. This is standard functionality. Media Composer will allow you to place the audio or video segment to a different track, but not both simultaneously. For more complex edits, it is best to patch tracks and perform a three-point edit.

Exercise Break: Exercise 4.1
Pause here to practice what you've learned.

Adding Narration with Drag-and -Drop Overwrite

Pictures may be worth a thousand words, but sometimes the story is best articulated (and advanced) by a concise bit of narration or a sound bite from an interview. To add voiceover to your project, you use Overwrite. Overwrite can be used with audio or video material, but it is especially well suited for audio edits. Unlike video tracks, which tend to be full from start to end, audio tracks often have gaps (see Figure 4.9).

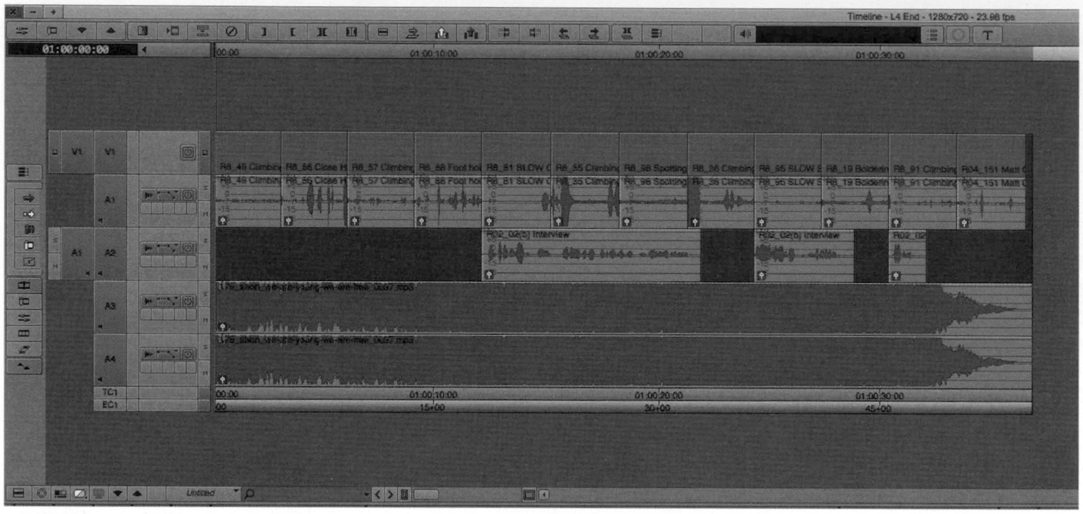

Figure 4.9 Unlike video tracks, audio tracks naturally have gaps of filler between segments, as on A2.

Depending on how you organize your tracks, one track may have large sections without any audio material while sounds or music from another track are heard. For example, a narration track in a travel show might be empty while you see and hear interviews and supporting b-roll with natural sound. Or, a track you are using for sound effects may be largely empty during a quiet, poignant conversation in a narrative film.

Overwrite is the right tool for these edits because with all that empty space, you may have segments elsewhere in the sequence that may or may not be visible at the moment. Splicing in a shot could move those other audio segments, which you carefully placed earlier in the edit—obviously not what you want. Overwrite will leave everything else in the Timeline locked in place. (This is true of all red-colored tools.)

> **Develop the habit now of editing your audio material onto tracks by audio type—i.e., dialogue, sound effects, music, etc. As your projects grow in scale and complexity, your sequences will remain well organized. Plus, you won't have any bad habits to unlearn later!**

The Overwrite segment mode is the Smart Tool's red arrow. When active, it enables you to overwrite shots into the sequence through drag and drop.

Well, almost. Here's the caveat: If both segment modes are enabled, the system will splice shots into the sequence when you drag them to the Timeline. This is a default setting. But don't worry, you don't need to go digging in the settings just to perform an overwrite. To override the setting, simply deselect the yellow arrow, shown in Figure 4.10. Whether you have other tools active or not is irrelevant right now.

Figure 4.10
To use Overwrite when you drag shots to the Timeline, disable the yellow arrow of the Splice-In segment mode.

Exercise Break: Exercise 4.2
Pause here to practice what you've learned.

Editing Audio in the Sequence

As you edit, you will come across clips that are too loud or too quiet. In Lesson 1, you made some rough adjustments to clips to get them to an audible level, but even slight differences in level become more obvious when segments are played in succession. This can distract you from the creative flow -- and your viewers from the story – every time you play them. It is best to adjust these during the editing process.

Many professional editors who mix their own audio (also known as "sweetening"), treat the audio-sweetening process as a dedicated stage of the editing workflow. These initial adjustments just move them closer to the final goal. In the companion course, MC110: Media Composer Fundamentals II, you'll dig into audio tools in greater detail and learn the basic tools and techniques for audio sweetening. For now, you will learn how to make basic adjustments so the music doesn't blow out your speakers and so you can hear everyone talking at the times you want to.

Setting Up for Audio Work

There are a few settings to turn on before you can see any audio information in the Timeline. Once enabled, they make changing audio levels quick and easy.

To enable audio data in the Timeline:

1. In the Timeline, click the **DISCLOSURE TRIANGLE** next to the green Timecode window to open the Track Control Panel. (See Figure 4.11.)

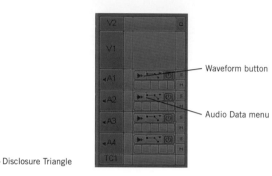

Waveform button

Audio Data menu

Disclosure Triangle

Figure 4.11   The disclosure triangle next to the Timecode window reveals the Track Control panel, which contains audio-related controls.

2. To turn on waveform display on all tracks, hold down the **ALT** (Windows) or **OPTION** (Mac) key and click the **WAVEFORM** button on one of the audio tracks.

    The waveforms on all audio tracks are enabled.

3. Click the **AUDIO DATA** button to open the Audio Data menu.

4. While pressing the **ALT** (Windows) or **OPTION** (Mac) key, select **CLIP GAIN** in the Audio Data menu.

    Clip Gain is enabled on all tracks.

 Holding Alt/Option in the Track Control Panel activates the item for all tracks. Otherwise, all selections are on a per-track basis.

The Timeline will now show the audio waveform patterns of the clips in your Timeline and a decibel graph overlay. Also, in the bottom-left corner of each segment, a very small button appears, marked with the icon of an audio fader. (See Figure 4.12.)

Figure 4.12 With Clip Gain enabled, the audio segments reveal a mini fader button.

 White waveforms indicate that the sample rate of that audio is different from the designated sample rate of the project. If you see these and find them distracting, change them. To do so, open the Audio Project setting. Then, on the Main tab, change the Show Mismatched Sample Rates as Different Color setting to No.

When working with audio, you may wish to look at more precise meters than those in the Timeline. Media Composer includes large audio meters that are easier to read than the Timeline meters. The large audio meters are called the Audio Tool. (The Audio Tool does do other things, hence the name "Tool," but it is mainly a big meter.) Use these meters when you need to measure audio levels.

To open the Audio Tool:

■ Press Ctrl+1 (Windows) or Command+1 (Mac).

■ Select Tools > Audio Tool.

So, what's the "right" audio level? As a rule of thumb, the audio in your sequences should bounce between −20dB and −8dB, as measured by the digital values on the left side of the meter.

Using Solo and Mute

The Timeline has dedicated Solo and Mute buttons for each track. The Solo and Mute buttons are shown in Figure 4.13. Activate Solo to play the audio on that track in isolation, silencing all other sounds. Activate Mute to silence the sounds on the track on which you activate it.

Figure 4.13
The Solo and Mute buttons are always visible and easily accessible in the Timeline tracks, whether the Track Selector panel is open or not.

Solo and mute give you a mechanism to hear just the audio tracks you want to at any given moment. Using these can eliminate frustration and wasted time fussing with controls just to isolate or silence a particular voice. Solo and Mute, however, do nothing to help you balance the relative loudness of different sounds. For that, you will need to adjust the clip gain of your sequence audio.

    It is possible to solo more than one track. This is ideal for isolating just a couple tracks out of the full mix, such as the music and sound effects without the dialogue or vice-versa.

Using Digital Audio Scrub

As you focus on editing the audio, you may find it useful to enable Digital Audio Scrub.

Digital Audio Scrub plays the digital audio samples associated with each frame as you move the position indicator through the sequence. This will allow you to hear the audio with each individual frame you are parked over, allowing for very precise audio editing. For example, you may have difficulty seeing on the waveform the exact point between spoken words, but could easily pick the exact frame on which to cut by slowly moving the position indicator over the audio segments with Digital Audio Scrub enabled. Digital Audio Scrub works the same whether you drag the position indicator, or use the Step Forward/Step Back buttons on the keyboard or interface.

To enable digital audio scrub:

■ Hold the Shift key while dragging through the Timeline to temporarily activate Digital Audio Scrub.

■ Use the Caps Lock key to toggle Digital Audio Scrub on and off.

Changing the Volume of a Segment

For most videos or film scenes, the audio levels, from shot to shot, should be consistent. As you edit, though, you will encounter audio segments that are too loud or too soft. It doesn't take a big difference in the levels to be distracting. To deal with this, Media Composer features the ability to change clip gain and volume directly in the Timeline. Clip gain can be adjusted on a per-segment basis using the mini fader, as shown in Figure 4.14.

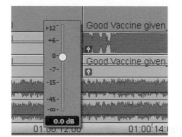

Figure 4.14
Mini-faders in the Timeline let you change the clip gain of segments individually.

To adjust the clip gain of a segment:

1. Click the **FADER** button in the corner of the segment you want to adjust.

    A pop-up fader window appears.

2. Click and drag the **FADER** to adjust the level.

    The fader pop-up window will close automatically when you click elsewhere in Timeline.

    Media Composer offers a number of useful shortcuts for adjusting the clip gain in the Timeline, once enabled. These appear in Table 4.1.

Table 4.1: Shortcuts for Adjusting Clip Gain

Action	Result
Click-drag the fader icon.	The fader opens and simultaneously adjusts. No separate action is required to open and then select the fader.
Click icon, then up/down arrow keys.	Adjusts gain in 0.1dB increments.
Click icon, then number keys (use minus sign to set negative value; works with both keyboard numbers and numeric keypad)	Gain is set to the value typed.
Alt/Option-click fader icon	Resets the level to 0 dB.
Shift +up arrow/down arrow (Windows)/ Shift +up arrow/down arrow (Mac)	Adjusts gain in 1dB increments without opening the mini fader. (Affects all segments on active tracks at the location of the position indicator.)

Exercise Break: Exercise 4.3
Pause here to practice what you've learned.

Review/Discussion Questions

1. What type of edit is performed by default when you drag a clip from Source monitor to the Timeline?

2. Look at the following figure. Why do images A and D appear identical? What type of edit is being performed?

3. Look at the following figure. With the Smart Tool configured this way, what determines the active tool while working in the Timeline?

4. Name two ways to add audio or video tracks to a sequence?

5. How can you enable solo on an audio track? What is the result?

6. If the music is too loud, how can you lower the volume of just the music?

7. Why is Overwrite mode well-suited for editing audio?

8. Why are audio waveforms useful to see while editing?

9. Name one method or shortcut to adjust the clip gain in the Timeline besides dragging the mini-fader.

10. What is Digital Audio Scrub? How is it enabled?

11.   Describe the steps to overwrite a segment to the Timeline using drag-and-drop.

Lesson 4 Keyboard Shortcuts

Key	Shortcut
Ctrl+Z (Windows)/Command+Z (Mac)	Undo
Ctrl+Shift+N (Windows)/ Command+Shift+N (Mac)	Create a new sequence
Ctrl+Y (Windows)/Command+Y (Mac)	Create a new video track
Ctrl+U (Windows)/Command+U (Mac)	Create a new audio track (mono)
Shift+Tab	Smart Tool toggle
Shift+L	Link Selection Toggle
Ctrl-drag (Windows)/Command-drag (Mac)	Snap headframe to edit point
Ctrl+Alt-drag (Windows)/ Command+Option-drag (Mac)	Snap tailframe to edit point
Alt-click waveform button (Windows)/ Option-click waveform button (Mac)	Enable/disable waveforms on all tracks
Alt+Ctrl+K (Windows)/Option+Ctrl+K (Mac)	Reduces the size of the waveform.
Alt-click Clip Gain in track menu (Windows)/ Option-click Clip Gain in track menu (Mac)	Enable/disable clip gain on all tracks
Ctrl+1 (Windows)/Command+1 (Mac)	Opens Audio tool
Shift-drag through the Timeline	Activates Digital Audio Scrub
Caps Lock key	Toggles Digital Audio Scrub on and off
Click mini fader > up/down arrow keys	Adjust clip gain in 1dB increments
Click mini fader > type the number	Set clip gain to specific value
Alt-click fader icon (Windows)/ Option-click fader icon (Mac)	Reset level to 0 dB
Shift +up/down arrow (Windows)/ Shift +up/down arrow (Mac)	Adjust gain in 1dB increments without opening the mini fader (affects all segments on active tracks at the location of the playhead)

Building a Montage with Segment Mode

In this exercise, you will be creating a rock climbing montage. You will use drag-and-drop editing to lay down a music track and edit a montage of images on top.

Media Used: Rock Climber

Duration: 45 minutes

GOALS

- Create a new sequence
- Add audio as a bed for your sequence
- Drag and drop shots into the sequence using Segment Mode
- Move shots around using Segment Mode

Exercise 4.1: Building a Montage with Segment Mode

We will create a new sequence and add the music first, then add shots to match the music, in the process learning the power of Avid Media Composer's Segment Mode. In this lesson, we will add shots in Avid Media Composer by using drag-and-drop techniques.

To create a new sequence:

1. Open the bin Sequences, or confirm that it is selected.

2. Press **CTRL+SHIFT+N** (Windows) or **COMMAND+SHIFT+N** (Mac); select Clip > New Sequence, or you can right-click in the gray area of the open bin and select New Sequence from the menu.

    The new sequence is created and appears in the bin with the default name "Untitled Sequence." This name is also visible in the title bar of the Timeline and above the Record monitor. The new sequence has 1 video track and 2 mono audio tracks.

3. Click on the name (not the icon) and call the sequence "Rock Climber Montage."

    Next, we are going to lay down a music bed to cut some climbing shots to.

4. Load the clip **179_SHORT_WE-ARE-YOUNG-WE-ARE-FREE_0037.WAV**.

    In this case, you'll use the entire clip, so rather than marking separate IN and OUT points, you can simply mark the whole clip.

5. Make the Source monitor active, then press **T** to mark the clip or click the Mark Clip button in the tool bar of the Source monitor.

    IN and OUT points appear at the head and tail of the position bar in the Source monitor.

    Notice that the source control buttons include two audio tracks (A1 and A2). We want to edit these onto tracks A3 and A4, so we need to create these first.

6. Press **CTRL+U** (Windows) or **COMMAND+U** (Mac), or right-click in the Timeline > New Audio Track > Mono.

    The A3 track appears in the Timeline.

7. Repeat, adding track A4.

8. Turn off the V1, A1 and A2 Timeline track selectors (if they are on). The source track selectors A1 and A2 move down ("Auto Patch") to A3 and A4.

9. Now instead of using Splice and Overwrite, click on the image in the Source monitor and drag down to the Timeline. Release the mouse button.

    The music segment is now in position on tracks 3 and 4 in your sequence.

10. Enable waveforms on all tracks, if they are not already showing. This will be useful to identify audio elements when you mark IN and OUT points. In the Timeline, click the **DISCLOSURE TRIANGLE** next to the timecode window to open the Track Control Panel. While pressing the **ALT** (Windows) or **OPTION** (Mac) key, click the **WAVEFORM** button on one of the audio tracks.

    The waveforms on all audio tracks are enabled (see Figure 4.15).

It is hard to see the waveforms in detail. So, let's start by making the audio track larger to see the waveform in more detail by choosing Edit>Enlarge Track or pressing Ctrl+L (Windows) or Command+L (Mac). Next, we want to reduce the modulation of the waveform display within the timeline track. (This has no effect on the actual level of the segment – remember we changed that with clip gain.)

11.   This time, while pressing the **ALT** (Windows) or **OPTION** (Mac) key, use **CTRL+K** (Windows) or **COMMAND+K** (Mac) to reduce the size of the waveform.

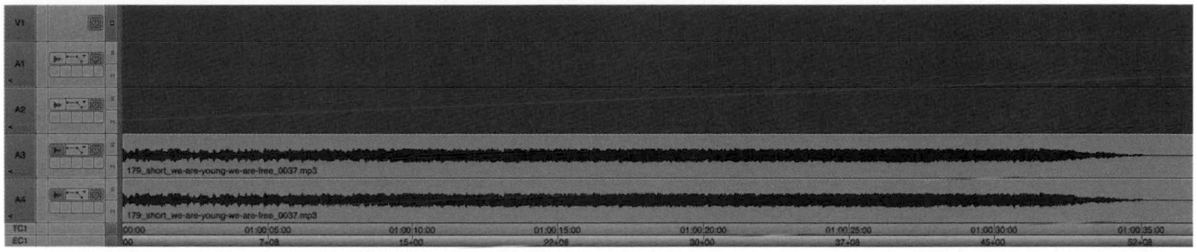

Figure 4.15 The Music track in place.

Now it's time to find a series of video clips that express the thrill of climbing and edit them above the music segment. You can choose to go for the wildest shots or try to follow the process of Matt getting up the climb.

12.   Start with **R8_49 CLIMBING**. Select 3 seconds of it using IN and OUT marks. Now instead of using Spice or Overwrite, click on the image in the Source monitor and drag down to the Timeline.

The clip moves freely back and forth, as well as up and down the Timeline and the Source/Record monitor display becomes four monitors. We are in Segment Mode. Unlike Source/Record mode (last lesson), Trim mode (next lesson) and Effects mode (Lesson 7 onward), which have mode buttons in both the Composer window and the Timeline, Segment mode is entered automatically when you perform certain actions. This is one of them.

13.   Remember Ctrl/Command snapping as we selected cuts in the Timeline? Here holding down the **CTRL/COMMAND** key will allow us to snap the head of segment to the beginning of the sequence.

That's our first shot in place.

14.   Load your second choice and mark three seconds. Drag it down to the Timeline while pressing the Ctrl/Command key to snap the head of the new segment to the tail (end) of the first.

We are using Segment Mode (Extract/Spice-in) and in drag and drop we are using the Splice-in part of the function.

15.   Undo your edit (Ctrl+Z/Command+Z), and lets experiment for a moment. Before making the edit this time, click on the red **SEGMENT MODE (LIFT/OVERWRITE)** button. Now, in drag and drop we are using the Overwrite part of the function.

16.   Keep adding three second shots until you reach the end of the music.

Of course if you change your mind and want to splice a shot in between two others, switch off the red Segment Mode (Lift/Overwrite) button, drag and drop reverts to slice-in and with the Ctrl/Command key held down you can drag the clip to any edit, just not the end of the last shot as we discovered earlier.

It is entirely up to you whether to edit shots into the Timeline using this method or three-point editing described in the previous lesson. Obviously, if you like using the keyboard, you should stick with the three-point editing method. Figure 4.16 shows the Timeline with more climbing shots in place.

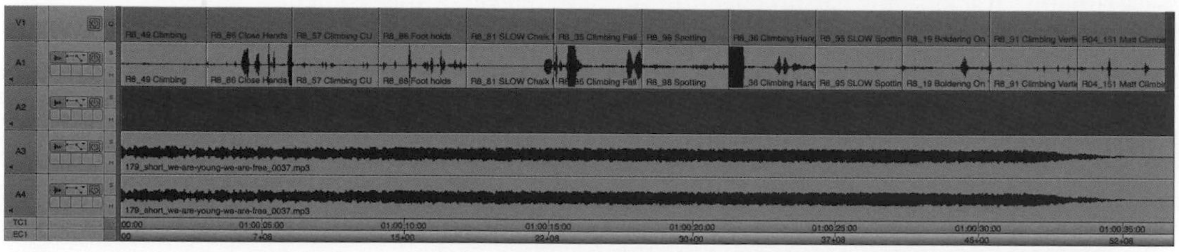

Figure 4.16 The climbing shots in place.

Exercise 4.2: Add Narration

Now that you have a solid montage, it's time to add the voiceover narration. For this, you will again use one of the interview clips.

To add the narration:

1. Double click the master clip **R02_02(B) INTERVIEW** to load it into the Source monitor, or drag it in using the icon (not the name).

2. Find the sentence, "There is a point in routes when you get to a really difficult part, but if you don't commit to it and know you are going to get it, you're not going to get it."

3. Click the **MARK IN** button in the Toolbar under the Source monitor or press the I or E key on the keyboard to mark an IN point at the beginning of the statement.

4. Click the **MARK OUT** button in the Toolbar under the Source monitor or press the O or R key on the keyboard to mark an OUT point after the statement.

    The highlighted section in the Timeline between the IN and OUT points shows the marked up section.

5. Click the **PLAY IN TO OUT** button in the Toolbar under the Source monitor or press 6 on the keyboard to listen to the section.

6. We only want his audio, so deselect V1 on the source side.

7. Make sure the yellow Segment Mode (Extract/Splice-in) is not enabled but that the red Segment Mode (Lift/Overwrite) is enabled.

8. Drag the clip to the Timeline to edit it in on A2.

9. Repeat this with two more sections from the same interview clip. Leave some filler between them.

    The two sound bites are: "When you mess up on a route and fall you just have to get back on it." and "You have to commit."

    In the next lesson we will move them around. We will also move the images they relate to.

Exercise 4.3: Adjust Sequence Audio

In Lesson 1, you learned to adjust the audio level of master clips while they were still in the Source monitor. Once you get those shots cut into a Timeline, you will inevitably need to adjust them further as you listen to them play back-to-back. Even small changes in audio levels can be distracting. Work to get the audio levels as consistent as possible. In Lesson 6, you will take a final step to improve the audio by adding audio crossfades.

To improve the audio mix:

1. If it is not already loaded, load your sequence, **ROCK CLIMBER MONTAGE**.

2. Play the sequence and listen to it.

   The music will be drowning out the narration you have just added.

3. In the Timeline, click the **DISCLOSURE TRIANGLE** next to the timecode window to open the Track Control panel.

4. Click the **AUDIO DATA** button to open the Audio Data menu.

5. While pressing the **ALT** (Windows) or **OPTION** (Mac) key, select **CLIP GAIN** in the Audio Data menu.

   Clip Gain is enabled on all tracks. A little audio slider icon appears on each clip.

6. Click on the slider icon and the slider control is displayed. Move the slider down a bit to reduce the level of the music.

7. Play through the sequence again to hear the improvements.

   There is some good "nat sound" (meaning the inherent, natural sound from the footage) of the climbers. Some of this we will want to hear and some we will not.

8. Go through the sequence again and reduce the gain of any "nat sound" you do not want to hear and increase what you want to stand out.

   Play the sequence through. It should look something like Figure 4.17. The transitions between audio segments may sound a bit rough at this stage, but later we'll show you how to smooth them out.

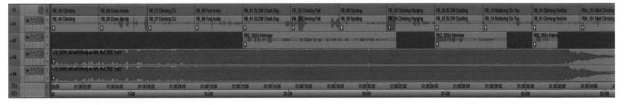

Figure 4.17 The narration in place.

That is our rough cut. In the next lesson we will learn how to refine it.

Refining the Sequence

Whether doing creative writing or visual storytelling, there is a similar process to getting your ideas out of your head first, however rough or messy, and then cleaning them up and making them presentable for viewing. It's the pivot from creating an idea to refining it. This happens on a macro level with the film, but at a micro level with every sequence, every scene. The real work of editing happens as you start to refine the rough cut.

In this lesson, you will improve your sequence by removing or replacing unwanted material, dividing segments, reordering shots, and finally trimming shots to improve the pacing.

Media Used: The Rock Climber

Duration: 45 minutes

GOALS

■ Reorder segments using Segment Mode (Extract/Splice-In)

■ Adjust the pacing of narration with Segment Mode (Lift/Overwrite)

■ Replace existing shots in sequence

■ Audition alternative shots

■ Delete unwanted segments

■ Divide segments with Add Edit

■ Remove unwanted frames with Trim

■ Adjust the pacing of the sequence with Trim

Moving Segments in the Timeline

Now that you have some material in the Timeline, let's look at how you can move and rearrange it.

Rearranging Video Segments

When cutting a montage, it is common to want to change the order of shots as you explore different creative options. Even when cutting other types of scenes, you may find yourself wanting to move a shot or series of shots from one location to another within the sequence. The yellow segment mode of the Smart Tool is the tool of choice for doing this kind of work. It is called Extract/Splice-In segment mode, and is shown in Figure 5.1.

Figure 5.1
The yellow arrow, Extract/Splice-In segment mode, is the best tool for reordering segments in the sequence.

Segment modes are used to move (or remove) segments in the Timeline. The yellow arrow, having the same color as Splice-In, performs a similar function:

- When you move a segment using Extract/Splice-In Segment Mode, the system will open a new space for it wherever you drop it.

  - If you drop a segment in the middle of another one, it will split the existing segment into two parts.

  - If you drop the segment exactly at an existing edit point between two shots (segments), the system will insert the segment at this new location, thereby reordering the clips.

As you have already seen, Media Composer dynamically updates the sequence as you drag, so it is easy to see what is going to happen in the sequence even before you release the mouse to execute the edit.

In the exercise, you will use the Extract/Splice-in segment mode to rearrange the shots in your montage.

 Press the Ctrl (Windows) or Command (Mac) key when you drag a segment to snap it to existing edit points. If you don't, it's easy to accidentally create a flash frame.

Link Selection Toggle

The button above the Smart Tool is called Link Selection Toggle (see Figure 5.2), and it is key to working efficiently with the Smart Tool.

Figure 5.2 The Link Selection Toggle button.

If the Link Selection Toggle button is active, when you select a video segment, the system will automatically select its audio segments, too, as shown in Figure 5.3. As you move, trim, or delete that video segment, the linked audio segments are equally affected. This is a tremendous help to keeping things in sync.

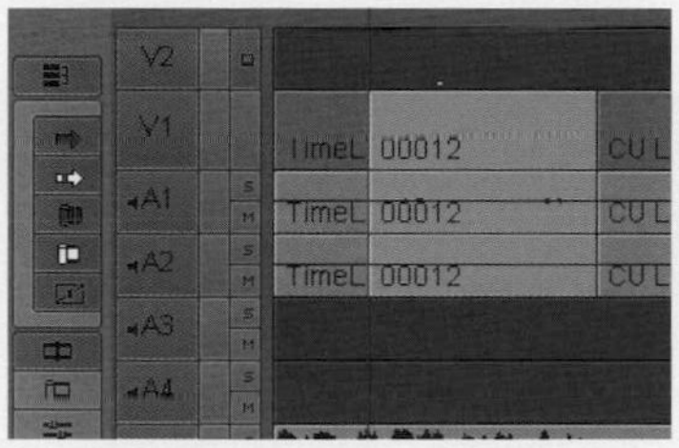

Figure 5.3 With Link Selection active, clicking the video segment also selects the audio segments, and vice-versa.

To edit the audio or video material independently of the other, disable the Link Selection Toggle button before selecting a segment. That way, only the segment you click will be selected. To select more than one—for example, both audio segments—click the first segment, then press the Shift key as you click each additional segment. (For fastest operation, use the keyboard shortcut. The default is Shift+L. To remember it, think "L for linking.")

Media Composer associates audio and video material based on the segments being ingested simultaneously from the same source. Material from different sources will be ignored by Link Selection.

Moving Audio Segments

Having edited the audio clips into the Timeline using Overwrite, you can similarly use the red arrow called, Lift/Overwrite Segment Mode, to move audio segments (see Figure 5.4). When moving segments with Lift/Overwrite Segment Mode everything in the sequence stays locked in place while the segment moves to the new location. This is perfect for adjusting the timing of the narration under the montage.

Figure 5.4 Lift/Overwrite segment mode.

To move audio segments:

1. Select the red **LIFT/OVERWRITE** arrow button in the Smart Tool.

2. Click and drag an **AUDIO SEGMENT** to the new location.

3. If both segment modes are active, click and drag in the top half of the **AUDIO SEGMENT**.

4. Release the **CLIP**.

    In the "Before" image in Figure 5.5, the blue position indicator is parked on a segment in A2 that is a spoken phrase. There is a pause (gap) before it that sounds unnatural. Using the red arrow (Lift/Overwrite Segment mode), the segment can be moved earlier in time to reduce the pause, making the narration sound more natural, as shown in the "After" image.

Before   **After**

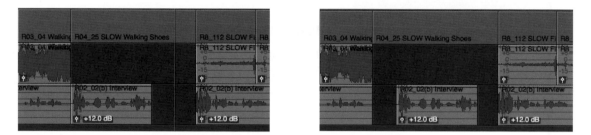

Figure 5.5 Lift/Overwrite enables you to reposition segments without affecting others.

Because there is already empty space, called filler, on the audio tracks, it may not be obvious what is happening when you use the Lift/Overwrite tool. To understand it better, take an extra minute here to do the following experiment with any sequence. After experimenting, you can simply undo the change.

Experiment by using Lift/Overwrite on a video track:

1. Select **LIFT/OVERWRITE** in the Smart Tool.

2. Click on any **VIDEO SEGMENT** to select it.

3. While pressing the **CTRL** (Windows) or **COMMAND** (Mac) key, drag the **SEGMENT** to a new location between two other segments.

4. Release the **SEGMENT**.

    The before and after images are shown in Figure 5.6. You did the same sequence of steps using the Extract/Splice-In tool, but you got a very different result here. With Extract/Splice-In, the segments just rearranged themselves. Now, using Lift/Overwrite, you have opened a gap at the original location and overwritten one segment on top of another.

Before   **After**

Figure 5.6 When you move a segment with Lift/Overwrite, you leave a space behind and overwrite the segment at the new location.

 If you perform this type of move by accident, remember you can always undo.

Moving Segments Between Tracks

You can easily move segments between tracks (up or down, vertically), without getting out of sync. In fact, moving a video- or audio-only segment is as simple as dragging it to the new track. Table 5.1 shows keyboard shortcuts that will help ensure that you move the segments exactly as you wish. A couple of these should be familiar by now.

Table 5.1: Useful Keyboard Shortcuts When Moving Segments

Keyboard Shortcut	Result
Ctrl-drag (Windows)/Command-drag (Mac)	Snaps the headframe to the edit point
Ctrl+Alt-drag (Windows)/Command+Option-drag (Mac)	Snaps the tailframe to the edit point
Ctrl+Shift-drag (Windows)/Command+Shift-drag (Mac)	Locks the segment to vertical movement only

When dragging a shot with paired audio and video segments, you can relocate the audio or video segment to a new track as you drag through the Timeline. (This is the same behavior you saw when splicing in clips using drag-and-drop.). As you drag a segment, if your mouse crosses from video to audio tracks, or vice versa, Media Composer will shift its focus to the corresponding segment you're dragging. This is easy to see in the Timeline. If you click on a video segment on V1 and drag up, for example, the video segment would move up to V2, and the linked audio segments stay on A1, as shown in Figure 5.7. If you were to drag down, on the other hand, Media Composer would move the linked audio segments to A2, and the video segment would stay on V1.

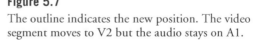

Figure 5.7

The outline indicates the new position. The video segment moves to V2 but the audio stays on A1.

Selecting Multiple Segments

There will be times when you want to move (or remove) multiple segments in the Timeline. Using segment mode (the red and yellow arrows in the Smart Tool), you can select multiple segments at once. There are several ways to do this, as you might expect. No doubt you will use each method at a different time.

Let's go through each method.

To select multiple segments:

- Enable one or both of the Segment mode arrows. Now, while pressing the **SHIFT** key, click on each **SEGMENT**.

    Each segment is highlighted to indicate it is selected. This is useful for selecting a few segments, whether they are contiguous or not. Use this "Shift-click" method to deselect segments as well.

To lasso segments:

1. Starting in the gray space above the top video track, click and drag the **POINTER** down and to the right. This creates a lasso.

    Lassoing from left to right is important in this case because lassoing right to left puts you into an entirely different type of editing called trimming (specifically a trim type called "Slipping").

2. Continue dragging to draw the **LASSO** around the **SEGMENTS** you want to select. The lasso must completely encompass a segment to select it.

3. Release the **MOUSE** button to select the segments.

    All segments completely inside the lasso when you release will be highlighted. This is useful for selecting a contiguous group on adjacent tracks.

 The direction in which you draw the lasso is important. Moving from left to right, as described here, selects the segments. Moving from right to left sets up an advanced, slip trim on the segments. More advanced trim techniques are taught in MC110: Media Composer Fundamentals II.

Finally, you can select a group of segments by track by using dedicated buttons in the Timeline rather than the Smart Tool. These are shown in Table 5.2.

Table 5.2: Buttons for Selecting Segments

Button	Name	Description
←	Select Left	Selects the segments under the position indicator and all segments to the left on active tracks
→	Select Right	Selects the segments under the position indicator and all segments to the right on active tracks
⟷	Select In/Out	Selects all segments between the IN and OUT marks on active tracks

To select segments by track:

1. Select the **TRACKS** containing segments you want to move by enabling their Track Selectors.

2. Optionally, add **IN** and **OUT** marks to define a region of the sequence.

3. Click the **SELECT LEFT**, **SELECT RIGHT**, or **SELECT IN/OUT** button to make your selection.

    The segments are selected in the same way as if you had selected them with the Smart Tool. You can now move or delete all those segments.

 Exercise Break: Exercise 5.1
Pause here to practice what you've learned.

Changing Shots in the Sequence

Your first choice for a shot won't always be the right one. Fortunately, you can use Overwrite to replace existing segments in the sequence—literally writing over them—or to add shots above existing material. The latter technique is useful for creating cutaways and for viewing alternate shots. Let's look at both.

 The techniques described here could also be accomplished with the same results using Overwrite with three-point editing techniques. We present them here in the context of Media Composer's drag-and-drop editing functions.

Replacing Existing Material

To replace existing material on the Timeline:

1. Activate the **LIFT/OVERWRITE** tool in the Smart Tool, and deactivate **EXTRACT/SPLICE-IN**.

2. Set **IN** and **OUT** marks around the material to replace, either an entire segment or a portion of one.

3. Load a replacement **MASTER CLIP** in the Source monitor.

4. Click the **SOURCE TRACK SELECTORS** to choose the tracks to include in the edit.

5. Set an **IN** mark in the Source monitor where you want the shot to begin.

6. While pressing the **CTRL** (Windows) or **COMMAND** (Mac) key, drag the **CLIP** to the marked region in the sequence.

    When the mouse pointer crosses into the marked region, you will see the segment outline constrained to the duration of the marked region instead of its original duration.

    This is effectively a three-point edit, similar to the Overwrite you performed in Lesson 2.

Creating Cutaways

Cutaways are great for hiding cuts, for example, in an interview. You can overwrite a cutaway shot onto V1 or onto a higher track.

Virtually all editing apps treat video tracks the same way in that layers of video are seen from the top down. If two video clips are in the same time location, as shown in Figure 5.8, the one on the higher track will be seen instead of the one on the lower track (assuming there is no effect used to blend them). Unlike with audio, you can see only one video stream at a time without an effect to blend or composite them.

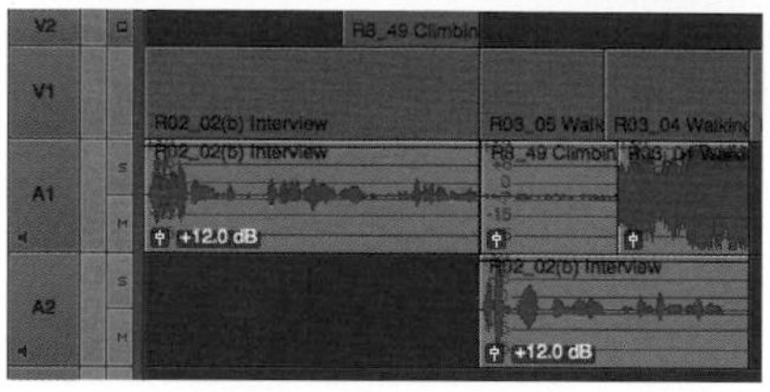

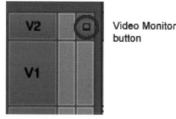

Figure 5.8 Upper-level video segments are seen instead of lower-level segments.

One way to add cutaways (also known as B-roll) to your sequence, then, is to add them to V2. This is an easy way to manage your video tracks when you are getting started editing, especially when it comes to adjusting the timing of the shot (which you will do later in this lesson).

To add a cutaway shot:

1. If necessary, right-click in the **TIMELINE** and select **NEW VIDEO TRACK**.

2. Load the **MASTER CLIP** in the Source window and set **MARKS** around the desired segment.

3. In the Smart Tool, enable **LIFT/OVERWRITE** and disable **EXTRACT/SPLICE-IN**.

4. Disable the **SOURCE AUDIO TRACK SELECTORS** in the Track Selector panel to create a cutaway.

5. Click the **IMAGE** in the Source window and drag it to the **TIMELINE**. Release it on **V2** at the desired location.

6. To be able to see the image on V2, click the **VIDEO MONITOR** button on V2, as shown in Figure 5.9.

Figure 5.9 The video monitor shows all tracks from that level down.

Useful Application: Auditioning Alternate Shots

As you work, you may reach a point where you are torn between two shots. Maybe the director has circled one take but you think another might actually play better. Or, the client really liked one shot of their product but you want them to consider another. A great way to solve this challenge is to add the "alternative" shot to a higher-level video track. You can then review the scene or sequence with them, moving the monitor icon each time to view the different choices. Just remember: Always show the director or client the one that they chose first before suggesting an alternative.

Note: If the alternate clip on V2 is from the same master clip, don't be surprised to see sync break numbers.

Deleting from the Timeline

Just because you put something into the sequence doesn't mean you want it to stay there. Just as you added material to the sequence using the Smart Tool segment modes—the yellow and red arrows in the Smart Tool—you can also delete using those same tools.

To delete a segment using Extract/Splice-In:

1. Click the yellow **EXTRACT/SPLICE-IN** arrow button in the Smart Tool to enable it.

2. Click on the **SEGMENT** you want to delete.

    It will appear highlighted.

3. Press the **DELETE** or **BACKSPACE** key on the keyboard.

    The segment is deleted from the Timeline and the gap is closed.

    When deleting a segment using this mode, Media Composer removes the material via the Extract function, which you used in Lesson 3.

 To avoid breaking the sync relationship between audio and video, use the Link Selection Toggle to delete both audio and video simultaneously. Deleting a MOS segment? Use Lift/Overwrite, described next.

You can delete segments using the red Lift/Overwrite in the same way. Simply select the segment and press Delete. Well, almost. Just like before when you had to disable Extract/Splice-In before you could overwrite a segment onto the Timeline, here again, you will need to disable the yellow Extract/Splice-In button before you can delete using Lift/Overwrite.

To delete a segment using Lift/Overwrite:

1. Enable the **SMART TOOL**.

2. If both segment mode tools are enabled, deselect the yellow **EXTRACT/SPLICE-IN** arrow button, leaving the red **LIFT/OVERWRITE** arrow button selected.

3. In the Timeline, select the **SEGMENT(S)** you want to remove.

4. Press the **DELETE** or **BACKSPACE** key on the keyboard.

If you have adjusted the clip gain on the audio segment, when you try to delete the segment, the gain adjustment will be deleted first. To remove the segment itself, you will need to select it a second time and press Delete again. This is both an advantage and disadvantage of using the segment tools to delete. The edit functions of Lift and Extract will remove the material in one fell swoop.

Adding Cuts

As you edit, you may find that you want to remove only a portion of a segment in the sequence, not the whole segment. To achieve this, just cut the segment in two, and then delete the part you don't want. Bada-bing! Problem solved.

In Media Composer, the command that allows you to divide segments in the Timeline is Add Edit. Its button is shown in Figure 5.10. By default, it appears under the Record monitor and in the Timeline's toolbar. Take a moment now to find it yourself.

 Figure 5.10 The Add Edit button.

To divide a segment:

1. Move the blue **POSITION INDICATOR** to the point at which you want to cut the segment.

2. Using the Record Track Selector buttons, enable the tracks to which you want to add the edit.

3. Click the **ADD EDIT** button.

    An edit point is added to all selected tracks, dividing any segments there.

    The edit point that is created by Add Edit is called a "match frame edit" in Media Composer. You may also hear people refer to it as a "through edit" or "false edit."

 Avid's Add Edit is equivalent to the Blade tool in Final Cut Pro and the Razor tool in Premiere.

If you are careless—well, let's say "less than precise"—with your track selection when adding edits, you may end up cutting tracks you don't want to cut. For example, if you forgot to disable the music tracks A5 and A6 when adding edit points to other tracks, the music track would have lots of unwanted edit points. Not to worry; it is just as easy to remove undesired match frame edits.

To remove add edits:

1. Select the **TRACKS** with the add edits.

2. Mark **IN** and **OUT POINTS** around the area with the Match Frame edits you want to remove; or clear **IN** and **OUT POINTS** to remove them from the entire sequence.

3. Choose **TIMELINE > REMOVE MATCH FRAME EDITS**.

 You can remove Match Frame edits only if the clips on each side of the add edit are in the same state (such as no effects or audio changes). If they are not in the same state, the add edit mark, which looks like an equals sign (=) in the Timeline, will be red.

Exercise Break: Exercise 5.2
Pause here to practice what you've learned.

Changing the Length of Timeline Segments

The Smart Tool contains two trim tools—the red and yellow rollers (below the Segment Mode arrows) — which can be used to change the length of segments within the Timeline. This is called *trimming*, another film-editing term used in Media Composer. Using the Smart Tool trim rollers, you can trim segments using the mouse.

To trim a segment is simply to shorten or lengthen it by a certain number of frames. When you lengthen a segment, you are simply revealing additional frames from the original master clip. When you reach the end of the master clip, you can't trim any further, and the standard system alert will sound.

 The unused portion of the master clip is called "handle." This is a common term that will be used throughout the book.

Both trim rollers allow you to change the length of a segment. To decide which one to use, ask yourself: What do you want to happen to the rest of the sequence material to the right ("downstream") of the clip you're trimming? For example, if you plan to shorten a segment and you don't want to leave an open space, you would use the yellow trim roller, called Ripple Trim. The system will "ripple" all downstream material up to keep it together with the new duration of the segment you trimmed. (See Figure 5.11.)

Figure 5.11 This image shows Ripple Trim being used to shorten shot "A" which moves all downstream material, represented by shot "B."

The same is true if you extend a segment by dragging the roller to the right. The segment you are trimming gets longer and all downstream segments get pushed to the right by the same number of frames that you added. Just as with all other yellow-colored tools, you need to be mindful of keeping things in sync.

On the other hand, if you want to leave everything downstream locked in place (to maintain sync) and you don't mind having empty space (filler) when you shorten the segment, use the red Overwrite Trim tool (see Figure 5.12). The red versus yellow paradigm holds true here, too.

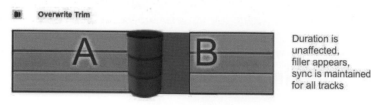

Figure 5.12 Overwrite Trim opens a gap, but leaves downstream material in place. Duration is unaffected, filler appears, and sync is maintained for all tracks.

Here again, you can use Overwrite Trim to extend a segment, too. As you drag the roller to the right, you will overwrite the adjacent segment, shortening it. For example, in Figure 5.12, above, suppose you drag the red, Overwrite Trim roller 13 frames to the right. The edit point itself will happen 13 frames later in time, and the first 13 frames that were visible in the B segment will no longer be there. But, as expected, everything downstream will still be in place.

Up to this point, you have used yellow tools with video and red tools with audio. That is a great way to start using the trim rollers, too. Of course, you are not limited to using them in this context. As you become more comfortable with how they work, you will branch out and use them both with audio and video.

A-Side Versus B-Side Trims

As a way to describe the two shots on either side of any edit point, we refer to them as the "A side" and the "B side" of the edit. (You can see this in Figure 5.11 and Figure 5.12.) The A side is the left side and can also be called the outgoing shot. The B side is the right side, which can also be called the incoming shot.

Trimming on the A-side is very intuitive. Figure 5.11 and Figure 5.12 both show A-side trims, where the trim roller appears on the tail of the outgoing shot. When you drag the roller to the left, the segment you are trimming gets shorter, and you end the shot earlier in time. When you drag the roller to the right, it gets longer and you reveal more of the action in that shot before the cut. When using Ripple Trim on the A side, all downstream material moves in the same direction as your mouse. Easy.

Trimming on the B-side is less intuitive, particularly with Ripple Trim. A B-side trim has the rollers on the right side of the edit point, on the head of the incoming shot. (See Figure 5.13.) As a result, it changes the first frame or image you see from that segment. With a B-side Ripple Trim, when you drag the roller to the left, you are revealing frames from the master clip that exist earlier in time, but now you are extending the material and making the segment longer. When you drag to the right, you are trimming away frames and starting the action of the shot later in time, As a result, the segment is shorter.

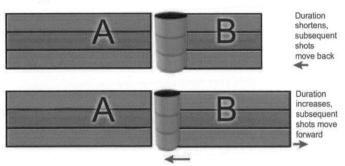

Figure 5.13 A B-side ripple trim changes the first frame in that segment and moves all downstream material to the right.

The concept of trimming is not that difficult, but the first few times you do it, you may find yourself getting turned around. Just be patient, and remember: Undo is your friend.

Dual-Roller Trim

When you have Smart Tool Trimming enabled, and you hover directly over an edit point, you will notice a white icon that doesn't appear as a button in the Smart Tool. It is Dual-Roller Trim, shown in Figure 5.14.

 Figure 5.14 The Dual-Roller icon.

Dual-roller trim "rolls" an edit point by changing both the A and the B sides at the same time. As one side is rolled out (lengthened), the other is rolled up (shortened), as shown in Figure 5.15. The result is that the edit point changes its location in time, and the A and B clips are longer or shorter, but no other clips downstream have been affected.

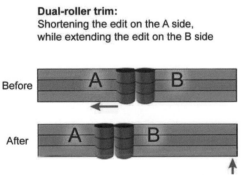

Figure 5.15
Dual-roller trim shortens the edit on the A side while extending the edit on the B side. Note that the duration of the track or sequence does not change.

Creating Split Edits with Dual-Roller Trim

Dual-roller trims are the tool of choice for creating J-cuts and L-cuts, generically referred to as split edits. Split edits are less noticeable because the audio and video don't change simultaneously. If all your edits are straight cuts, the editing will be rather obvious to the viewer, which is usually not good. Instead, it is better to interweave the audio and video with split edits. The only trick to creating these is to use a dual-roller trim on just the audio or video, not both.

To create a split edit:

1. Deselect the LINK SELECTION TOGGLE.

2. Enable one of the trim modes in the Smart Tool.

3. Position the cursor over the video or audio edit point you wish to roll. When the white Dual-Roller Trim icon is visible, then click and drag the edit point to the desired location.

 Before performing a dual-roller trim to create a split edit, it is very helpful to first use Ripple Trim on the A-side and/or B-side of the edit to adjust the pacing / timing.

Using Sync Locks

Ripple Trim, as you have learned, moves all downstream material in a track. So, if you use Ripple Trim on audio or video alone, you run the risk of breaking sync of that downstream material. To eliminate that risk, use Sync Locks.

Sync Locks do exactly what the name implies. They lock the sync relationship between audio and video on any tracks for which they are enabled. They do not depend on the material having been input from the same source, like Link Selection Toggle. If you enable them on tracks you want to keep in sync, no trim will break sync. (See Figure 5.16.)

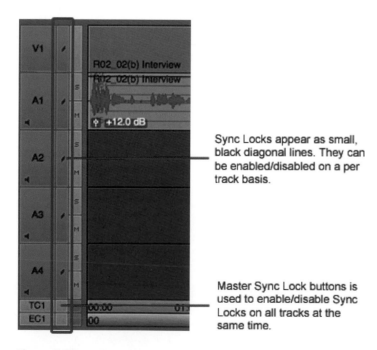

Sync Locks appear as small, black diagonal lines. They can be enabled/disabled on a per track basis.

Master Sync Lock buttons is used to enable/disable Sync Locks on all tracks at the same time.

Figure 5.16 Sync Locks are enabled on tracks V1 and A1–A4.

To enable Sync Locks:

- Click the Sync Lock button on each track you wish to lock together.

- Click the Master Sync Lock button next to the TC1 track to lock all tracks.

   So, how do they work? Sync Locks maintain sync by preventing you from removing any frames from a locked track without removing frames from the other locked tracks. If there is filler close to where you are performing the trim, Media Composer will intelligently remove frames from the filler. If you add frames by trimming a segment longer on one of the locked tracks, the system will add blank filler frames to the other tracks. This is a logic that comes from the physical act of editing celluloid film.

Sync Lock Trim Rollers

When trimming with Sync Locks enabled, you will see gray wireframe trim rollers on the sync-locked tracks that show you exactly where, and how the other tracks are being affected. This can be particularly handy if Media Composer has stopped you from going further in a trim because of a segment on a different track. With Sync Lock Rollers enabled, you will be able to identify the culprit because the wireframe roller changes from a straight line to a bracket icon.

Like many things, you can disable Sync Lock Trim Rollers if you don't like them.

To disable Sync Lock Trim Rollers:

1. While in Trim mode, right-click on either Trim monitor (Composer window), and select **TRIM MODE SETTINGS**.

2. In the Trim Settings window, click the **FEATURES** button at the top.

3. Uncheck the box **SYNC ROLLERS FOR SYNC LOCKED TRACKS**.

 Be aware, that even with Sync Locks enabled, you can break sync in other ways, such as using the Extract/Splice-In segment mode.

Exploring Trim Mode

If you have been following along in the Media Composer interface, you may have noticed some changes happening to the interface as you use the trim tools. These changes, shown in Figure 5.17, are the result of entering and exiting Trim mode. Media Composer enters Trim mode whenever you activate a trim roller on an edit point. Media Composer exits Trim mode when you click on the timecode ruler or track to move to a different location or when you click elsewhere in the sequence with a segment mode or the Transition Manipulation tool.

Figure 5.17 The Trim mode interface.

Take a moment to find each of the interface features identified in Figure 5.17:

- **A-side monitor:** This shows the last frame of the outgoing shot.

- **B-side monitor:** This shows the first frame of the incoming shot.

- **Pre-roll/post-roll durations:** These display the amount of time before and after the edit point included in the loop. By default, the duration is 2.5 seconds before and after the cut point, which totals a five-second loop. You can change this by typing in a new value.

- **Trim buttons:** The trim buttons that look like << and >> enable you to trim one frame or 1/3 second in either direction. In a 30 fps project, 1/3 second = 10 frames; in a 24 fps project, 1/3 second = 8 frames.

- **Trim counters:** These indicate the number of frames that have been trimmed on each side of the edit (A-side and B-side). Negative numbers mean you've trimmed to the left, while positive numbers indicate you've trimmed to the right.

■ **Play Loop button:** This plays a loop around the edit point. It allows for focused attention on the edit point you are trimming at the moment. Play buttons on the keyboard, like space bar, also convert to Play Loop when in Trim mode.

■ **Trim Mode toggle:** This activates and deactivates Trim mode. It is mapped to the U key by default.

You will use these tools as you work through the exercise.

Entering and Exiting Trim Mode

There are several different ways to enter and exit Trim mode. The first method is to use the Trim Mode button, shown in Figure 5.18. The Trim Mode button is found at the bottom-center of the Composer window, in the Timeline Palette (under the Smart Tool), and on the U key of the keyboard.

 Figure 5.18 The Trim Mode button.

To enter Trim mode:

■ Click the **TRIM MODE** button on the interface in the Timeline Palette or between the Source and Record monitors. Alternatively, press the **U** key on the keyboard.

Media Composer will enter Trim mode, the position indicator will jump to the nearest edit point, and trim rollers will appear on all selected tracks. By default, the system selects both the outgoing and incoming material for the transitions on the selected tracks (Dual Roller Trim). After you enter Trim mode, if necessary, select or deselect Record Track Selector buttons.

You can also enter Trim mode by lassoing an edit point in the Timeline, as shown in Figure 5.19. The advantage of this method is that by lassoing, you are simultaneously selecting the tracks you wish to trim. Media Composer will activate the tracks for any transitions you lasso and deactivate all other tracks.

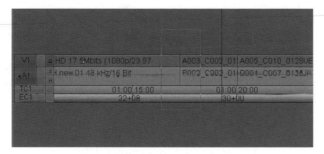

Figure 5.19..Lasso the edit points you wish to trim.

To lasso transitions in the Timeline:

1. Position the **CURSOR** in the gray area above the top video track displayed in the Timeline.

2. Click and drag a **LASSO** around a transition (on one or more tracks).

   Make sure the lasso totally surrounds the cut point(s).

   The position indicator snaps to the lassoed transition.

 You can start a lasso in the middle of the Timeline tracks by holding the Alt (Windows) or Option (Mac) key when you click and drag.

There are several ways to exit Trim mode.

To exit Trim mode and return to Source/Record mode:

- Press the U key to toggle off Trim mode.

- Press the Y key.

- Press the Esc key.

- Click anywhere in the Timecode (TC1) track or the Timeline ruler. The position indicator is positioned where you click in the TC1 track. It's efficient to click before the previous edit so you can play back the trim you just made

Trimming with the Keyboard

The Smart Tool is well-suited for rough trimming, performed quickly by dragging. For more precise control, it is better to use the trim keys, either in the interface or on the keyboard.

Let's begin by learning to perform the different single-roller trims using the keyboard.

To perform a single-roller trim:

1. Select the tracks you want to trim, and then enter TRIM mode.

2. Select the SIDE you wish to trim doing one of the following:

   - Click the picture of the outgoing (A-side) or incoming (B-side) frame.

   - Press one of the default keys: P, [, or] to select the side you wish to trim (see Figure 5.20).

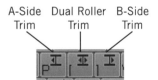

Figure 5.20 Select which side of the edit (A-side or B-side) you want to trim using these keys.

The Trim mode rollers in the Timeline switch to the corresponding side to be trimmed and the corresponding Trim Counter display box (in the Trim window) is highlighted, and a green light turns on as well.

3. (Optional) If no Smart Tool rollers are enabled, single-roller trims default to yellow (Ripple Trim). To change the MODE of the single-roller trim, use the following keyboard shortcuts:

   - Press Shift+D to toggle Ripple Trim

   - Press Shift+F to toggle Overwrite Trim

4. Click the **TRIM BUTTONS** under the A-side monitor, or press the **TRIM BUTTONS** on the keyboard to add or remove frames from the selected material at the selected transition. (See Figure 5.21.)

Trim 8/10   Trim 1
Frames Left   Frame Right

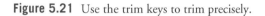

Trim 1   Trim 8/10
Frame Left   Frames Right

Figure 5.21 Use the trim keys to trim precisely.

5. When you're in Trim mode, the Play function automatically changes to Play Loop. So, you can loop by pressing any of the Play shortcuts (for example, the space bar or the 5 key).

   The system plays the number of outgoing and incoming frames currently set in the Preroll and Postroll boxes in the Trim mode window.

6. To stop the loop playback, use any **PLAY** shortcut again.

7. Trim **FRAMES** and play the **LOOP** until you are satisfied with the trim.

 In Trim mode, the Play function automatically converts to Play Loop.

Moving Between Edit Points

As you get into the groove of trimming, it can be nice to move from edit to edit, making adjustments as you go. You can do this with the mouse by simply clicking on another edit point when in Trim mode, and the trim rollers will move to that edit point, without exiting Trim mode.

This is faster and easier still on the keyboard. By default, the A and S keys on the keyboard perform the Go to Previous Edit and Go to Next Edit functions (see Figure 5.22).

 Go to Previous Edit

 Go to Next Edit   **Figure 5.22** The Go to Previous Edit and Go to Next Edit buttons.

These functions allow you to very quickly move between edit points when trimming and will *put you into Trim mode* if you are not there already. (It could just as accurately be called "Trim Previous Edit" and "Trim Next Edit" since they always put you into Trim mode.)

Tracks matter here. The Go to Previous/Next Edit functions respond to track activation by looking for a *common* edit point on all the tracks that are enabled. If all tracks are active, that may very well be the beginning or end of the sequence.

 If you press the Alt (Windows) or Option (Mac) key when you use A or S, Media Composer will ignore the Track Selectors and jump from edit point to edit point on every track.

Scrubbing Audio While Trimming

Digital Audio Scrub works the same in Trim mode as it does in Source/Record Editing mode.

To scrub audio while you trim, press the Caps Lock key and solo the track you want to scrub. Then trim using the Trim buttons or by dragging the trim rollers. If you only want to hear the audio scrub momentarily, hold the Shift key instead of using Caps Lock.

Exercise Break: Exercise 5.3
Pause here to practice what you've learned.

Useful Tools

The following tools will be useful as you work through the exercises.

Clip Name Menus

As you edit, you may find yourself wanting to return to a clip you were using just a minute ago. Instead of finding it in the bin again, you can easily reload it in the monitor from the Clip Name Menu.

At the top of each of the Composer window monitors, Source and Record, you will see the name of the clip you are using. The name field is actually a drop-down menu, called the Clip Name menu. (See Figure 5.23.)

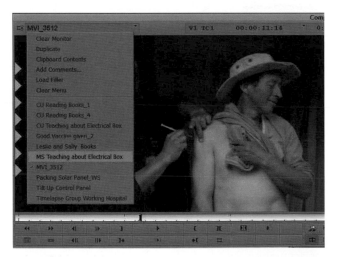

Figure 5.23 The Clip Name menu.

The Clip Name menu is divided. Above the line are commands to clear the monitor and the menu; while below the line is a list of the last items loaded into the monitor. On the Source side, these are source clips. On the Record side, these are sequences. The Clip Name menu holds the names of up to 20 items; and by default are presented in alphanumeric order.

Using Undo in the Creative Process

The previous lesson briefly mentioned how to undo. In case you missed it, here it is again.

To undo the last action:

■ Press **CTRL+Z** (Windows) or **COMMAND+Z** (Mac). Alternatively, select **EDIT > UNDO**.

The creative process is messy, though. There may be times when you realize you headed down the wrong path and you want to undo a series of actions rather than just one or two. In the same menu as the Undo command—the Edit menu—there is another item of note: Undo/Redo List. The Undo/Redo list contains a historical list of up to 100 actions. As shown in Figure 5.24, the actions are listed by name and include almost every action in the Timeline. If you select an entry in the list, your sequence will revert to the state it was at that point in history.

Figure 5.24 The Undo/Redo list displays actions you've performed and your current position within that sequence of steps, as indicated by the line

 You cannot undo / redo a single event in the middle of the list. Selecting an action to Undo from the list will also Undo all other actions above it.

Although the entries are just the generic name of the action, it is usually enough to give you a good sense of where to go. Decide how far back you want to undo and then select that point from the Undo/Redo list. You will see the Timeline updates very quickly as those actions are reversed.

If you went too far in the Undo/Redo list, or perhaps not far enough, just reopen the list. You will now see a line in the list below which the actions read "Undo" and above which they read "Redo." From here, you can choose which direction is best. You can move freely forward and backward in the list until you find the right spot. The Undo/Redo list is cleared when you change sequences, or close the project.

 Redo has its own keyboard shortcut: Ctrl+R (Windows) and Command+R (Mac).

Duplicate

As you edit, it is helpful – even necessary sometimes – to create multiple versions of a sequence. You may need multiple versions to meet the delivery requirements or to create multiple versions of a news story, but versioning is important even just to track the evolution of the sequence through the edit process. (Not every idea is brilliant, so sometimes it's helpful to have one to go back to.)

In Media Composer, versioning is done with the Duplicate command.

To duplicate a sequence you are editing:

■ Right-click in the Record monitor and select **DUPLICATE**.

The sequence is duplicated, and the new copy, whose name is appended ".copy.01" is automatically loaded in the Timeline, ready for you to edit. You can change the name of the sequence in the bin.

To duplicate a sequence in the bin:

1. Select the sequence in the bin.

2. Select **EDIT > DUPLICATE** or use the keyboard shortcut Ctrl+D (Windows) or Command+D (Mac).

The new sequence appears in the bin, with the name appended with "*name*.copy.01"

It is important to note, you are only duplicating the metadata, not the media. The duplicated copies share the same media. So you don't need to worry about taking up more space on your drive (the added metadata is negligible).

Exercise Break: Exercise 5.4
Pause here to practice what you've learned.

Review/Discussion Questions

1. How can you remove a shot from the sequence and leave a gap (or filler)?

2. What does this button do?

3. What does this button do?

4. Why is the yellow segment mode often well-suited for video and the red for audio?

5. What is the danger of performing a Ripple Trim?

6. What are Sync Locks? How can you enable/disable them?

7. What is the shortcut for Undo?

8. What are match-frame edits? How can you remove them?

9. What impact does Ripple Trim have on a track and/or the sequence?

10. What are the steps to remove a segment from the sequence using Lift/Overwrite Segment Mode? What is the result?

11. You try to remove an audio segment from the sequence using either the yellow or red Segment Mode arrows, but the first time you hit delete, the segment remains in place. The second time, it is removed as expected. Why?

Lesson 5 Keyboard Shortcuts

Key	Shortcut
Alt (Windows)/Option (Mac) and click the Select Right button.	Selects the segments but not the filler between
Ctrl-drag (Windows)/Command-drag (Mac)	Snap headframe to edit point
Ctrl+Alt-drag (Windows)/ Command+Option-drag (Mac)	Snap tailframe to edit point
Ctrl+Shift-drag (Windows)/ Command+Shift-drag (Mac)	Locks the segment to vertical moves only
U or Esc	Toggle off Trim mode
Shift+D	Toggles Ripple Trim
Shift+F	Toggles Overwrite Trim
Ctrl+Z (Windows)/Command+Z (Mac)	Undo
Ctrl+R (Windows)/Command+R (Mac)	Redo

Refining Your Sequence

In this exercise, you will work on your montage and opening sequence from "Rock Climber."

Media Used: Rock Climber

Duration: 45 minutes

GOALS

- Rearrange shots using Segment Mode (Extract /Splice-in)
- Replace shots using Overwrite
- Delete unwanted bits of audio
- Adjust the pacing of the narration using Segment Mode
- Trim unwanted frames from segments
- Improve the pacing using Trim functions

Exercise 5.1: Reorder shots in the Montage

Whatever method you use to cut shots into the sequence, Segment Mode has a lot to offer for moving shots around in the sequence.

Let's explore this functionality:

1. Click on the **YELLOW SEGMENT MODE** (Extract/Spice-in) button. Now click on a segment.

    That segment and its clip are highlighted.

2. With the yellow arrow cursor, start to drag the segment to move its position in the Timeline.

    The Source/Record monitor display becomes four monitors.

    The middle two displays are the first and last frames of the shot we are moving and the first and last show the frame that will precede and the frame that will follow the segment we are moving if we were to release it. As you slide the segment left or right, the first and last frames will look identical, they will actually be successive frames.

3. Now hold down **CTRL** (Windows) or **COMMAND** (Mac) as you drag the segment.

    The segment will jump to a cut and the first and last frame will be different shots. If you let the segment go it will Splice-in at that point and be extracted from where it came. Other shots will ripple and there will be no gap in the sequence.

4. Switch **OFF YELLOW SEGMENT MODE** (Extract/Spice-in) using the button at the left of the Timeline and switch **ON RED SEGMENT MODE** (Lift/Overwrite). Now try moving segments with the red Segment Mode arrow.

    When you let the segment go, it will overwrite what is below it and it will be lifted from where it was originally leaving a gap of gray filler.

5. Use both of the Segment Mode tools to move some of your shots around. You can move more than one segment at a time if you Shift-click them, or lasso them moving from left to right.

6. If you leave both buttons enabled, you can make use of the Smart Tool function and choose between the two segment modes with the cursor. Try it out. If you hover over the upper part of the segment in the Timeline you get the red Segment Mode arrow and if you hover over the bottom you get the yellow one.

Exercise 5.2: Working on the Narration in the Montage

In this exercise, you will both add and remove some narration. Load the previous sequence you were working on, called "Rock Climber Montage", if it is not already loaded.

To add the narration:

1. Double click the master clip **R02_02(B) INTERVIEW** to load it into the Source monitor, or drag it in using the icon (not the name).

2. Find the sentence, "To me rock climbing is not necessarily how hard you can climb or what grade of rock you can climb."

3. Click the **MARK IN** button in the Toolbar under the Source monitor or press the I or E key on the keyboard to mark an IN point at the beginning of the statement.

4. Click the **MARK OUT** button in the Toolbar or press the O or R key on the keyboard to mark an OUT point after the statement.

5. Click the **PLAY IN TO OUT** button in the Toolbar under the Source monitor or press 6 on the keyboard to listen to the section.

6. Patch **A1 TO A2** and deselect the other video tracks.

7. Click **OVERWRITE** or press B on the keyboard.

8. Repeat this with the sections from the same interview clip where he says, "It's about the whole experience." Leave filler between these sections and between these and the first section you added in Lesson 4.

   The Director points out that the viewer may not know what a grade of rock climb is and wants this bit removed. You could Mark IN and Mark OUT at the beginning and end of the offending piece and use Lift, but let's try another way.

9. Play through the first segment and stop after he says "can climb." Click on the **ADD EDIT** button.

   This divides the segment into two

10. Enable **RED SEGMENT MODE** (Lift/Overwrite).

11. Click on the second segment where he says "or what grade of rock you can climb."

12. Press the **DELETE** key.

    This removes the Clip Gain we applied to the whole clip back in Lesson 2.

13. Press the **DELETE** key again.

    This time the segment is removed.

14. While you are in red Segment Mode (Lift/Overwrite) you can move the next couple of shots around to adjust for the new space in the sequence.

Your Montage sequence should look something like Figure 5.25.

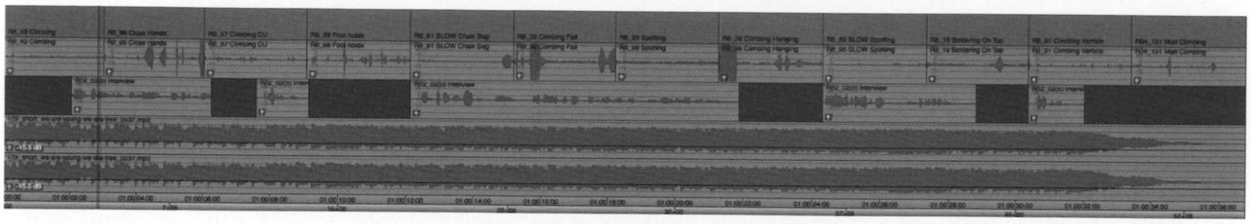

Figure 5.25 The Rock Climber Montage before trimming 1.

Exercise 5.3: Trimming the Montage

In this exercise, you will use the trim tools to improve the pacing of the lifestyle branding piece.

Pacing your video with Trimming:

Finally, let's put a bit more rhythm and finesse into the montage by trimming all the shots. Use dual roller trims to make one longer or shorter affecting the duration of its neighbor or single roller trims to shorten or lengthen shots while moving everything downstream.

1. Obviously you will review each trim by pressing the Spacebar to loop play the selected transition point. By default the Pre-roll times are 2 seconds 12 frames before and after the cut. If you want to change this you can. In the Composer window, below the A-side (left) monitor, click the **PREROLL FOR PLAY LOOP** field. Type 400 and press Enter.

   The preroll changes to 4:00 (four seconds).

2. Try different methods of trimming. Drag the rollers. Use the keys. See what suits you best.

Exercise 5.4: Combining Trim and Segment Moves to Refine the Opening

Cleaning up narration to create some space:

1. Load the **Rock Climber Opening** sequence

2. Play the second **R02_02(b) Interview** segment. The end of this when he says "... as I get to the rock," is a bit weak.

    We are going to remove trim this off. A dual-roller trim would extend the next interview segment by the amount we reduce this one, so that won't work. We need a single-roller trim. A yellow ripple trim on all segments would remove this and pull everything else in the sequence (and shorten the sequence). We want this to introduce a pause in his narration and so a red Overwrite trim in his audio segment will do the trick.

3. Click on the **Red Overwrite Trim** button to the left of the Timeline and then click just inside the audio segment we want to shorten.

    A red roller will appear at the end of the segment.

4. Make the trim by any of the methods you have been taught (or indeed review all of them). Drag the red roller to the left with an eye on the waveforms, or use the J key, or trim backwards, or use the trim ten frames back, trim single frames back to get to where we want. Phew, what a lot of ways Avid gives us to trim! Find which suits you.

5. At the beginning of the third R02_02(b) Interview segment there is a "So," that we would like to remove. This time click the **Red Overwrite Trim** button to the left of the Timeline to switch it off, click on the **Yellow Ripple Trim** button and then click just inside the audio segment we want to shorten.

    A yellow roller will appear at the start of the segment. This will move the whole of the audio segment earlier in the sequence, which may have an adverse effect on sync points later on, but let's try it and see. With the power of Avid Media Composer's undo function this approach is fine.

6. Trim the "So" by using any of the methods mentioned in Step 4 above.

7. Now, use **Red Segment Mode** (Lift/Overwrite) to move the second R02_02(b) Interview segment later in the sequence so that there is a pause between it and the previous segment.

8. We would like to move the statement "Sometimes it gives you like chills. It's pretty cool." But it is all one segment. Place the position indicator just before "Sometimes" and use the **Add Edit** button.

    This splits the segment in two.

9. Now we can move that section independently. Use **RED SEGMENT MODE** (Lift/Overwrite) to move it later in the sequence.

    Your Opening sequence should look something like Figure 5.26.

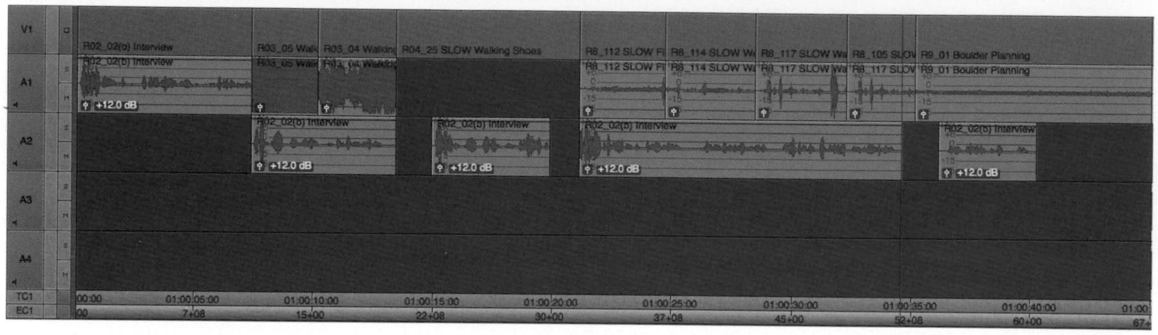

Figure 5.26 The Opening sequence before final trimming.

Finally let's put a bit more rhythm and finesse into the montage by trimming all the shots. Use dual-roller trims to make one longer or shorter affecting the duration of its neighbor or single-roller trims to shorten or lengthen shots while moving everything downstream.

10. Try different methods of trimming. Drag the rollers. Use the keys. See what suits you best.

11. Review each trim by pressing the Spacebar to loop play the selected transition point.

12. Click the Fast Forward and Rewind buttons or press the A and S keys to move up and down the Timeline staying in Trim mode.

Introduction to Transition Effects

Even in the most straightforward of projects, visual effects can play an important role in the timing and dramatic feel of a sequence. As an editor, it's just as important for you to learn *why* you add effects as it is to learn the steps to apply them. In this lesson, you'll start with the fundamentals and cover a few "whys" along the way. Then you can apply your knowledge on a real sequence using the exercise at the end.

Media Used: Running the Sahara

Duration: 45 minutes

GOALS

- Apply Quick Transitions
- Modify transitions in the Timeline
- Remove effects
- Create audio cross-fades to smooth audio edits

Creating Transition Effects

Visual transitions – the most common being dissolves and fades – affect the rhythm of a sequence. They can add drama, resolve a difficult cut point, or convey the passage of time or even a change in consciousness. Media Composer uses the same basic method to create crossfades for audio and dissolves for picture. Because these are the most commonly used effects, they get special privileges, like a super-quick way for adding them to a sequence.

 A dissolve blends together the images between adjacent shots in the sequence. A fade blends the image to, or from, black. Fades are commonly used only at the beginning or end of a scene.

Adding Quick Transition Effects

The Quick Transition button is the fastest way to add a dissolve to a cut point (see Figure 6.1).

Figure 6.1 The Quick Transition button.

To quickly add a 1-second dissolve:

1. Click the **QUICK TRANSITION BUTTON**, or press the **BACKSLASH KEY** [\].

   The Quick Transition window opens, as shown in Figure 6.2.

2. Click **ADD**, or press the **ENTER** key.

   The system will close the dialog box and the default transition—a one-second dissolve—will be applied to the edit points on all active tracks that contain edits close to the position indicator.

   After you click the Add button, a 1-second dissolve will appear on all edit points under (or very near) the position indicator on all active tracks. Of course, you won't always want a 1-second dissolve for a transition, so let's explore the other controls.

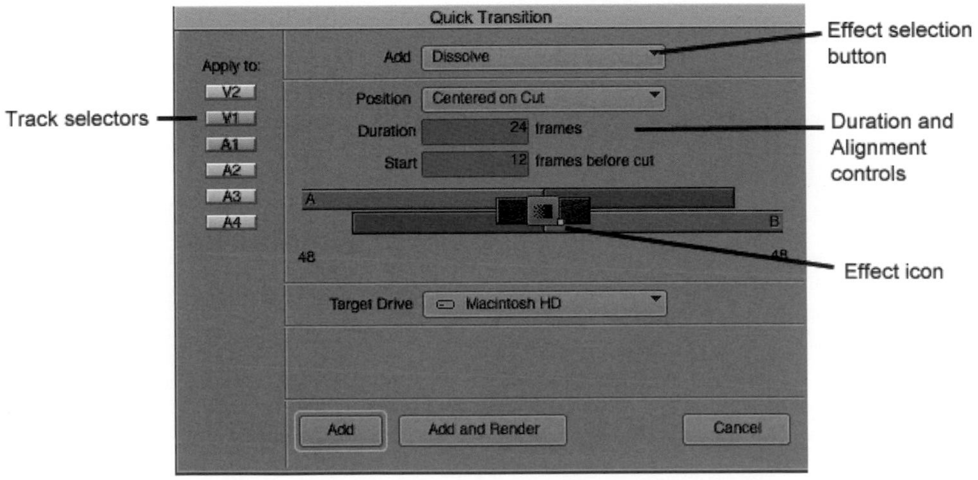

Figure 6.2 Using the Quick Transition dialog box is the easiest way to create a transition effect.

Understanding Quick Transition Effects

The Quick Transition window is divided into a number of sections. The top section enables you to select from a few other dissolve-related transition effects using the Add menu.

Below the Add menu are a few choices for modifying the duration and alignment of the transition. Included in this section is a scaled graphical display of the transition that shows the alignment and handles (see Figure 6.3). This can help you to understand the duration and any handle problems that may occur.

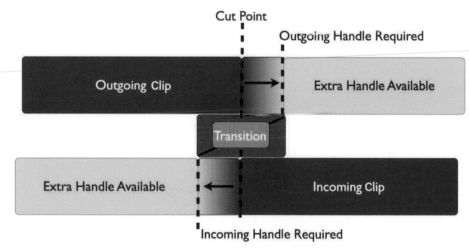

Figure 6.3 Alignment section of the Quick Transition dialog box.

To create a transition, you must have source media beyond what is edited into the sequence because the outgoing segment (the A-side shot) and the incoming segment (the B-side shot) will overlap for the duration of the transition (see Figure 6.4). This extra media is referred to as *handle*.

Or, in other words, *handle* is the unused portion of the master clip.

Figure 6.4 Handle diagram.

If you type a duration in the dialog box that requires more handle than is available, Media Composer automatically adjusts the duration to give you the longest possible transition.

By default, the Quick Transition dialog box attempts to apply a dissolve transition that is centered on the cut point, meaning an equal number of frames for the dissolve effect happens before and after the cut points. This requires the outgoing and incoming segments to have enough handle for half the duration of the transition (see Figure 6.5).

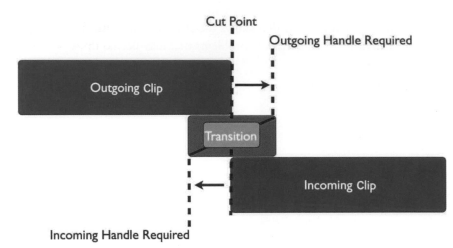

Figure 6.5 Transition alignment diagram.

Changing the alignment so the transition starts on the cut, instead of being centered on the cut, means the outgoing segment needs to have a handle length equal to the entire transition but the incoming shot doesn't need any extra handle. The incoming shot already "starts at the cut."

 Another way to adjust a transition is to drag the left or right edge of the purple graphical effect icon to change its duration or drag within the purple effect icon to change its alignment.

Quick Transitions are real-time effects, so you only need to click the Add button. If you were to click the Add and Render button, Media Composer would render the transition, creating a new media file on your hard drive. This can be helpful to guarantee real-time playback on early computer systems, but otherwise is largely unused.

The left section of the dialog box is used for track selection. The tracks selected before you click the Quick Transition button determine the track(s) that will get the effect. For convenience, if you forget to select the correct tracks ahead of time, you can select the here.

Once you have added a transition, the Timeline displays a transition icon over the cut point. A diagonal line indicates the duration of the transition (see Figure 6.6).

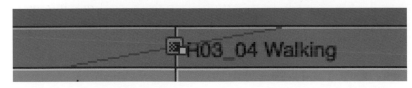

Figure 6.6 Timeline transition icon.

Adding Multiple Transition Effects

Watch your favorite films and TV shows, and you will see that most edits are straight cuts. But, when you start looking at music videos, movie and game trailers, and other short, highly stylized pieces, you can find plenty of examples where transition effects are used on many cuts.

Media Composer allows you to easily add Quick Transition effects to a series of edits. This is a great little time-saver in those instances, like in a montage, where you may want to add dissolves to three or four edits in a row. (Media Composer doesn't limit you to the number of transitions you can include, but good aesthetic judgment and common decency should.)

To add a dissolve to multiple cuts:

1. Select the **TRACK(S)** in the Track Selector panel on which you want to apply the effect.

2. Mark the cuts with a **MARK IN** point and a **MARK OUT** point.

3. Click the **QUICK TRANSITION** button or press the **\ (BACKSLASH)** key to open the Quick Transition dialog box.

4. Select the **APPLY TO ALL TRANSITIONS (IN->OUT)** checkbox, as shown in Figure 6.7.

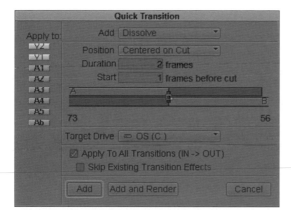

Figure 6.7 The Apply to All Transitions (IN -> OUT) option.

5. Click the **ADD** button.

Removing Quick Transition Effects

Experience from viewing your uncle's home movies tells you that not every transition you add will improve your sequence. Often, a straight cut can set a better tone and keep a better rhythm than a transition effect. So as important as it is to know how to add a transition, it is just as important to know how to remove one. The Remove Effect button is adjacent to the Quick Transition button below the Record monitor, as shown in Figure 6.8. Clicking it will remove the effect that is under the position indicator, based on your track selection.

Figure 6.8 The Remove Effect button.

To remove a transition effect using Remove Effect:

1. Park the **POSITION INDICATOR** near the transition effect(s).

2. Select the **TRACK(S)** that contains the transition effect(s) to be removed. (Deselect any tracks you want to leave unaffected.)

3. Click the **REMOVE EFFECT** button.

To remove a transition effect using the Smart Tool:

1. Using the **TRANSITION MANIPULATION** tool, click on the transition **EFFECT ICON**.

2. Press **DELETE**.

Exercise Break: Exercise 6.1
Pause here to practice what you've learned.

Modifying Transition Effects in the Timeline

Once you have transitions in a sequence, you don't have to open the Quick Transition dialog box to make modifications. Some changes, like duration and alignment, can be done directly in the Timeline using the Transition Manipulation tool. The Transition Manipulation tool, located in the Smart tool in the Timeline Palette (see Figure 6.9), enables you to shorten, lengthen, or move the alignment by dragging the effect icon directly in the Timeline.

Figure 6.9 The Transition Manipulation tool.

When the Transition Manipulation tool is enabled, moving the pointer over a transition in the Timeline will cause the pointer to change into a hand icon, as shown in Figure 6.10. The hand icon indicates that you can move the alignment of the effect by dragging it.

Figure 6.10 The Transition Manipulation tool's hand icon.

To move a transition's alignment:

1. In the Smart Tool Palette, click the **TRANSITION MANIPULATION** button.

2. Position the pointer over a transition until a hand icon appears.

3. Drag the effect's icon to the right to reposition the transition to start at the cut point. Drag it to the left to reposition the transition to end at the cut point.

   You can also use the Transition Manipulation tool to change the duration of a transition effect. Moving the pointer over the lower-left or upper-right transition handle, as shown in Figure 6.11, enables you to modify exactly where the transition starts and ends, respectively. The Transition Corner display appears to assist you in selecting the frames to include in the dissolve. The duration of the transition is displayed under the left side of the Transition Corner display.

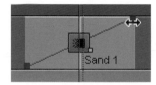

Figure 6.11 The pointer changes to a resizing arrow when you adjust a transition's duration.

 You cannot drag an effect beyond the cut point, nor can you drag an effect beyond the ends of the handles.

To modify a transition's duration:

1. Position the **POINTER** over the lower-left or top-right corner of a transition until the pointer changes to a resizing arrow.

2. Drag the **TRANSITION HANDLE** to shorten or lengthen the duration.

 You can press the Alt key (Windows) or the Option key (Mac) before you drag a transition handle to lengthen or shorten the transition equally in both directions.

As you drag, the Record monitor changes to the Transition Corner display, which shows the first, middle, and last frames of the outgoing and incoming sides of the transition (see Figure 6.12). You can use these frames to guide you as you modify the effect.

Figure 6.12 The Transition Corner Display is activated anytime you use Transition Manipulation in the Timeline.

The Transition Corner Display is not a new feature. It was designed for a tape-based world in which images on videotape could change instantly, such as when the videographer stopped and restarted the recording. Because tapes are often captured as one long master clip, these shot changes can exist in the master clip as well. If the segment has undesired frames in the handle near the cut point in the sequence, then adding a dissolve could reveal them. When this happens, it looks like a flash frame.

Flash frames are still a common challenge on programs where an *edit master* is used as one of the sources. (An edit master is a tape or file that contains the full, edited program.) Also, in broadcast news, editors regularly use source material from satellite feeds. The feed is captured very much like a tape, with shots changing in the middle of the clip.

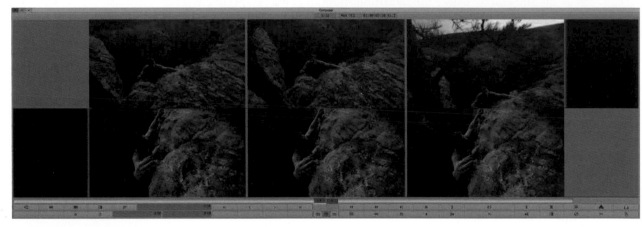

Figure 6.13 A flash frame at the end of the outgoing shot is easy to see here.

Even when production is done on file-based cameras, which is now standard, you will find Transition Corner Display useful for spotting unwanted elements in the transition. For example, look at Figure 6.13. Notice that the last frame on the A side (the image in the top right) is different. In this case, the dissolve is revealing a camera move. You can fix this by shortening the dissolve or moving it to the left to include less handle material.

 Videotape is still present in many productions due to the use of archival material, even as its popularity wanes as an acquisition format.

 Exercise Break: Exercise 6.2
Pause here to practice what you've learned.

Accessing Effects from the Effect Palette

You can access even more effects from the Effect Palette. To open the Effect Palette choose Tools > Effect Palette or press Ctrl+8 (Windows) or Command+8 (Mac).

 You can save time managing palettes (as well as screen real estate) by using the Effect Palette tab within the Project window.

The Effect Palette displays a list of effects you can apply (see Figure 6.14). Notice across the top are buttons to display "Filters" (also known as Segment Effects), Transition Effects, Audio Track Effects, and Audio Clip Effects. These help to keep things organized and easier to find.

Figure 6.14 The Effect Palette.

The left side of the Effect Palette lists effect categories, and the right side lists the effects within the selected category. When you select a category on the left side of the Effect Palette, all the effects in that category are displayed on the right.

 A green dot next to an effect icon indicates that the effect does not require rendering and will play back in real time.

To add a transition effect from the Effect Palette:

1. Open the **EFFECT PALETTE**.

2. Select the **BLEND, PEEL, CONCEAL, PUSH, SPIN, SQUEEZE** or one of the many **WIPE** categories to access the transition effects.

3. Drag a **TRANSITION EFFECT** from the right side of the Effect Palette over a cut in the Timeline.

4. When the cut highlights, release the mouse to apply the effect.

To replace an existing transition effect with an effect from the Effect Palette:

1. Drag a **TRANSITION EFFECT** from the right side of the Effect Palette over an existing transition in the Timeline.

2. When the Timeline effect highlights, release the mouse to replace the effect.

Modifying Effects in Effect Mode

To access all the adjustment parameters for any given effect, enter Effect mode.

The Effect Mode button is located in the bottom-center of the Composer window and in the Timeline Palette, as shown in Figure 6.15.

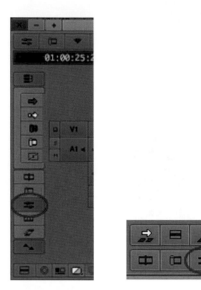

Figure 6.15 The Effect Mode button appears in the Timeline Palette (left) and in the Composer window (right).

To enter Effects Mode, do one of the following:

- Click the Effect Mode button in the bottom-center of the Composer window.

- Click the Effect Mode button in the Timeline Palette, below the Smart Tool.

- Select Windows > Workspaces > Effect Editing.
  This workspace nicely optimizes the window layout for effects editing.

  When you enter Effect mode, a few changes will occur. First, the Effect Editor is displayed. The Effect Editor organizes effect parameters in collapsible groups. The types of parameters available vary according to the effect you are modifying. Clicking a triangle opens the group and displays parameters, as shown in Figure 6.16. Any changes are instantly previewed in the monitor.

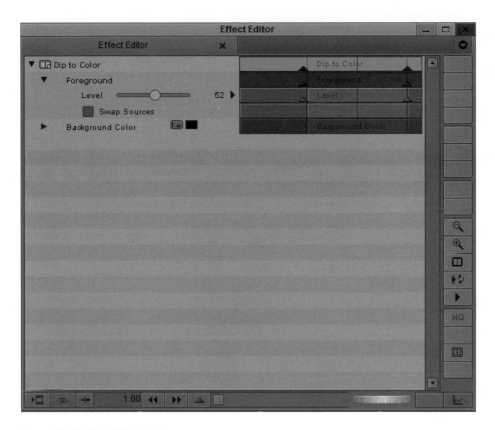

Figure 6.16 The Effect Editor.

The second change you need to be aware of is more subtle, but very critical. Your old friend the Record monitor has now morphed into the Effect Preview monitor. (This is Effect mode, after all!) The Effect Preview monitor displays only the selected effect, which is highlighted in the Timeline. The position bar under the monitor, which used to shuttle through the entire sequence, now shuttles only through the selected effect.

When working in Effect mode, get in the habit of using the position bar to scrub through the effect – NOT the Timecode tracks in the Timeline. If you click the Timecode track, the Effect Editor will close. This is normal behavior.

When working in Effect mode, you can use either the Effect Editor or the Effect Preview monitor to loop playback through the effect, view the effect duration, and even render the effect if needed (see Figure 6.17).

 For quick access to Effect mode, map the **Effect Mode** button to a key on your keyboard. This is especially handy if you keep closing it accidentally by clicking on a timecode track in the Timeline.

Figure 6.17 The Effect Editor and Effect Preview monitor.

To modify effects in Effect mode:

1. Select the **TRACK(S)** containing the effect.

2. Place the **POSITION INDICATOR** over the effect.

3. Click the **EFFECT MODE BUTTON** or Choose **WINDOWS MENU> WORKSPACES > EFFECT EDITING**.

4. Click a triangle next to a **PARAMETER GROUP** to view the parameters.

5. Drag the sliders to modify the parameter's value.

6. To preview the transition, click the **PLAY LOOP** button.

Creating an Effect Template

After creating a great effect, you may want to reuse it in other parts of your sequence. For those occasions, you can save effects as templates and use them repeatedly without having to re-create them. The icon in the upper-left corner of the Effect Editor (see Figure 6.18) is used to save effect templates into a bin. When the pointer is over the icon, it changes to a finger. You can then drag the icon to any bin, thereby saving it as a template for later use.

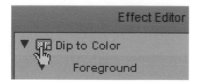

Figure 6.18 The Effect icon, for saving effect templates.

To save an effect template from Effect mode:

■ From the upper-left corner of the Effect Editor, drag the **EFFECT ICON** into a bin.

To apply effects templates from a Bin:

■ From the bin, drag an **EFFECT TEMPLATE** for a transition effect onto a transition or a previously applied transition effect in the Timeline.

 Any open bin that contains an effect template will be displayed as a category at the bottom of the Effect Palette. Selecting the Bin category will display all the effect templates from that bin on the right side of the Effect Palette.

You'll probably use transition effects more than other effects. Pause here to practice what we've covered to this point. In the next section, we'll look at how you can use transition effects for audio as well.

 Exercise Break: Exercise 6.3
Pause here to practice what you've learned.

Creating Audio Crossfades

Straight cuts in the audio track can sometimes sound abrupt, or introduce a click or pop. These problems can usually be resolved by creating an *audio crossfade*. An audio crossfade blends the audio segments together on either side of the edit, just like a dissolve in video.

In Media Composer, there is no separate audio crossfade effect. Instead, crossfades are created by literally applying a dissolve to an audio edit point. The buttons and controls are identical to those for applying dissolves to video, so at this point, you already know how to add and modify audio crossfades.

In terms of workflow, an editor may choose to apply audio crossfades as they build the sequence, or as a step in the "finishing" process. It is largely a matter of preference and individual working style. Since this lesson already covered the tools to create video dissolves, now is as good a time as any to learn to use those same tools and techniques for audio.

Audio crossfades are commonly used to:

■ Smooth out pops and clicks at audio cut points

■ Fade or blend music segments and sound effects

The principal difference between applying an audio crossfade to smooth out a dialogue edit vs fading out music is the length of the dissolve effect. As a rule of thumb, use very short dissolves for smoothing dialogue edits—typically one to four *frames*. Anything longer and you risk having other words in the handle become audible during the transition. Figure 6.19 shows audio crossfades on dialogue segments.

Figure 6.19 Crossfades on dialogue need to be short to avoid revealing unwanted words at the edit.

For music, it tends to be the opposite. You usually want long dissolves—one second or more—to slowly fade the music in or out of the scene. You may also use long crossfades with nat sound (ambience).

 Many editors prefer to use audio keyframes to fade music out over a longer period of time because this gives them more control over how the music fades.

Media Composer allows you to apply dissolves to every edit point in an entire region of the sequence in one fell swoop. Applying dissolves to every video edit can seem amateurish, but it is a real lifesaver when used with audio. If you have a section of the sequence with lots of dialogue edits, you can quickly smooth them all out at once, instead of applying one dissolve at a time, 10, 20, or 30 times over.

To apply audio dissolves (crossfades) to multiple edit points:

1. Select the **TRACKS** to which you want to apply the dissolves. Deselect all others.

2. Move the **POSITION INDICATOR** to the beginning of the region and click **MARK IN**.

3. Move the **POSITION INDICATOR** to the end of the region and click **MARK OUT**.

4. Move the **POSITION INDICATOR** near an edit point, and open the **QUICK TRANSITION** dialog box.

5. Adjust the **DURATION** and **POSITION** (effect alignment) settings. All transition effects will be created identically.

6. Click the **APPLY TO ALL TRANSITIONS (IN -> OUT)** check box to select it, as shown in Figure 6.20.

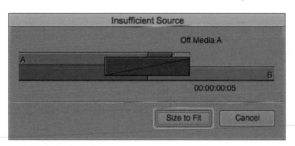

Figure 6.20
You can use the Quick Transition window to apply the same transition to multiple edits. The settings shown would work well to smooth choppy audio edits.

7. Click the **ADD** button.

It is entirely possible that one of the clips within that region doesn't have enough handle to apply an effect. This is especially true if you are adding longer dissolves. In this case, the system will warn you that there is "insufficient source." (See Figure 6.21.)

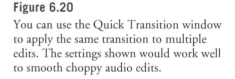

Figure 6.21 This dialog box warns you that there is not enough handle to create the transition effect.

If you click the Size to Fit button, the system will create a shorter transition to fit the available handle material, and then continue creating the rest of the batch. If you click Cancel, the system will skip only that one transition and apply the rest. A report dialog box will appear, telling you how many transitions were created and how many were skipped or cancelled.

Exercise Break: Exercise 6.4
Pause here to practice what you've learned.

Review/Discussion Questions

1. If you want to add multiple dissolves to a series of cut points using the Quick Transition dialog box, how do you identify the cuts that will get the dissolves?

2. What is a handle, and why is it important in the context of effects?

3. What must you do to ensure a Quick Transition is added only to a video cut point, and not an audio cut point?

4. True or False: The Transition Corner display shows the first, middle, and last frames of the A-side and B-side of the transition.

5. True or False: Dragging a transition from the Effect Palette onto an existing transition in the Timeline replaces the existing transition.

6. True or False: To save an effect template, you drag the effect icon from the upper-left corner of the Effect Editor into the Effect Palette.

7. What function must be enabled before dragging a transition effect in the Timeline to change its duration or position?

Lesson 6 Keyboard Shortcuts

Key	Shortcut
\ (backslash)	Opens the Quick Transition dialog box
Ctrl+8 (Windows)/Command+8 (Mac)	Opens the Effect Palette

Applying Transition Effects

In this first exercise, you'll use your newly developed knowledge to apply a few transition effects, modify one, and then save it as an effect template. You will also apply transition effects to smooth out audio edits.

Media Used: Running the Sahara

Duration: 30 minutes

GOALS

- Apply Quick Transition effects
- Add multiple transition effects
- Replace an existing transition effect
- Modify and save effects as an effect template
- Create audio crossfades

Exercise 6.1: Apply Quick Transition Effects

Before you add transitions, watch the "RTS Trailer 50 Start" to get a feel for the project. This portion of the trailer is the opening montage for the *Running the Sahara* documentary. This montage introduces the setting: the Sahara. For such a mysterious opening, it lacks a bit of drama. You'll start by adding a transition to the first video cut in the project.

1. Using the **Quick Transition** button, add a 1.5-second dissolve, centered on the first cut point between the Sun Panning shot and the Sand1 shot (see Figure 6.22). Be aware that this is a 24 fps project.

    If your audio tracks are enabled, you will not be able to center the transition. You can deselect them in the Quick Transition Window.

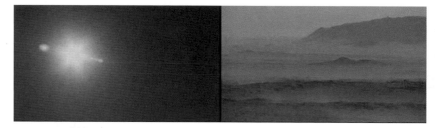

Figure 6.22 Add a dissolve between the Sun Panning shot and the Sand 1 shot.

2. Play through to see if the transition improved the cut. The transition smoothes out the cut, but because this is a major introduction point where the narration starts, it might be better with a dramatic pause.

3. Use the **Quick Transition** dialog box to change the effect from a Dissolve to a Dip to Color.

4. Review the transition, then press the **Esc** key to leave Trim mode.

    The first cut is much better with the Dip to Color transition effect. It sets the right tone for the trailer. Maintaining the right tone or feel in a project is certainly a major factor to keep in mind when you are deciding to add any effect!

    Now that you have a firm grasp of using the Quick Transition dialog box, let's try our hand at adding multiple transitions from the Quick Transition dialog box.

5. Apply 24-frame dissolves to the three cuts that happen between 01:00:07:00 and 01:00:14:00 in the sequence (see Figure 6.23). Do this by opening the Quick Transitions dialog box only once.

Senegal, Aerial 1	Senegal, Aerial 3	Sand 3

Figure 6.23 Apply one-second dissolves to these three cuts.

The dissolve from the Senegal Aerial 3 shot to the Sand 3 shot is too long. It takes away from the already short Senegal Aerial 3 shot. To correct this, shorten the transition's length and change its alignment to see more of the Senegal Aerial 3 shot. Make those changes directly in the Timeline using the Transition Manipulation tool following the steps below.

6. In the Smart Tool Palette, click the **Transition Manipulation** button.

7. Drag the transition between the **SENEGAL AERIAL 3** shot and the **SAND 3** shot right until the effect starts at the cut point (see Figure 6.24).

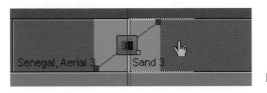

Figure 6.24 Drag the transition to start at the cut point.

Next, use the Transition Manipulation tool to change the duration of a transition.

8. Shorten the duration to about 12 frames. The duration of the transition is displayed under the left side of the Transition Corner display, as shown in Figure 6.25.

Figure 6.25
Use the Transition Manipulation tool to shorten the duration to 12 frames.

9. Click the **PLAY LOOP** button to view the transition. Click it again to stop playback after you have reviewed the transition a few times.

10. Click the **TRANSITION MANIPULATION** button to disable the tool.

11. Click the Timecode Track or Timecode Ruler to return to Source/Record Mode.

Exercise 6.2: Replace a Transition

The last transition effect ends a paragraph in a sense. It should be emphasized using a Dip to Color effect just like the start of the sequence. You could go back into the Quick Transition dialog box to switch the last dissolve to a Dip to Color effect, but another option is to use the Effect Palette to replace the last dissolve with a Dip to Color effect and then modify the color that is dipped into using the Effect Editor in Effect mode.

To do so:

1. Access the Effect Palette using the button in the Project window.

2. Locate the **DIP TO COLOR** effect from the **BLEND** category in the **TRANSITIONS TAB**.

3. Drag the effect from the Effect Palette to the last transition you added in the Timeline.

    As shown in Figure 6.26, the transition in the Timeline becomes highlighted when you drag the effect over it. The new effect will replace the old one, but keeps the same alignment and duration.

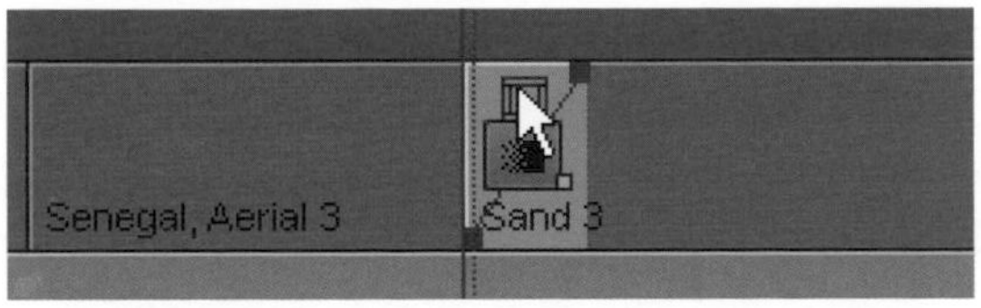

Figure 6.26
Dragging an effect onto an existing Timeline effect.

The Dip to Color transition replaces the original dissolve transition, and a Dip to Color icon appears on the transition.

4. Press the **SPACE BAR** to play the sequence. Press it again to stop playback after Matt Damon says, "With people and cultures as unpredictable as the landscape."

Having a Dip to Color transition on both ends works better to encapsulate the short montage. Now that your effect is applied, positioned, and aligned, you will use the Effect mode to further customize it.

Exercise 6.3: Modify and Save Effects

Customizing an effect can produce results that better fit the feeling of your program. In Effect mode, the Effect Editor displays all the parameters you can use to customize any given effect. Let's modify the Dip to Color transition so that instead of dipping to black, it dips to a more appropriate desert color.

1. Place the **POSITION INDICATOR** over the last Dip to Color transition.

2. Enter **EFFECT MODE**.

The Effect Editor appears with a list of parameter categories available for the Dip to Color effect (see Figure 6.27).

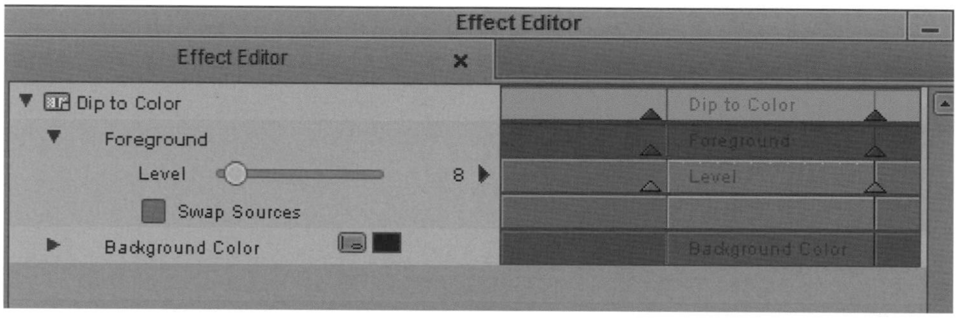

Figure 6.27 Dip-to-color parameters in the Effect Editor.

3. Adjust the background color to a brownish red using the **BACKGROUND COLOR** HSL parameters or by double-clicking on the black square to access a color palette, the Select Color window.

Note that a single click opens a different tool, the Color Info window.

4. To preview the transition, click the **PLAY LOOP** button.

5. This change works well, and you might want to use it later. (Trust me, you will.)

Instead of re-creating this exact Dip to Color effect, you can save it to a bin that you'll use just for customized effects.

6. Create a new bin and name it **EFFECTS**.

7. From Effect mode, drag the **DIP TO COLOR** icon (see Figure 6.28) into the newly created Effects bin.

   A new bin item is displayed, named Dip to Color.

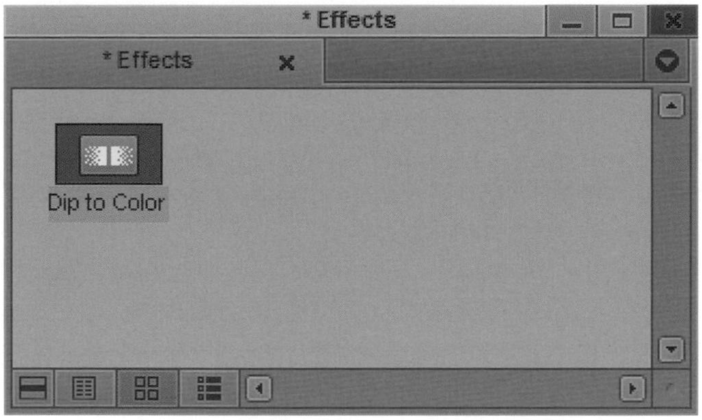

Figure 6.28
The Dip-to-Color effect
template saved to a bin.

An editor should always use good labeling and naming conventions. Instead of saving the effect with the default name, it is better to label it with a descriptive name that will make it easier to find when you search for it.

8. Name the Dip to Color effect template **DIP TO RAW UMBER (12 FRAMES)**.

   That's much more exciting than Dip to Brown! The name alone makes you want to use it again, right? Now let's reuse the effect template on the first Dip to Color transition so the start and end of the scenic montage match.

9. Drag the **DIP TO RAW UMBER** template onto the first **DIP TO COLOR** icon in the Timeline.

   Note, the template changes the alignment and duration of the transition effect.

10. (Optional) Adjust the alignment and duration of the transition effect, if desired.

11. Play the sequence to review all your transition.

Exercise 6.4: Create Audio Crossfades

Media Used: Rock Climber or RTS

Before you add transitions, watch the "RTS Trailer 57 Start" to get a feel for the project. We want to smooth out the audio underneath the five clips on V1 in the middle of the sequence where the runners discuss their commitment to the run. We will do this by adding a short dissolve between each shot. This is a common use of adding multiple dissolves. A very short dissolve is used to avoid removing important audio from each segment or bringing in extraneous audio from an adjacent segment.

To add multiple audio crossfades:

1.   Deselect **V1**, **A3** and **A4**.

2.   Place a **MARK IN** before the first cut and a **MARK OUT** after the last cut. (See Figure 6.29.)

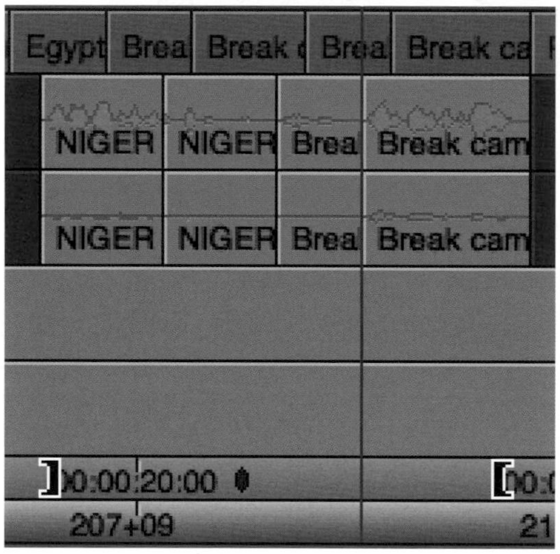

Figure 6.29   Using IN and OUT marks to select multiple transitions.

3.   Click on the Quick Transition button.

     This opens the Quick Transition dialog box now displaying the option, "Apply To All Transitions (IN > OUT)."

4.   Set the Position to **CENTERED ON THE CUT**.

5.   Set the Duration to **2 FRAMES**.

6.   Select **APPLY TO ALL TRANSITIONS (IN > OUT)**. (See Figure 6.30.)

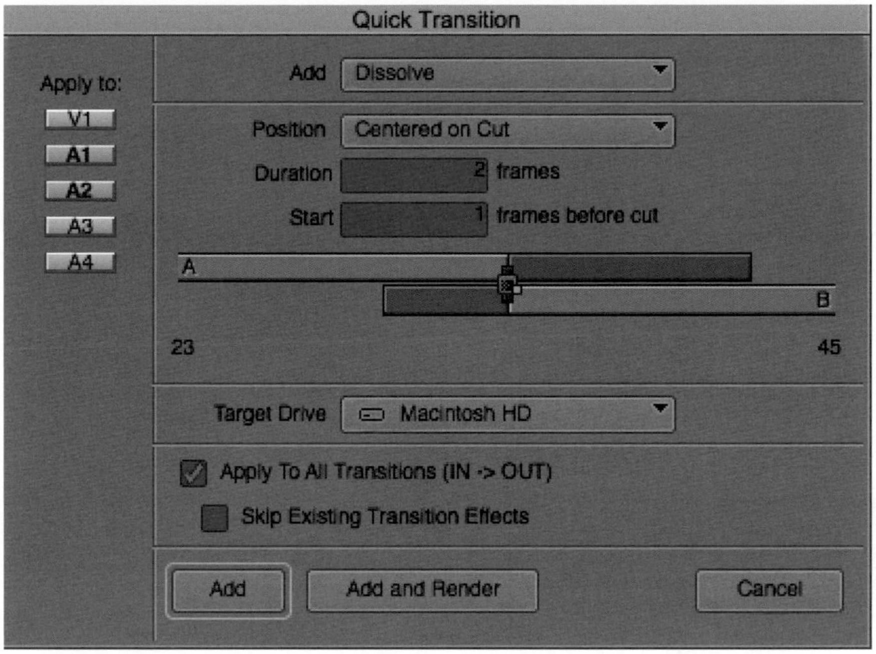

Figure 6.30 The Apply To All Transitions (IN > OUT) option in the Quick Transition dialog.

7.   Click Add.

The transitions will be added to the segments in the sequence. (See Figure 6.31.)

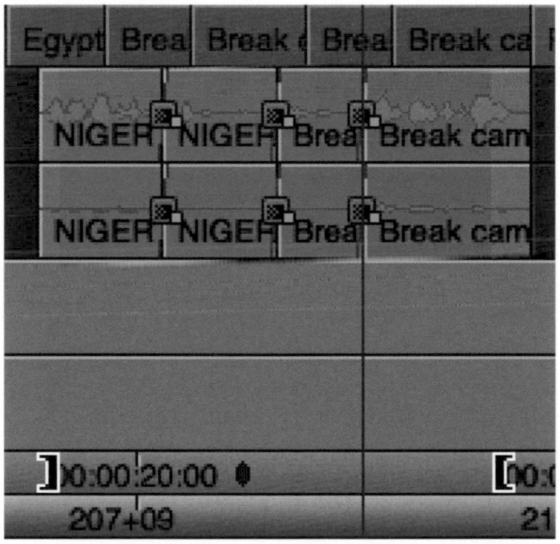

Figure 6.31 Multiple transitions have been added to the sequence.

Introduction to Segment Effects

When we talk about visual effects, we often think about spectacular spaceships, wand-wielding wizards, and the always-popular flesh-eating demon. Those are fantastic visual effects, but more often, effects are used to correct shots that have problems. These "hidden" effects are used to remove unwanted elements, improve the color or smooth out a shaky shot, or even subtly warp jump cuts into one seamless shot. As an editor, you will probably be called on to create these corrective effects more often than to create a flesh-eating demon. This lesson covers a few of the common tools used to improve a variety of imperfect shots.

Media: Running the Sahara

Duration: 45 minutes

GOALS

- Learn to work with segment effects, a.k.a. Filters
- Flop a shot to reverse screen direction
- Stabilize a shot
- Apply Automatic Color Correction
- Hide jump cuts with Fluid Morph
- Resize clips
- Set standard keyframes

Adding Segment Effects

In Media Composer, visual effects can be broken down into three different types:

- **Transition effects**: As you've learned, these are applied at the transition point between two clips, often to emphasize a change of time or theme. Transition effects include dissolves, dip-to-color effects, wipes, pushes, squeezes, spins, etc.

- **Segment effects**: These are applied to an entire segment within a sequence to change the look of a shot. Segment effects include color effects, masks, resizes and more.

- **Motion effects:** These are applied to entire clips within a sequence or to source clips to vary the frame rate or motion of the footage. Motion effects are covered in more depth later in this book.

Media Composer offers more than 200 customizable transition and segment effects. Like transitions effects, segment effects are accessed through the Effect Palette, see Figure 7.1.

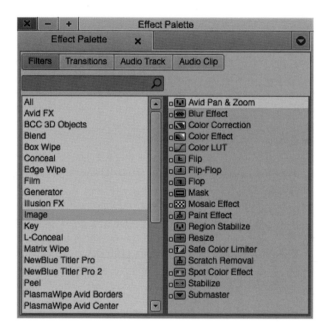

Figure 7.1
Displaying effects in the Image category.

The Effect Palette has a series of buttons across the top – Filters, Transitions, Audio Track, and Audio Clip – which organize the effects by type. Each type of effects are further organized into categories listed in the left column, with individual effects appearing in the right column. Arguably, most common video effects are found in the Image category, which is where you will find most of the effects for this lesson.

The Effect Palette also has a search field at the top, which you can use to filter the effect list by type.

To search for an effect:

1. Select the organizational pane (e.g. Filters).

2. Type the name in the Search field.

    When you start typing the name – Flop, for example. Media Composer dynamically filters the effects displayed in the Effect Palette as you type, as seen in Figure 7.2. Even before you finish typing the full word, the list of effects is dramatically shorter.

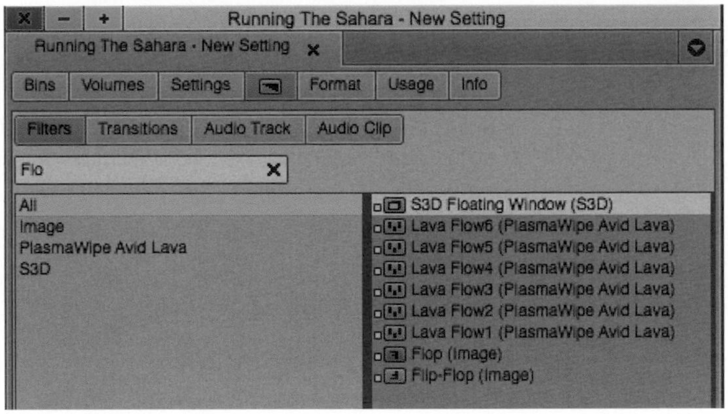

Figure 7.2: Search results update dynamically as you type; the category in which the effect resides is shown in parenthesis.

Once you find the effect you want to add, there are a couple ways you can quickly add it to the Timeline.

To add a segment effect, do one of the following:

■ Drag a **SEGMENT EFFECT** icon from the Effect Palette on to a segment in the Timeline.

■ Enter **EFFECT MODE**, select the **SEGMENT(S)** in the Timeline to which you want to add a segment effect, and then double-click the **SEGMENT EFFECT** in the Effect Palette.

■ Select a segment with either a red or yellow Segment Mode, then double-click the segment effect in the Effect Palette.

After you have added a segment effect, the Timeline displays a segment effect icon over the segment (see Figure 7.3).

Figure 7.3 Timeline segment effect icon.

Similar to removing transitions, the Remove Effect button can be used to remove segment effects.

To remove segment effects:

1. Make sure the **TRACK** is selected in the Track Selector panel.

2. Place the **POSITION INDICATOR** directly over the clip with the effect applied.

3. Click the **REMOVE EFFECT** button.

Exercise Break: Exercise 7.1
Pause here to practice what you've learned.

Learning to Love Effects Mode

New users can sometimes find working with the Effects Mode frustrating. Two behaviors in particular take some getting used to, especially if you are working on a single display, like a laptop or iMac. First, if you scrub the timecode track / ruler in the Timeline to review an effect, the Effects Editor disappears. Second, if you remember to scrub the position bar (at the bottom of the Effects monitor), the Effects Editor may be hidden behind the Composer window. (If you are working with dual displays, these are less of a problem because you can simply move the Effects Editor to the second display.)

There are easy solutions to both of these behaviors.
1.) Use the Effects Editing Workspace, instead of just opening the Effects Editor, and map it to a key on your keyboard.
2.) Map the Effects Mode button to a key on your keyboard.

To open the Effects Editing workspace, select Windows > Workspaces > Effects Editing.
To map it to your keyboard, you can find it in the Command Palette > Workspaces tab > W3 [EE].

The Effects Editing workspace is an arrangement of tools and windows for working with effects. This includes opening the Effect Editor when you activate the workspace, and positioning it on the main display right next to the Composer window, which also changes to a single monitor. (Presumably, you will not be looking for new source footage at the moment you are editing effects.)

By mapping the Effects Editing workspace to a key on the keyboard, you can call up this window arrangement with a single keystroke.

Secondly, by mapping the Effects Mode button to a key on your keyboard, if you accidentally close the Effects Editor, you can very quickly reopen it – again, with a single keystroke.

Stabilizing Shaky Footage

A common problem you will encounter as an editor is unstable camera work. In a documentary, it's not always possible to use a tripod. And sometimes, you want the look and energy of a handheld shot, but just want it toned down. Media Composer has a flexible stabilization effect that can either lock down an unstable shot, removing all camera motion, or just eliminate the erratic bumps and jitters but keep the general camera movement. The beauty of the Stabilize effect is that is practically "auto-magical."

To smooth out a bumpy, shaky shot:

1. From the **IMAGE** category in the Effect Palette, drag the **STABILIZE** effect onto a segment in the Timeline.

   Almost immediately, the Tracking Window opens (see Figure 7.4), and the process of stabilization begins automatically. You will see green dots appear and disappear over the image as Media Composer uses its advanced 3D tracking engine to automatically identify and track reference points in the image, and then use that information to stabilize the shot.

2. Close the Tracking window, and play the clip to view the results.

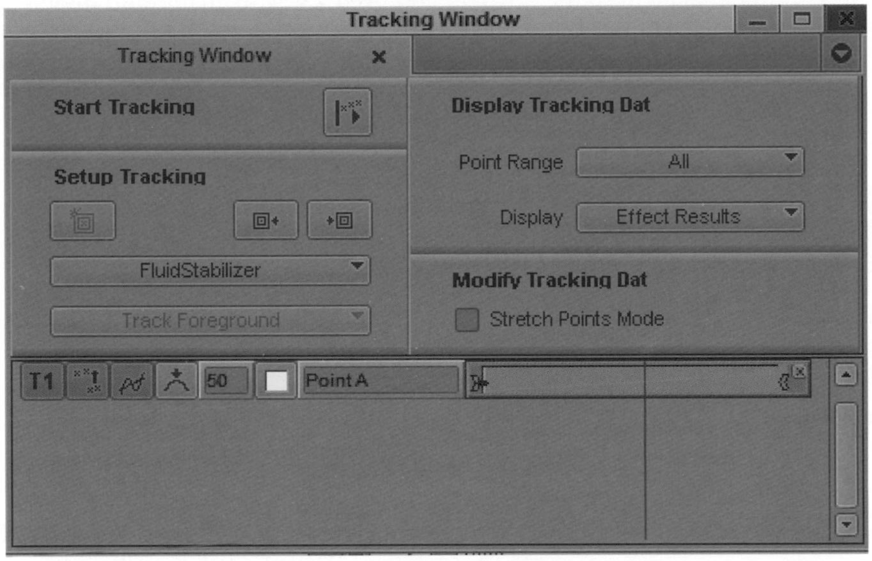

Figure 7.4..The Tracking Window.

The effect initially steps through the segment one frame at a time, analyzing and comparing the frames to extract the motion data of the camera. Once the entire segment is analyzed, the Stabilize effect inverts the motion data and applies it to the clip, leaving only the smooth movement of the camera. For instance, when the camera suddenly jerks down to the left, the motion data offsets it by repositioning the frame up to the right. The amount the frame has to be offset determines how much it also has to be scaled up so the image still fills the frame. The end result is a clip that appears smooth because it is repositioned in the opposite direction by the same amount.

Stabilize: The Rest of the Story

Stabilize is a fantastic effect for its speed, ease of use, and very good results. But, like any fully automated effect, it has its limitations. Media Composer actually includes three effects that can stabilize a shot, which you can learn more about in advanced courses, or through the Media Composer Help menu.

Stabilize: In general, the Stabilize effect should be your first choice. It is the most flexible choice and usually does a good job automatically. If necessary, you can also try it in Manual mode to take more control over the process.

Regional Stabilize: This effect is "old school." It does not have an automatic mode, so it's up to you to select a region to analyze in order to calculate the stabilization. It is also not a real-time effect, so it must be rendered. It does, however, provide a Progressive Source option, so you can use it on progressive material in an interlaced project.

3D Warp: The 3D Warp effect has the Stabilize effect built into it, so you can stabilize a segment with all the other features included in the 3D Warp effect. Nice, but overkill if you just need to stabilize a shot.

You can learn more about working with more of these effects in additional courses in the Avid Learning Series.

To compare the smoothed segment to the original, you need a way to enable and disable parameter groups within the effect. The Effect Editor includes blue highlighted "enable" buttons for active parameters, as shown in Figure 7.5. You can disable the Stabilize effect by disabling the active parameters in the Effect Editor. The Parameter group's settings are still retained, so they can be enabled again at any time.

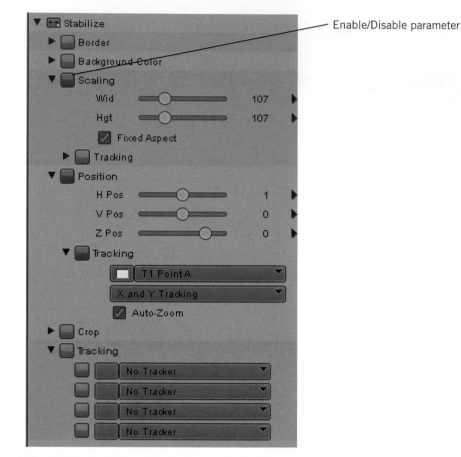

Figure 7.5 The Effect Editor's blue enable/disable buttons.

 If you disable the Scaling parameter on a stabilized segment, you can see how the motion data is applied to the clip. When you play the effect, the frame moves around within the Effect Preview monitor. This is the motion data, offsetting the camera movement.

Locking Down a Shot

That covers just one method of stabilizing, the smoothing method. A more traditional type of stabilization technique aims to create a locked-down shot. All camera movement is removed, and the clip appears as if the camera were on a tripod. The Stabilize effect can be used quite effectively for this, with one slight modification.

By default, the Stabilize effect utilizes the SteadyGlide feature. SteadyGlide is designed to allow movement on one axis – up/down, left/right – while eliminating movement on the other. For example, it will allow for a horizontal pan, but eliminate any vertical wobbles introduced by the camera operator. If you disable SteadyGlide, in many instances, it can produce a result that looks tripod-steady.

To lock down a shot with Stabilize:

1. From the **IMAGE** category in the Effect Palette, drag the **STABILIZE** effect onto a segment in the Timeline.

2. Allow the effect to process as normal, but do not close the Tracking Tool window.

3. In the Tracking Tool window, toggle off the Steadyglide button, as shown in Figure 7.6.

Figure 7.6 Disable the SteadyGlide button to eliminate all movement.

Exercise Break: Exercise 7.2
Pause here to practice what you've learned.

Using Automatic Color Correction to Improve the Footage

There are many times that you will work with footage that is poorly exposed, has low contrast, or color balance problems. Automatic color correction can do a lot to solve these common problems and improve the look of your program. Figure 7.7 shows a before and after look at a shot with automatic corrections applied.

Figure 7.7 A before and after look at how automatic correction can improve your shots.

Setting Up the Color Correction Effect

The Color Correction effect, found in the Image category, is an automated effect, much like Stabilize. The only difference is that there are a variety of actions that the effect will perform to improve the image so you have to set it up before you can use it.

You can choose up to three actions to be run every time the effect is applied, and you can apply the effect to multiple segments at once. The extra minute it takes to configure is well worth the time it saves you later.

Each action uses one of the two color correction toolsets in Media Composer, HSL or Curves, and can affect brightness or contrast, as well as color balance.

To setup the Color Correction effect:

1. Select the **PROJECT WINDOW > SETTINGS** pane.

2. Find the Correction setting, and double-click it to open.

3. Click the **AUTOCORRECT** button at the top.

4. Click the drop down menu that reads "Nothing," and select an action.

   After selecting one, another drop-down menu appears.

   (Optional) Click the drop-down menu again, and select another action as shown in Figure 7.8.

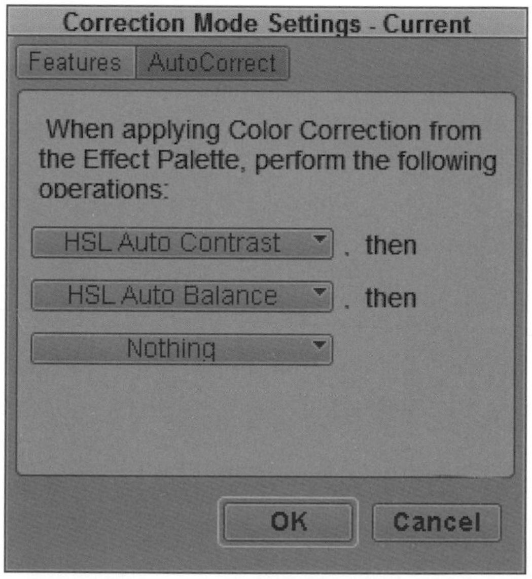

Figure 7.8 The Correction Mode setting is configured and ready for use.

5. Click **OK** to save the settings.

6. In the Settings window, click to the right of "Correction" to open the text field, as shown in Figure 7.9, and type in a descriptive name. For the example, above in Figure 7.8, you might type "HSL Contrast/Balance."

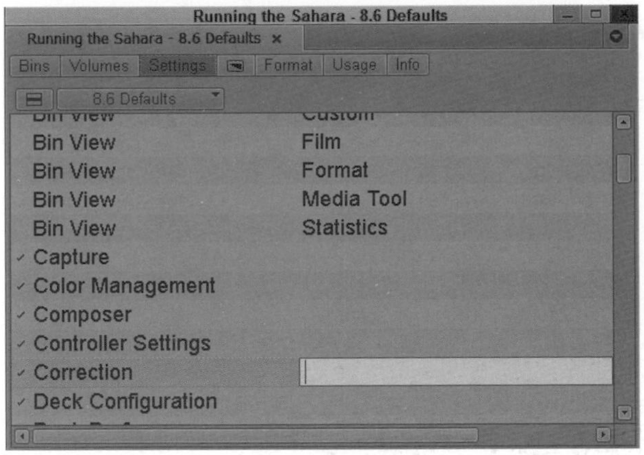

Figure 7.9 Click to open the name field, and enter a descriptive name.

7. (Optional) Create an alternate version of the setting by doing the following:

    a. Select the Correction setting in the list, and press Ctrl+D (Windows) or Command+D (Mac) to duplicate the setting.

        The duplicated will appear in the list and the name will be appended with ".1".

    b. Rename the duplicate setting, and then open it.

    c. Modify the settings to create a different auto-correction workflow, e.g. for Curves, and then click OK.

    d. Click to the left of the new setting to move the check mark from the original Correction setting, to the new one.

        This activates the new setting.

        Anytime you wish to change the active setting, open the Settings window and switch the location of the checkmark.

Applying Automatic Color Corrections

Once configured, you can simply drag the Color Correction effect to a segment in the Timeline. The image will immediately show the results.

At the top of this lesson, you learned that you can apply segment effects by selecting a segment in Segment Mode, and then double-clicking an effect. Put that together with what you learned in the previous lesson about selecting multiple segments, and you apply automatic corrections to the entire sequence in just a few clicks.

To apply the Color Correction effect to a whole sequence at once:

1. Press the **HOME** key, or move the position indicator to the first segment in the sequence.

2. Select the track(s) to apply the effect.

3. Click the **SELECT RIGHT** button in the Timeline toolbar to select all segments in Segment Mode, as shown in Figure 7.10.

4.   Double-click the **COLOR CORRECTION** effect.

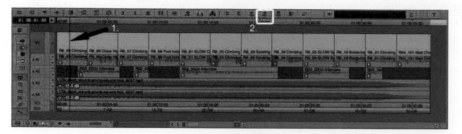

Figure 7.10   You can very quickly setup the Timeline to apply Color Correction to all clips.

There may be a momentary pause before you see the effects appear in the Timeline and the changes are visible. After all, your system is calculating the changes for all the clips in one fell swoop. But then, they appear! (See Figure 7.11.)

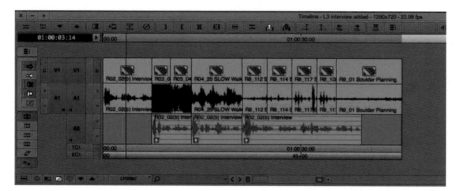

Figure 7.11   Color Correction effects appear on every segment in the Timeline.

Limitations of Automatic Color Correction

Automatic color correction is a useful tool to solve basic image problems very quickly. Like any fully automatic function, it won't produce a perfect result in every situation.

The major drawback of automatic color corrections is that the system cannot see what's in the scene. It doesn't see landscape or faces; it can't differentiate between foreground and background; it only knows that there is some white, yellow, blue, and so on. It will make assumptions about the colors in the frame—assumptions that may or may not be correct. Also, automatic corrections do not compare one shot to another. Each shot is "corrected" based on the first frame.

There are many color-correction problems that are not appropriate for automatic correction. Automatic color corrections might not provide useful results with the following:

Extreme light conditions: If a significant area of an image is deliberately overexposed or underexposed, automatic color corrections may misunderstand the intent and produce an undesired result.

Extreme color-balance problems: Automatic color corrections might not provide the expected result on images that show extreme white-balance issues or in mixed-lighting conditions where part of the image is white balanced while other parts of the image are not.

> **Images lacking the appropriate distinct white or black regions:** Automatic color corrections are effective only with images that have the appropriate content for calculating either white, black, or both, such as areas of strong highlight (white or close to white) and areas of strong shadow (black or close to black).

Exercise Break: Exercise 7.3
Pause here to practice what you've learned.

Hiding Jump Cuts with FluidMorph

Although most corrective effects are segment effects, Media Composer does have a unique transition effect that can also be used to hide problems in a sequence. FluidMorph, located in the Illusion FX category (see Figure 7.12), specifically helps solve the problem of jump cuts, where two shots of the same subject are edited back to back with only slight differences between them. It's a jarring cut because elements within the frame suddenly pop up on screen in a different place. FluidMorph can warp the two images to better align with each other, so they perform a more seamless transition.

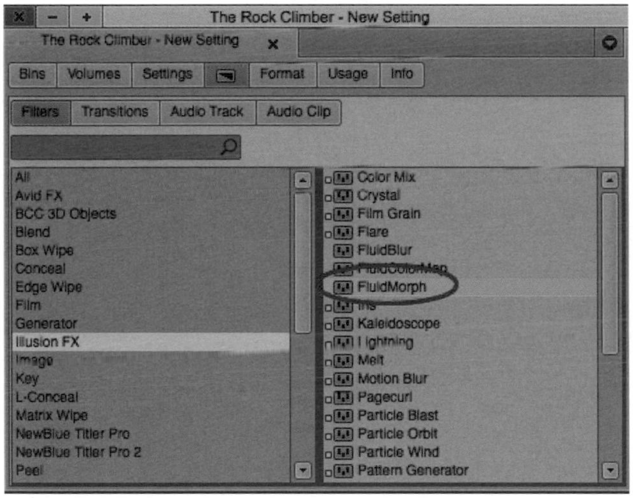

Figure .7.12
Fluid Morph is located in the IllusionFX category of the Effect Palette.

To hide jump cuts using a FluidMorph effect:

1. From the **ILLUSION FX** category, drag the **FLUIDMORPH** effect onto a cut point.

2. Choose **SOURCE > STILL > STILL**.

3. Enable the **FEATURE MATCH** option.

4.   Click **RENDER EFFECT** at the bottom of the Effect Editor.

The Fluid Morph does not require any user input to work, although there are a few options in the Effect Editor. Feature Match (see Figure 7.13) should be the first option you change if the default settings don't produce accurate results. By default, FluidMorph warps both images based on the luminance of the images. Feature Match improves the warping by aligning feature patterns as it warps both images.

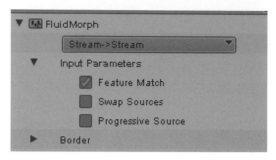

Figure 7.13   The Fluid Morph Feature Match option in the Effect Editor.

 Fluid Morph works best when the majority of the image is the same and the difference in the object that moves is not too severe.

The Source menu (see Figure 7.14) is the next level of assistance for improving FluidMorph's results. By default, FluidMorph takes the safest approach and uses a freeze frame in place of moving video during the morph transition. The simplicity involved in warping two freeze frames to create the morph produces more reliable results but doesn't always look the most realistic. An alternative is to set the Source menu to warp each side of the transition frame by frame. This is the Stream > Stream setting. It is the most complicated of the settings, but will produce the most realistic results if—and this is a big if—the movement doesn't vary all that much. This setting is more likely to result in artifacts because you have two images moving that must be aligned. Setting one side or the other of the transition at Still instead of Stream sort of splits the difference; these half-and-half settings lower the complexity by creating a freeze frame for one of the shots but produces a more realistic result because one shot still has normal motion.

Figure 7.14   The FluidMorph Source menu option in the Effect Editor.

After you have chosen all your settings, you can use the Effect Preview monitor's position bar to click through the various stages of the effect, but the subtlety of this effect can really only be judged by playing it, which requires rendering.

 Exercise Break: Exercise 7.4
Pause here to practice what you've learned.

Resizing a Shot

If you've ever have taken a photo and used a crop tool to cut out unwanted scenery around the edges, you'll understand the value of resizing clips in Media Composer. The difference is that instead of cropping down a photo, you scale up the shot to focus the viewer's attention on a specific area. The result is the same: Unwanted material around the edges of a shot can be removed, and the attention of the viewer can be focused on the important area.

To use the Resize effect:

1. Select the **IMAGE** category in the Effect Palette.

2. Drag the **RESIZE** effect onto a segment in the Timeline

3. Open the **EFFECT EDITOR**.

4. Use the parameters to modify the **RESIZE** effect.

5. (Optional) To avoid distorting the image while you resize it, check the box next to "Fixed Aspect."

    This ensures the width and height are adjusted in proportion when using the parameter sliders.

    Unlike the effects you have used up until now, the Resize effect can be manipulated directly in the Effect Preview monitor. You can reduce the size of the viewing area in the Effect Preview monitor using the Reduce button (See Figure 7.15), making it easier to work outside the boundaries of the visible frame.

 Before you resize the image, it can be helpful to open the Scaling parameter group in the Effect Editor so you can see the scale values as you change them in the Effect Preview monitor.

Figure 7.15 Use the Reduce button to zoom out on the Effect Preview monitor.

A white outline surrounds the frame after you apply the effect and enter Effect mode, as shown in Figure 7.16. This outline allows you to directly manipulate the Resize effect in the Effect Preview monitor. Resize changes are made by dragging the white handles. The handle in the upper right is used to maintain the aspect ratio.

Figure 7.16 The white outline in the Effect Preview monitor allows for direct manipulation.

Additionally, by dragging within the white outline, you can reposition the scaled image to re-center the shot or eliminate unwanted parts around the edges of the frame.

 Any time you directly manipulate the image, Media Composer adds a keyframe. If you don't want the keyframe, hit Delete on your keyboard to remove it.

The only parameters within the Resize effect that do not have controls in the Effect Preview monitor are the crop parameters. The crop parameters in the Effect Editor enable you to cut out unwanted areas around the edges of the frame without scaling. Since Resize is not a compositing (blending) effect, when you crop it does not create a transparent area. Instead a colored background is revealed. You can adjust the background color using the background parameters similar to the parameters you used when adjusting the Dip to Color effect.

When you resize, reposition, or crop the image, the effect is set for the entire segment's length. This works in some cases, but in other cases you may want the scale value or the repositioning to change over time. That's where keyframing comes in.

Using Standard Keyframes

In many effects, Resize being one of them, you may need to have a parameter change value over time. With a Resize, for example, you may need to reposition or increase the scale at a particular point within the shot. To solve this type of problem, Media Composer allows you to animate the change in values over time using a technique called *keyframing*. Here, you'll use the standard keyframing built into the Effect Preview monitor.

Under the Effect Preview monitor is a position bar that represents the duration of the segment. *Keyframes* are added at the location of the blue Position Indicator when you click the Add Keyframe button. Selected keyframes are displayed in purple, while unselected keyframes are gray (see Figure 7.17).

Figure 7.17 Keyframes located under the Effect Preview monitor.

Once a keyframe is added, selecting it and then changing any parameter sets the parameter value for that frame. Selecting another keyframe and changing the same parameter causes an interpolation between the different parameter values on the keyframes. This interpolation creates the animation of the parameters. So, creating animation is the process of selecting keyframes at various points in time and adjusting parameter values differently for each keyframe.

There are two ways to add keyframes:

- Direct manipulation of the image in the Effect Preview Monitor.

- Clicking the keyframe button in the interface or pressing the keyframe button on your keyboard (semicolon).

   Using the Add Keyframe button under the Effect Preview monitor, as shown in Figure 7.18, you can add as many keyframes as required anywhere within the position bar.

Figure 7.18 The Add Keyframe button.

To use keyframing:

1. Either select an existing **KEYFRAME** in the Effect Preview monitor's position bar, or click the **ADD KEY** button to add a keyframe on the current frame.

2. Adjust a **PARAMETER** in the Effect Editor.

3. Move to, or add, another keyframe at a different moment in time.

4. Change the value of the same parameter you adjusted in Step 2.

5. Play the clip from the first keyframe to the second to view the resulting animation.

 Dragging the position indicator in the Timeline will cause you to exit Effect mode. Use the position bar beneath the Effect Preview monitor to move the position indicator within the effect and stay in Effect mode.

You can add any number of keyframes to animate different parameters, but if you want a parameter adjustment to be applied across the entire effect, you must select all the keyframes in the position bar before making the parameter change. You can do this by clicking in the Effect Preview monitor to activate it, and then pressing Ctrl+A (Windows) or Command+A (Mac) or choosing Select All Keyframes from the Edit menu.

 Exercise Break: Exercise 7.5
Pause here to practice what you've learned.

Review/Discussion Questions

1. How do you apply an effect to multiple segments?

2. Once a clip is stabilized, how can you compare the stabilized result with the original video?

3. How do you "lock down" a shot with the Stabilize effect?

4. When using Automatic Color Correction, what is the suggested order of corrections in HSL?

5. When using Automatic Color Correction, what is the suggested order of corrections in Curves?

6. Under what category is the Fluid Morph located in the Effect Palette?

7. Is Fluid Morph a real time effect? What are two ways you can know this?

8. What do the Enlarge and Reduce buttons do in the Effect Preview monitor?

9. Using a Resize effect, how can you scale a clip in the Effect Preview monitor but maintain the aspect ratio?

10. How do you delete a keyframe?

Lesson 7 Keyboard Shortcuts

Key	Shortcut
Ctrl+8 (Windows)/Command+8 (Mac)	Opens the Effect Palette
Ctrl+A (Windows) / Command+A (Mac)	Selects all keyframes in the Effect Editor or Effect Preview monitor, depending on which is active

Making Corrections to Shots

This is a different section of the **Running the Sahara** trailer that you worked with in the previous lesson. Whenever you begin working on a project, you should always view it to know what you are dealing with, so that's how you should start this exercise. As you view the sequence, there are a number of problems in this section of the trailer that could benefit from some corrective visual effects work. The problems are already identified using markers.

Media Used: Running the Sahara

Duration: 60 minutes

GOALS

- Apply a Flop
- Stabilize a shot
- Apply Automatic Color Correction
- Hide a jump cut with FluidMorph
- Resize a clip to eliminate distractions

Exercise 7.1: Flop a Shot

To apply a Flop Effect:

1.   Load the **RTS TRAILER 57** sequence.

2.   From the Tools menu, open the **MARKERS** window, (see Figure 7.19).

     The Markers window has many features. One feature is that when you double-click on a marker in the window, the Position Indicator jumps to that location in the Timeline. In the Markers Tool you'll see a column of red markers that indicates where effects need to be applied in the exercise.

3.   Double-click on the marker in the Markers window to go directly to the segment where you will apply a Flop effect.

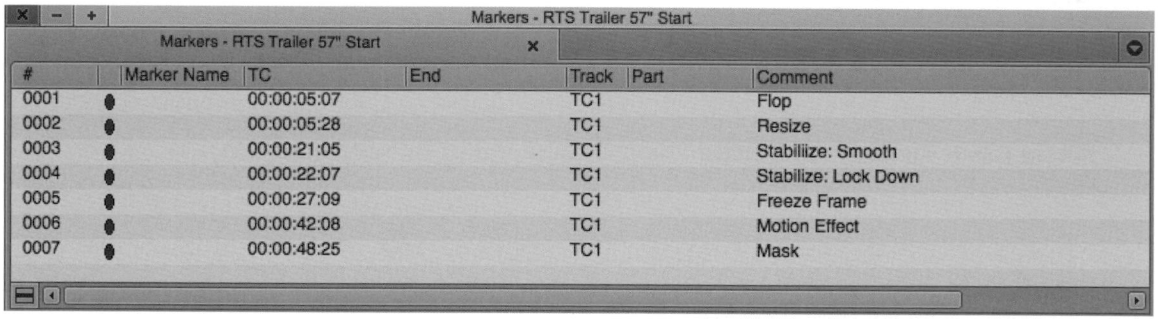

#	Marker Name	TC	End	Track	Part	Comment
0001		00:00:05:07		TC1		Flop
0002		00:00:05:28		TC1		Resize
0003		00:00:21:05		TC1		Stabiliize: Smooth
0004		00:00:22:07		TC1		Stabilize: Lock Down
0005		00:00:27:09		TC1		Freeze Frame
0006		00:00:42:08		TC1		Motion Effect
0007		00:00:48:25		TC1		Mask

Figure 7.19 Markers Window.

The director feels that the flow of images would be better here if the clapping crowd were facing the other way. You'll use the Flop effect to achieve this.

4.   Locate the **FLOP** effect in the Image category of the Effect Palette and drag it to the **MAU, WOMEN CLAPPING** segment in the Timeline.

     When you release the mouse button, the effect is applied, and the Flop icon appears on the clip.

5.   Play the sequence to review the Flop effect.

6.   Open the Effect Editor and check out the Flop parameters (see Figure 7.20). That's right, there aren't any.

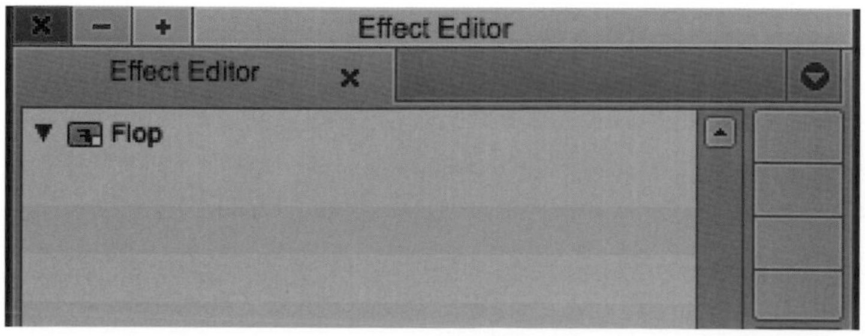

Figure 7.20 The Flop Effect in the Effect Editor.

Now we will go through the steps to apply a segment effect to a series of shots, namely the three "injury" shots about 13 seconds into the sequence.

7. Select the shots by doing one of the following:

   - Lasso all three making sure the lasso is outside the segments.

   - Enable one of the Segment Mode buttons and click on the first "Injury" segment. Then, Shift-click on the other two.

8. Again, locate the **FLOP** effect in the Image category of the Effect Palette and this time double-click it.

   The effect is applied and the Flop icon appears on all the selected segments.

9. Play the sequence to review these three Flop effects. The director doesn't like the last one.

10. Place the position indicator in that third segment and click on the **REMOVE EFFECT** button.

Exercise 7.2: Use the Different Types of Stabilization

1. From the Markers window, double-click the marker with the comment "Stabilize:Smooth." (See Figure 7.21.)

   You will jump to the segment named "Break cam 1A" (see Figure 7.21).

Figure 7.21
The Stabilize: Smooth shot.

This shot has a little camera move going on, which gives it that nice documentary feel, but there are a few bumps that make it jarring.

2. Drag the **STABILIZE** effect from the **IMAGE** category onto the segment in the Timeline.

   Almost immediately after you apply the effect, the Tracking Window opens, and tracking points appear in the Effect Preview monitor as the clip steps forward frame by frame. You can review the results by playing the segment.

    If you accidentally interrupt the tracking process, you can simply restart it by clicking the Start Tracking button in the upper-left corner of the Tracking Window.

3. Compare the before and after by disabling the active parameters (**SCALING** and **POSITION**) in the Effect Editor.

   Now you'll use Stabilize to fix a shot that would look better locked down as opposed to moving around.

4. Directly following the shot you just stabilized is the segment named "Break cam 2" (See Figure 7.22).

Figure 7.22 The Break Cam 2 segment, to be locked down.

5. Drag the **STABILIZE** effect onto the clip in the Timeline.

6. Allow the automatic tracking process to complete.

7. In the Tracking Tool window, disable the **STEADYGLIDE** option, as shown in Figure 7.23.

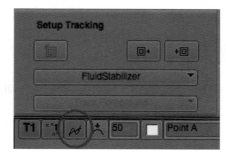

Figure 7.23
Disabling the SteadyGlide option creates a locked-down shot.

The segment should have virtually no camera movement.

 Media Composer has three different tracking engines built-in, and is capable of advanced multipoint tracking. Learn more about tracking in the next course MC110: Media Composer Fundamentals II.

Exercise 7.3: Using Automatic Color Corrections

Color Correction mode provides controls that manipulate the colors and tones of the shots in a sequence. It also includes a number of automatic adjustments that may save you a lot of time. These are set up using the Autocorrect tab of the Correction Mode settings.

1. Click on the **SETTINGS TAB** in the Project window.

   Find and open the **CORRECTION** settings.

   The Correction Mode settings window opens.

2. Click on the **AUTOCORRECT TAB**.

3. Create a sequence of actions.

   Automatic contrast correction and color balance adjustments are available using two different methods called HSL (Hue, Saturation and Luminance) and Curves (R,G,B). Because of differences in the way these two correction groups work, it is highly recommended that when using HSL we select Auto Contrast first and Auto Balance next (see Figure 7.24) while in Curves we use Auto Balance first and Auto Contrast next (see Figure 7.25). It is generally not advisable to mix HSL and Curves functions.

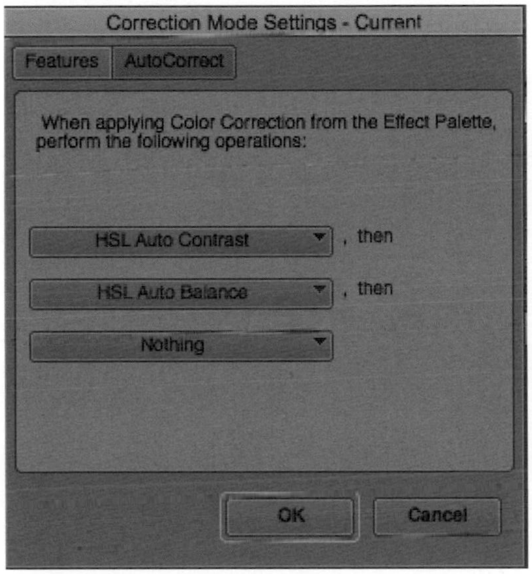

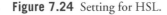

Figure 7.24 Setting for HSL. 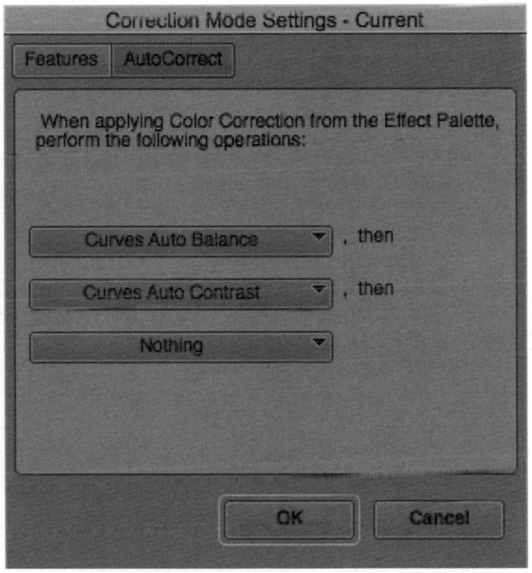   **Figure 7.25** Setting for Curves.

4. Set up the Correction Mode Settings for HSL adjustments, as seen in Figure 7.24. Then, click **OK**.

5. Duplicate the sequence twice. Name them **RTS TRAILER 57 CC-HSL** and **RTS TRAILER 57 CC-CURVES**.

6. Load the sequence **RTS TRAILER 57 CC-HSL**.

7. Park the position indicator over the first segment in the sequence, be sure V1 is active, and then click the Select Right buttons.

8. Double-click the **COLOR CORRECTION EFFECT** (not the Color Effect) in the Image category.

   A separate color correction is placed on every segment, based on an analysis of the first frame of every segment.

9. Configure the CORRECTION MODE SETTINGS for CURVE adjustments, as shown in Figure 7.25.

10. Load the sequence RTS TRAILER 57 CC- CURVES, and repeat.

Depending on the calibration (or lack thereof) of the display you are looking at, you may notice that the HSL auto corrections appear to be warmer, and the Curves corrections appear to be cooler.

It could be argued that the HSL group's auto corrections did a better job, but that's not always the case. It really depends on the nature of the shots to be corrected and the material that is visible in the frame. When in doubt, try them both!

Exercise 7.4: Hide Jump Cuts with Fluid Morph

For this exercise, you'll return to the sequence RTS Trailer 50 to improve a jump cut that happens during one of the interviews. The problem is identified using a marker.

1. Load the RTS TRAILER 50.

2. Open the MARKERS WINDOW if it isn't already open.

3. From the Markers window, double-click the marker with the comment JUMP CUT (see Figure 7.26).

This is a jump cut between two interview segments.

Figure 7.26 The marker identifies the jump cut in the sequence.

4. Play over the two CUTS to see the problem.

At the end of the sentence "It's never been done," the man's head pops to a different place on the screen. Everything else is exactly the same, making this a perfect candidate for a Fluid Morph.

5. From the **ILLUSION FX** category, drag the **FLUID MORPH** effect onto the Jump Cut transition.

   You may recall from Lesson 1 that the default duration for a transition is one second. That's much too long for a Fluid Morph, so you'll first change the duration to something shorter.

6. Click the **EFFECT MODE** button to open the Effect Editor.

7. At the bottom of the Effect Editor, type **10** into the **DURATION** field to create a 10-frame Fluid Morph transition, as shown in Figure 7.27.

Figure 7.27 The duration of a transition can be entered in the Effect Editor.

The Fluid Morph does not require any user input to work, but it does require rendering.

8. Click the **RENDER EFFECT** button at the bottom of the Effect Editor, as shown in Figure 7.28.

Figure 7.28
The Render Effect button in the Effect Editor.

9. In the Render Effect dialog box, select the **HARD DRIVE** where you want the effect media to be stored, and click **OK**.

10. Leave Effect mode and play the **EFFECT** to evaluate it.

11. To get a feel for the various options, enter Effect mode and change the **SOURCE** settings from **STREAM > STREAM** to another setting. Try rendering a few options to see the difference.

   When you get the results you want, consider yourself done with this exercise!

Exercise 7.5: Resize a Shot and Animate

In this exercise, you will resize an image and use standard keyframes to animate a move.

To resize the image.

1. From the **TOOLS** menu, open the **MARKERS WINDOW**. Use it to jump directly to the Resize segment.

   In this segment, the focus of the viewer should be on the runner, but you just can't help being drawn away by the woman turning and looking into the camera. To focus the audience on the runner you'll use the Resize effect to scale the image up until she is out of the picture.

2. Drag the **RESIZE EFFECT** from the Image category in the Effect Palette onto the segment and enter Effects mode.

3. Reduce the size of the frame by using the **REDUCE** button as shown in Figure 7.29.

   This makes it possible to work outside the boundaries of the image.

Figure 7.29 Reduce and Enlarge buttons.

4. Using the DIRECT MANIPULATION HANDLES on the frame outline, resize the image to 150%, Maintain the aspect ratio by dragging the top right direct manipulation handle so you don't end up with a distorted image (see Figure 7.30).

Figure 7.30 Direct Manipulation Handle outside the bounds of the image.

5. So that we don't resize the image larger than necessary, click inside the direct manipulation rectangle to reposition the frame as far as possible to the right so the woman is cut out.

6. When you have completed the resize, click the ENLARGE button to scale the display back to normal. Then, close the Effect Editor to return to Source/Record mode.

    You've successfully refocused the audience's attention onto the runner. In doing so, however, you have seriously reduced the quality of the image. The director would like you to zoom out to the full picture as soon as the woman has ceased to look at the camera. We achieve this with keyframes.

7. When you used the direct manipulation handle you will have created a keyframe, a purple triangle. Click on this holding down the OPTION key (Mac) ALT key (Windows) and drag it to the first frame of the shot.

8. Now make a new keyframe on the last frame by moving the Position Indicator to the end of the effect, and then clicking on the ADD KEYFRAME button (purple triangle) in the toolbar below the Composer window. Click on that frame and make sure that the keyframe at the beginning is gray. Now reset the SCALING X AND Y parameters to 100 and the POSITION X and Y parameters to 0.

9. This creates the feel of a camera pan and a zoom out as it animates back to the full original frame It works well because by the time we include the woman she has stopped looking at the camera.

Combining Multiple Effects

Until now, you've applied only one effect to a single segment. There are times, however, when more than one effect is required. For example, perhaps you want to apply a Color Correction effect to a shot and also resize it. Of course, Media Composer allows you to do this. The combining of effects is called nesting effects.

Media: Running the Sahara

Duration: 20 minutes

GOALS

- Apply more than one effect to a clip
- Change the order of nested effects

Nesting Effects

As you've learned previously, effects can be placed on any segment in the Timeline. But if an effect is already applied to that clip, the new effect replaces the existing effect. This is fine when you are experimenting to see which type of effect works best. But what if, for example, you want to both resize a clip and improve the contrast? Or add a mask?

Avid Media Composer allows you to apply multiple effects to a single segment via a process known as *nesting*. A good analogy to describe nesting effects is the Russian nesting dolls. When you open one, there's another, and another, etc. At the most basic level, a nest contains multiple effects on a single video segment. Nests, however, can be much more complex, with multiple tracks of video all nested within a single segment.

Autonesting

If you need to apply more than one effect to a clip, the easiest approach is to use a technique known as *Autonesting*. This technique allows you to add a new effect on top of an existing effect, such as a Resize on top of a Color Correction.

To Autonest one effect on top of another:

1. Place the position indicator over a **SEGMENT** that already has a segment effect applied.

2. Choose **TOOLS > EFFECT PALETTE** to open the Effect Palette.

3. Click on a **CATEGORY** on the left side of the window.

4. Hold down the **ALT** key (Windows) or **OPTION** key (Mac) and apply a **SEGMENT EFFECT**.

    The effect icon changes. Instead of the original segment effect icon, you now see the newly applied effect icon. The second effect was placed on top of the original effect.

    You can Autonest any number of effects. This can be very beneficial, especially in advanced effects operations where you need to apply multiple treatments to a clip using, for example, both Color Correction and third-party plug-in effects.

    Other than the visual results of having two effects applied, you can use the Effect Editor or the Timeline to see the multiple effects.

    There are a few effects that cannot be used with nesting, such as a Timewarp. If you attempt to create a nest with one of these, Media Composer will alert you with a message.

Seeing Multiple Effects in the Effect Editor

If you have nested multiple effects on a single clip, the parameters for every effect applied are available in the Effect Editor.

To see and manipulate nested effects in the Effect Editor:

1. Park on a **CLIP** with nested effects.

2. Click on the **EFFECT MODE** button to enter Effects Mode.

   The Effect Editor shows the parameters for the nested effects, as shown in Figure 8.1.

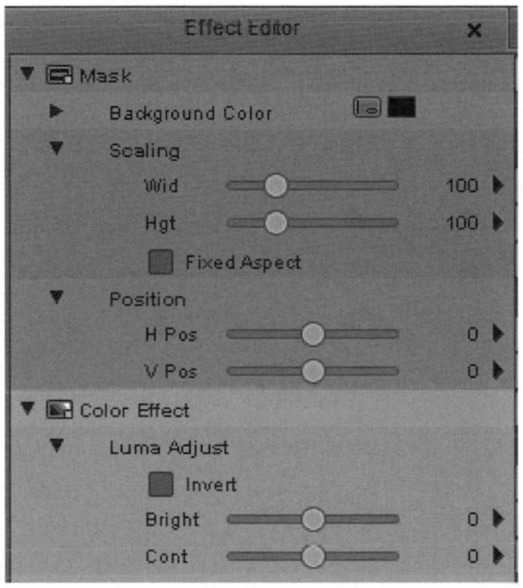

Figure 8.1 The Effect Editor with two effects displayed.

If nested effects have used standard keyframes in the effect's Preview monitor, their parameters will not be viewed in the Effect Editor. Some effects, such as the Blur effect, already have keyframes applied, so those parameters will not show alongside other nested effects in the Effect Editor.

The bottom-most effect in the Effect Editor is at the bottom of the nest – that is, closer to the video segment. All other effects are listed, traveling upward, in the order they reside on the segment. The top effect in the Effect Editor is the same effect you see at the top level in the Timeline.

Effects are always processed from the bottom of the nest up. This order of processing is significant and can have an impact on the final effect. It is easy to change the order of processing, though, as you will see in a moment.

Displaying a Nest in the Timeline

The second way you can view effects within a nest is to display the nest in the Timeline. Two methods are available: simple nesting and expanded nesting.

Method One: Simple Nesting View

In this method, you travel down inside a nest, and the video Track monitor travels with you, allowing you to view the lower effects in isolation from the effects above them. This is a very useful technique, especially for complex nests with numerous effects and/or video tracks, because it enables you to "dive underneath" higher effects so that you can focus on the effects beneath. To move down through each effect and back up to the top effect, you use the Step In/Step Out buttons (see Figure 8.2).

Figure 8.2 The Step In/Step Out buttons.

To step into an effect nest using Simple Nesting View:

1. Park on a **CLIP** with nested effects.

2. Make sure the track is active.

3. Click the **STEP IN** button at the bottom of the Timeline.

    When you step into a nest, the Timeline view changes, and only the contents of the nest (that is, what's beneath the top effect) are visible, as shown in Figure 8.3.

Figure 8.3 A nested effect's contents.

When you are inside a nest, you can access only the contents of that nest. That means that not only are the clips before and after the effect you stepped into not accessible while you are inside the nest, but neither is audio.

You can continue to step in as long as there are effects to step into. To tell how deep you are in a nested effect, you can look at the Track Patching panel. Beneath the video tracks appears a nest depth indicator, shown in Figure 8.4.

Figure 8.4 The N2 on the Nest depth indicator tells us we've stepped into two effects.

Method Two: Expanded Nesting View

Compared to simple nesting, expanded nesting lets you see the sequence and the nest contents simultaneously. It also allows you to listen to audio and access all material in the sequence before and after the effect nest you are working with.

In addition, unlike with simple nesting, the video monitor is always positioned at the top of the nest and cannot travel into the nest. As a result, with expanded nesting, you can edit the contents of a nest but still see the composite of all effects within the nest.

To expand an effect nest:

1. Park on a **CLIP** that is Autonested with effects.

2. Make sure that the track is active.

3. **ALT+CLICK** (Windows) or **OPTION+CLICK** (Mac) the **STEP IN** button.

    The Timeline displays the tracks inside and outside the nest, with the tracks inside the nest appearing directly above the track that contains the nest, as shown in Figure 8.5. This can be somewhat confusing at first. With the Expanded Nesting view, Media Composer slides the underlying layers up from behind. In Figure 8.5, the Color Effect is actually underneath the Mask effect in terms of compositing order. However, in the Expanding Nesting view it has been raised from behind the mask so we can see it.

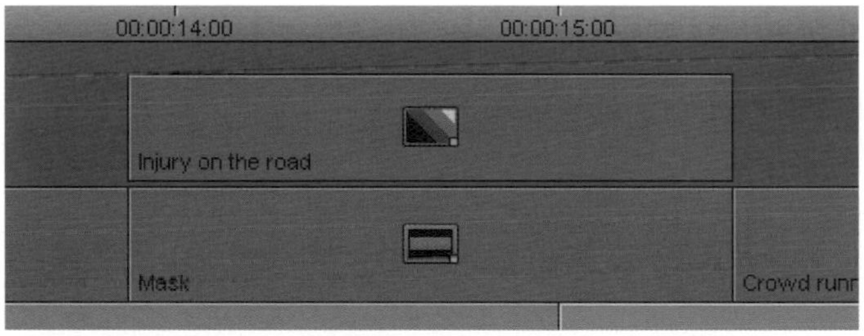

Figure 8.5 Expanded nesting.

 You can also enter and exit expanded nesting by double-clicking a segment with an effect on it. This can be disabled via the Timeline setting.

As with simple nesting, the Track Patching panel indicates the nest level for each element within the nest, this time using two numbers separated by a period instead of just one. (See Figure 8.6.)

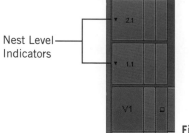

Nest Level Indicators

Figure 8.6 Expanded nesting track indicators.

The first number indicates the nest level of the track. The number 1 indicates the track is on the first level of the nest, and the number 2 indicates that you have stepped in twice (the source of an effect within an effect). The second number indicates the track number at that layer of the nest (i.e., video track 1 at that nest layer, video track 2 at that nest layer, and so on). In addition, each level of the nest is assigned a different track color to help differentiate it from other nest levels.

Exercise Break: Exercise 8.1
Pause here to practice what you've learned.

Changing the Order of Nested Effects

Although it isn't the case for all effect combinations, there are times when the order of the effects in the nest is important.

When more than one effect is applied to a clip, the composited result of each effect is fed up to the next effect in the nest. So in some cases, you may need to reorder the effects in a nest to get the desired results.

To reorder effects in a nest:

1. Park on a **CLIP** that is Autonested with effects.

2. Drag an **EFFECT ICON** in the Effect Editor to change its position in the nest. (See Figure 8.7.)

Figure 8.7 Reordering effect icons in Effect mode.

For the most part, effects that can be nested can also be reordered. There are some exceptions to this, and the system will display a dialog box explaining why, when you encounter one.

Exercise Break: Exercise 8.2
Pause here to practice what you've learned.

Review/Discussion Questions

1.   How do you add an effect to a clip in the Timeline on top of an existing effect?

2.   What is that procedure called?

3.   What are the two different methods you can use to view the effects inside of a nest?

4.   What is an advantage of simple nesting?

5.   What is an advantage of expanded nesting?

6.   How do you change the order of effects within a nest?

Lesson 8 Keyboard Shortcuts

Key	Shortcut
Alt (Windows)/Option (Mac)	To AutoNest a segment effect
Alt+click (Windows)/Option+click (Mac)	Opens an effect nest in the Timeline using Expanded Nesting on the Step In button
Alt+click (Windows)/Option+click (Mac)	Closes the Expanded Nesting view on the Step Out button

Nesting Effects

Until now, you've applied no more than one effect to a given clip. There are times, however, when more than one effect is required. Media Composer allows you to do this by nesting effects.

Media Used: Running the Sahara

Duration: 20 minutes

GOALS

- Nest effects
- Step in and out of an effect
- Rearrange the order of nested effects

Exercise 8.1: Nesting Effects

In this exercise, you're going to look at "nesting" effects. This is Avid Media Composer's way of allowing you to use multiple effects on the same shot.

1. Load the sequence you named **RTS TRAILER 57**.

   The director would like this final shot to have a mask on it to give that movie feel.

2. Open the Markers tool by selecting **TOOLS MENU > MARKERS**.

3. Double-click the last marker in the column to jump to the segment named "Runners, out of the sun."

4. Open the Effect Palette, and drag the 1.66 Mask from the Film category onto the segment.

   Since it's a preset, we can immediately see it masking the shot, as shown in Figure 8.8.

Figure 8.8 The shot with the 1:66 Mask applied.

5. Open the Effect Palette and apply the **RESIZE** effect from the Image Category.

   Our mask disappears as the Resize effect has replaced the Mask effect. To stop it behaving this way we need to nest the effect.

6. **UNDO** to restore the mask.

7. Now hold down the **ALT** key (Windows) or **OPTION** key (Mac) as you apply the Resize effect.

   The clip in the Timeline now shows the Resize effect, but in the Record monitor the mask clearly remains. This is called "Autonesting."

8. To see what has happened click on the **STEP IN** button in the toolbar at the bottom of the Timeline window.

    The Timeline changes and we are looking at one video track with the Mask effect on it. The Timecode track reads N1, which stands for Nest 1. (see Figure 8.9).

Figure 8.9 Simple Nest Step In 1.

9. If we click on the **STEP IN** button **AGAIN** we now see one video track with no effect on it.

    This is the segment itself. Notice that the mask does not show in the Record monitor and the Mask Effect is no longer visible on the segment. The Timecode track reads N2, which stands for Nest 2. (see Figure 8.10).

Figure 8.10 Simple Nest Step In 2.

10. Click the **STEP OUT** button **TWICE** to return to the normal view of the Timeline.

    This is called "Simple Nesting." Now let's examine the same nest with the Expanded Nesting view.

11. This time double-click the segment in the Timeline (or hold down the **ALT** key (Windows) or **OPTION** key (Mac) as you click the Step In button).

    The segment appears in a layer above V1, but under V2, named 1.1.

12. **DOUBLE-CLICK** on that segment on the 1.1 track showing the Mask effect icon (or hold down the Alt key (Windows) or Option key (Mac) as you click the Step In button again) and an additional layer, named 2.1 appears with no effect on it.

    This is the video segment itself (see Figure 8.11).

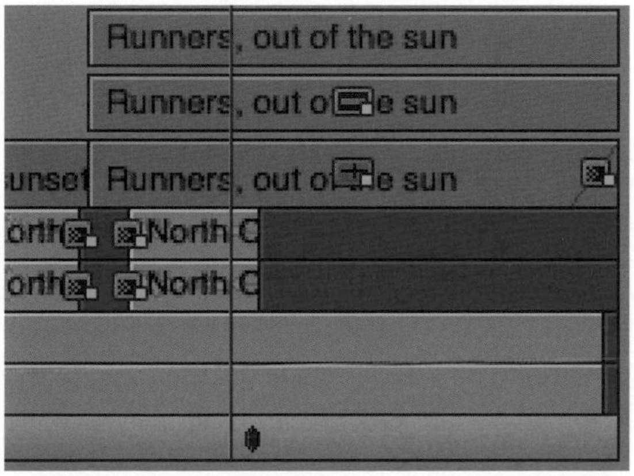

Figure 8.11 Expanded Nest.

13. To get out of the whole thing, double-click on the segment in the V1 layer with the Resize effect icon (or hold down the Alt key (Windows) or Option key (Mac) as you click the Step Out button.)

You have now used two different ways to view the same nest.

The disadvantage of Expanded Nesting is that you cannot monitor the individual video layers.

The disadvantage of Simple Nesting is that you cannot see other parts of the sequence or hear the audio.

You'll use both views in your work, depending on which one helps you accomplish your goal at that moment most efficiently.

Exercise 8.2 Rearranging the Order of Nested Effects

In this exercise, you will learn how the order of processing can affect effect results.

In the Effect Editor you can see that both effects are present when nested (see Figure 8.12).

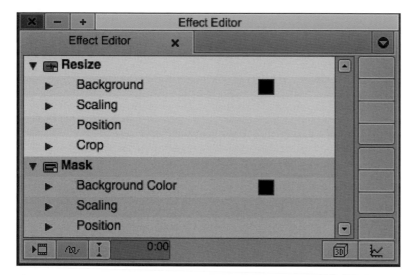

Figure 8.12 Both effects present in the Effect Editor.

1. In the Resize, open the **SCALING PARAMETER** group, enable fixed aspect and scale up the image.

As you do this the mask will disappear. This is because the resize is on top of the mask so that you are effectively rescaling both the image and the mask.

2. To fix this, simply drag the resize down in the Effect Editor to underneath the mask.

The mask is restored in the Record monitor but the Resize is still applied to the image.

Freeze Frames and Motion Effects

When putting a scene together, sometimes the original timing of the shot needs to be adjusted. For example, you may want a shot to last longer than what was actually shot. This chapter introduces you to motion effects that enable you to vary the playback speed of a clip or freeze the clip entirely.

Media Used: Running the Sahara

Duration: 20 minutes

GOALS

- Explore the different types of motion effects
- Create a freeze frame
- Create a motion effect

Types of Motion Effects

Motion effects vary the speed at which frames from clips play. Avid editing systems can create three different types of motion effects:

- **Freeze frames:** These are created using a master clip or subclip in the Source monitor and create a new clip containing only the desired frame.

- **Motion effects:** These are also created using a master clip or subclip in the Source monitor. In these types of effects we can speed up or slow down the video. The new clip that is created plays faster or slower than the original, but still at a constant speed.

- **Timewarp effects:** These are applied to a segment in the Timeline in the same way you have applied other segment effects, like Mask or Resize. The rate of motion can be keyframed and varied over time within a single clip. This means we can create motion effects where, for example, a shot of a person running can fluidly ramp from normal speed into slow motion to add drama or tension.

The key difference between the three different types is that two of them—freeze frames and motion effects—are created from the source side of the Composer window, while Timewarp effects are created from footage that already exists in your Timeline. Depending on the stage of your edit, one may be more convenient than the other.

Creating Freeze Frames

A freeze frame displays a single frame from a clip on the screen for a duration you choose. As with Motion Effects, these effects are generated from a master clip or subclip in the Source monitor and creates a brand new clip. Then, as with all other types of clips, a portion of the freeze frame clip is edited into your sequence.

If the clip from which you are generating the freeze frame is from a full-resolution clip, you must tell Media Composer how you want it generated. The system can generate freeze frames using two different rendering types (see Figure 9.1):

- **Both fields:** Uses both fields. Good for shots without interfield motion, e.g. a person running or someone swinging a bat. Shots with interfield motion will show noticeable jitter due to the temporal differences between the two fields. Additionally, while it is not intuitive, this is the render type you want to use when your source footage is progressive, i.e. 24p, 25p, etc.

- **Interpolated field:** Good for shots with interfield motion because it deletes the second field and uses the adjacent first field to calculate new data for the second field. For Freeze Frames made from interlaced footage, this produces a high-quality result that does not jitter.

 Be aware that your computer monitor does not display both fields of interlaced footage. If working with interlaced footage, be sure to view your freeze frames and motion effects on a broadcast monitor to be able to evaluate the results and quality.

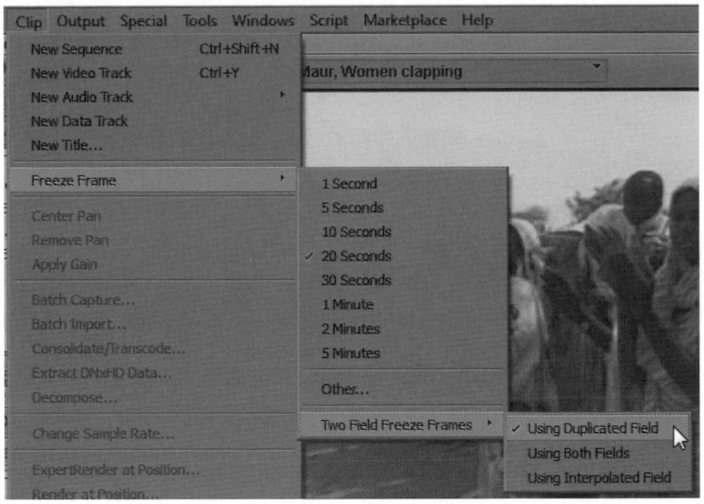

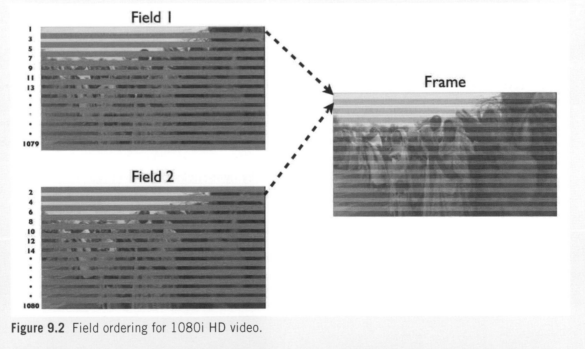

Figure 9.1 Freeze frame render types.

Understanding Fields and Frames

Back when television was being invented, the goal was to draw the entire picture on the screen, one line at a time, from top to bottom. Unfortunately, the technology of the time wouldn't allow that quickly enough to prevent unacceptable motion artifacts. So what they did instead was to draw half of the frame at once, skipping every other line, then draw the second half of the frame, filling in the skipped lines. This is known as *interlacing*, as the frame is made of two interwoven—or interlaced— parts. These two parts are known as *fields*. Figure 9.2 shows the interlacing order for high definition video, with the fields numbered. (Even though interlacing could have been bypassed when high-definition video was created, it was kept for backward compatibility.)

Figure 9.2 Field ordering for 1080i HD video.

The NTSC, PAL, and 1080-line interlaced (often written as 1080i) formats use interlaced fields. 720-line HD is always progressive, and there are progressive versions of 1080-line HD as well.

You should follow these general rules when selecting the render type:

- Use the interpolated field rendering type when working with NTSC 29.97i, PAL 25i, or 1080i media.

- Use the both fields rendering type when working with NTSC 24p/23.976p, PAL 25p/24p, 720p, or 1080p media.

Although using the interpolated field rendering type with progressive media will not necessarily get you into trouble (but could result in a slightly softer image), using the both fields rendering type in an interlaced project will almost always get you into trouble due to interfield motion that is present if not noticeable prior to creating the freeze frame. A good example of this is the blinking of an eye. A blink will appear as a visible flutter in a freeze frame created from interlaced media using the both fields rendering type.

When creating a freeze frame, it is generally a good idea to make these a little longer than you think you'll need so they're easier to edit into the sequence. The duration isn't critical, though, as you can always trim the clip to make it longer after editing it into the sequence. It would just need to be rendered after trimming

To create an interpolated field freeze frame:

1. Choose CLIP MENU > FREEZE FRAME > TWO FIELD FREEZE FRAME > USING INTERPOLATED FIELD.

2. Choose CLIP > FREEZE FRAME > 20 SECONDS.

   Creating a freeze frame creates a small media file, so Media Composer displays a dialog box asking where to store the media (see Figure 9.3).

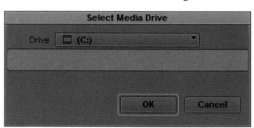

Figure 9.3 Render drive selection.

It is generally a good idea to store the rendered media on the same drive as the rest of your media, although there are some exceptions to this rule, particularly when working with shared storage.

You can also access the Freeze Frame menu by right-clicking on the image in the Source monitor.

If you have at least one bin open, Media Composer next asks where to store the freeze frame clip. (See Figure 9.4.) It is best to create a dedicated bin to store your Freeze Frames and Motion Effect clips, and name it accordingly, to keep yourself organized.

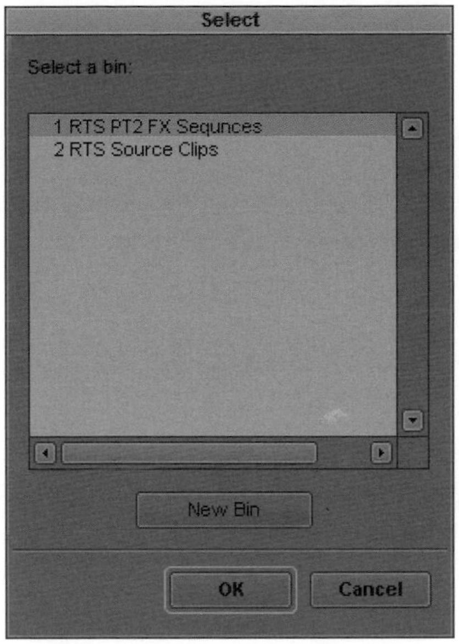

Figure 9.4 Bin selection.

After you save the Freeze Frame, it is automatically loaded into the Source monitor and appears in the bin. Freeze Frames can be easily distinguished from other clips in the bin by their unique icon. (See Figure 9.5.) Also note that after the name of the clip, Media Composer has added "FF" to indicate that it's a freeze frame.

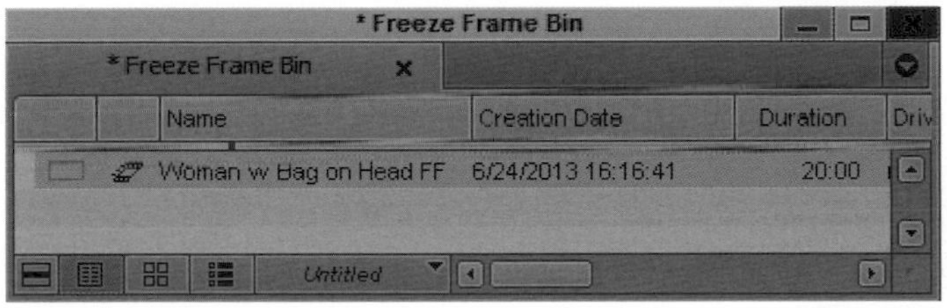

Figure 9.5 Freeze frame in bin.

Exercise Break: Exercise 9.1
Pause here to practice what you've learned.

Creating Motion Effects

With motion effects, you control the frame rate at which a clip plays, resulting in fast or slow motion. It's even possible to purposefully add a stuttered look to the video, called *strobing*. When creating motion effects, the more noticeable the motion is in a clip, the more careful you should be when you choose a frame rate or render method. For example, if someone is running quickly through the frame, not all frame rates and render methods will create acceptable results.

As with freeze frames, motion effects are generated from clips in the Source monitor using the Motion Effect button (shown in Figure 9.6) rather than clips already edited into a sequence.

Figure 9.6 Motion Effect button.

The Motion Effect button can actually open two different tools, depending on which monitor is active when you click it. If the Source monitor is active, then the "Motion Effect" window opens, as shown in Figure 9.7. If the Record monitor or Timeline is active, then the "Motion Effect Editor" window opens, used with Timewarp effects, which we will discuss shortly.

Figure 9.7 The Motion Effect dialog box.

You cannot use the Motion Effect button in the Timeline Palette to create a motion effect. This button is used only to modify a motion effect that has already been created in the sequence.

You have the option in the Motion Effect dialog box to change the playback speed in a few ways. You can enter in a new duration, a new frame rate, or a percentage of the actual playback speed, as shown in Figure 9.8.

You can compare the values you enter in the Frames field and FPS fields with the current value for each. Entering a larger number in the Frames field will create a slower motion, and entering a smaller number will create faster motion.

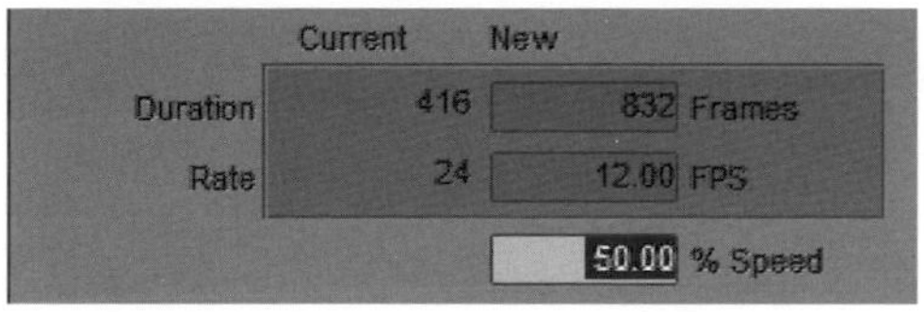

Figure 9.8
Enter the speed change by changing the number of frames, the frame rate, or the percentage of speed.

The percentage of speed works similarly: A number lower than 100% will create slow motion and a number greater than 100% will create fast motion. Entering a negative value in either the Rate or the % Speed field will create reverse motion.

With the exception of reverse motion effects and very high-speed motion effects, it is not typically necessary to render motion effects if you are editing on modern computer hardware and drives. If you are slowing down a clip or speeding it up by a factor of three or five, you will not have to render the clip; you can just click the Create button.

To create a motion effect:

1. Load a **CLIP** into the Source monitor.

2. Choose **MOTION EFFECT** from the Composer window's **FAST** menu.

3. Choose **OPTIONS** in the Motion Effect dialog box.

4. Click **CREATE** or **CREATE AND RENDER**.

   When you click Create or Create and Render to generate the motion effect, an additional dialog box will be displayed, allowing you to choose the bin to store the newly created motion effect. In the bin, motion effect clips have the same clip icon as a freeze frame but are named to indicate the change in frame rate applied to the clip. (See Figure 9.9.) As with freeze frames, the newly created clip is automatically loaded into the Source monitor.

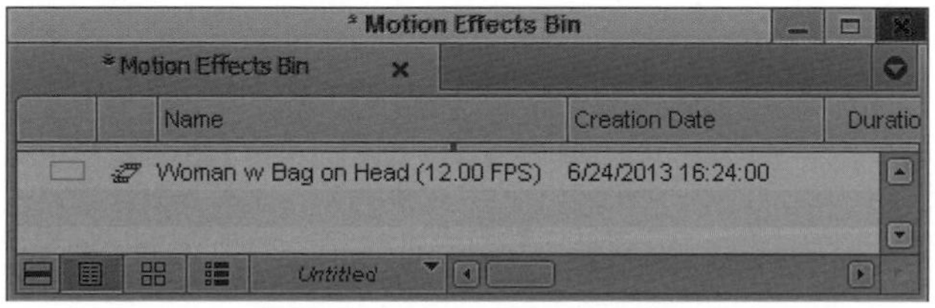

Figure 9.9 Motion effect in bin.

Setting the Proper Render Method

As with freeze frame, you need to set the render method. Because the final effect will be moving, the differences in render methods here may be more noticeable than it is with freeze frames. The good news is that if you try one and don't like the result, just re-render with a different method.

The following options are available:

Duplicated field: The default choice. This option reduces the vertical resolution by half because it drops one field of the image, resulting in a lower-quality image. This option does not require rendering (which is probably why it's the default). Be aware that the duplicated field rendering option should never be used in a project intended for broadcast (unless it is deliberately used to create a stylization), as it cuts the video's vertical resolution in half. It is intended only for offline use.

Both fields: Good for shots without interfield motion, progressive video, and still shots. For best results, with interlaced video, you should also use evenly divisible frame rates with this option. This is especially true when slowing a clip down.

Interpolated field: Calculates the motion effect at the field level rather than the frame level by combining field line pairs. This is used with interlaced video containing motion (e.g. a person running).

VTR-style: Calculates the motion effect at the field level rather than the frame level by shifting field information by a scan line. This creates very smooth motion effects without any reduction in detail. At very slow speeds, a slight vertical jitter (due to the field shifts) may be noticeable.

Motion Effects Segment Icons

Like other effects, and unlike freeze frames, when motion effects are edited into a sequence, they have an icon. The motion effect icon not only indicates that the clip is a motion effect, but it also relates the render method used to generate it. This extra bit of information is extremely useful in the later stages of editing, especially if a previous editor used the wrong type of motion effect. Table 9.1 shows the different icons and what they indicate.

Table 9.1: Motion Effects Segment Icons

Icon	Render Method
	Duplicated field
	Both fields
	Interpolated field
	VTR-style

Creating Motion Effects Using Fit to Fill

Another useful option when creating a motion effect is the Fit to Fill check box. Use this option when you have a specific part of a source clip that you want to fit to a specific region (or duration) in your sequence.

Unlike a typical three-point edit, using Fit to Fill requires that you have four marks set: two in Source and two in the Timeline. The four marks define two different durations. Media Composer calculates the difference and will speed up or slow down the source material so that the new clip that is generated fits exactly into the marked region of the sequence.

To use an oversimplified example, if the duration marked in the Source were 1 second, and the duration marked in the Timeline were 2 seconds, the resulting rate would be 50%. Play the material half as fast and it takes twice as long to go through.

Or, if the duration marked in the Source were 1 second, and the duration marked in the Timeline were ½ second, the resulting rate would be 200%. Twice as fast plays in half the time.

Real examples are never so precise, so be aware that creating motion effects in this way can cause fractional frame rates that may not produce as good a result as even frame rates. Despite this, they can still be an efficient way to generate things like a very high-speed version of a long, slow shot.

To create a Fit to Fill motion effect:

1. Mark an **IN** and **OUT** in the sequence where you want to place the motion effect clip.

2. Load a **CLIP** in the Source monitor.

3. Mark an **IN** and **OUT** on the source clip.

4. Open the Composer window's **FAST** menu and click the **MOTION EFFECT** button.

5. Enable the **FIT TO FILL** check box in the Motion Effect dialog box.

6. Press the Return or Enter key (or click the **CREATE AND RENDER BUTTON**).

   Media Composer creates the new Motion Effect clips, places it in the bin you have selected and also automatically loads it into the Source monitor for you.

   Since the new motion effect clip's duration exactly matches the duration marked in the sequence, and because the blue position indicator is placed at the beginning of the clip by default, all you have to do now is use the Overwrite function to edit it into the Timeline.

7. Press the B key on the keyboard (or click the Overwrite button in the Composer window).

Exercise Break: Exercise 9.2
Pause here to practice what you've learned.

Review/Discussion Questions

1. What are the three types of motion effects?

2. How are freeze frames created?

    a. They are generated from a source clip.

    b. They are applied to a clip in the sequence.

3. Why is it important to set the freeze frame render type?

4. How are motion effects created?

    a. They are generated from a source clip.

    b. They are applied to a clip in the sequence.

5. How many marks in total are required to create a Fit to Fill motion effect?

6. What are three types of rendering methods for creating motion effects? When should you use each one?

Creating Freeze Frames and Motion Effects

In this exercise, you will create freeze frames and motion effects to add drama and visual interest to your sequence.

Media Used: Running the Sahara

Duration: 20 minutes

GOALS

- Create a freeze frame
- Create a motion effect
- Create a motion effect with Fit To Fill

Exercise 9.1: Create a Freeze Frame

You will create a Freeze Frame and edit it into the sequence. You'll quickly jump to the correct location in the sequence using markers that have been set.

To create a Freeze Frame:

1. Load the **RTS TRAILER 57** sequence, if it is not already.

2. Using the Markers window, go to the segment marked **FREEZE FRAME**, (see Figure 9.10).

    The shot of the Minaret is a very small part of a crane shot, and the director would rather it had no movement. We are going to substitute a freeze frame.

Figure 9.10 Create a Freeze Frame to replace this segment.

3. Turn off all tracks except V1.

4. Click the **MARK CLIP** button or press T key on the keyboard.

5. Open the **RTS SCENERY** and **LOCAL PEOPLE** bin.

6. Load the **MINARET CLIP** into the Source monitor.

7. Place the position indicator in the middle of the clip.

8. Right-click to access **FREEZE FRAME**.

    The cascading menus allow you to choose a duration and a render method.

    For this clip, 5 secs is sufficient and the material is progressive so Both Fields is the render method to use.

9. Choose the render method.

10. Select the duration.

11. At this point, the Select Media Drive dialog asks us to choose which drive we want to place the new media in. Select one (your instructor will advise you) and click **OK**.

    The system prompts you to select a bin. If new media is being created, new metadata will be created as well. You are being asked which bin you want the freeze frame clip to be placed in.

12. Select a bin and click **OK**.

    A dialog window shows the progress of creating the media file of the freeze frame clip.

    Above the Source monitor in the Clip Name menu, the name of the clip has changed from **MINARET** to **MINARET FF** and the master clip icon beside it has been replaced by the Motion Effect clip icon, (see Figure 9.11).

Figure 9.11 Both icon and name indicate a Freeze Frame.

13. Place a **MARK IN** near the beginning of the FF clip, leaving some handle at the head of the shot to make it easier to trim or add a transition effect if you ever needed to in the future.

14. Click the **OVERWRITE** button or press B on the keyboard to overwrite the Minaret shot in the sequence with the freeze frame you just created.

15. Review the result.

Exercise 9.2: Create a Motion Effect

You will create a Motion Effect and edit it into the sequence. You'll quickly jump to the right location in the sequence using markers that have been set.

1.   Open the Markers Tool, if it is not already open.

2.   Double-click on the marker labeled **MOTION EFFECT**.

    This will jump you to the shot seen in Figure 9.12.

    The shot of the sunset has very little action, as is usually the case with sunsets. The director would like the shot to speed up so that we can actually see the sun setting.

Figure 9.12   Create a Motion Effect to replace this segment.

3.   Check that all tracks except V1 are disabled.

4.   Click the **MARK CLIP** button in the Record monitor toolbar or press T on the keyboard.

    The segment is now marked, ready for replacement.

5.   Open the **RTS SCENERY** and **LOCAL PEOPLE** bin.

6.   Load the **MAUR, SUNSET CLIP** into the Source monitor.

7.   **MARK IN** roughly 20 seconds from the start of the clip, and then **MARK OUT** roughly 20 seconds from the end of the clip.

8.   Choose **MOTION EFFECT** from the Tool Palette in the Composer's **FAST** menu.

9.   Add an element of drama by speeding up the setting of the sun by **1500%**.

10.   Choose **BOTH FIELDS** as the render option for the motion effect.

11.   Select a Target Drive for the media (your instructor will advise you).

12. Select **CREATE AND RENDER**.

    The system prompts you to select a bin.

13. Select a bin and click **OK**.

    A dialog tells us we are creating the video media for the motion effect.

    In the bin, the motion effect clip is named to indicate the change in frame rate and is automatically loaded into the Source monitor.

14. Perform an **OVERWRITE EDIT** to replace the shot. Play through and view the result.

    The director wants more. He wants to add as much drama as possible by speeding up the setting of the sun as much as is possible. The more frames we are compressing into the segment in the Timeline the faster the sun's movement will be.

15. Once again with only **V1** selected, click the **MARK CLIP** button in the Record monitor toolbar or press T on the keyboard.

16. Reload the original **MAUR, SUNSET** master clip into the Source monitor.

17. Click the Mark Clip button under the Source monitor or press T on the keyboard.

18. Choose **MOTION EFFECT** from the Tools Palette in the Composer's **FAST MENU**.

19. In the Speed section, check the box for **FIT TO FILL** and choose **BOTH FIELDS** as the render option.

20. Select a Target Drive for the media (your instructor will advise you).

21. Click **CREATE AND RENDER**.

    The system prompts you to select a bin.

22. Select a bin and click **OK**.

    A dialog tells us we are creating the video media for the motion effect.

    The motion effect clip is named to indicate the change in frame rate and is loaded into the Source monitor. Above the Source monitor in the Clip Name menu, the name of the clip has changed from **MAUR, SUNSET** to **MAUR, SUNSET (773.14 FPS)** and the master clip icon beside it has been replaced by the Motion Effect clip icon, (see Figure 9.13).

Figure 9.13 Both icon and name indicates a Motion Effect 2.

Finally, let's edit the motion effect into the Timeline. As you did with the freeze frame, you are going to replace a clip in the sequence.

23. Everything is already marked, so click the Overwrite button or press B on the keyboard to overwrite the Sunset shot in the sequence with the Motion Effect clip you just created.

24. Play through and view the result.

Creating Titles

Media Composer includes several title creation tools to accommodate your titling needs, whatever they may be. Whether static text or complex 3D motion graphics, there are tools to create them.

In this lesson, you will begin using the Avid Title Tool to create a simple, informational title.

Media Used: Rock Climber

Duration: 20 minutes

GOALS

■ Create and add a basic title to the sequence

■ Edit existing titles

Title Creation Tools

Most videos require a title. A title might consist of a static title card at the beginning, a Web site address, a phone number, or film credits at the end. Media Composer includes a variety of titling applications to suit any titling needs, including two built-in apps plus third-party titling plug-ins that come bundled with the application. These include the following:

- **Avid Title Tool:** The Avid Title Tool is a study in efficiency and simplicity. It is well-designed for creating the simple, high-quality titles that editors are commonly called upon to create. You will work with the Title Tool in this section.

- **Avid Marquee:** Avid Marquee is a more complex application, used for designing animated, 3D titles with scene-based lighting and more.

- **NewBlue Titler Pro:** NewBlue Titler Pro is bundled with Avid Media Composer for animated titles in SD, HD and larger than HD formats. (The version included with Media Composer depends on which bundle was purchased.) NewBlue Titler Pro offers sophisticated titling options with a range of presets and templates and real-time preview of your titles over the background video. Later versions (v2 and above) has added camera and lighting features, support for EPS logos, and more.

 For more info, check out the tutorial videos on New Blue FX's Web site (www.newbluefx.com/avid-titler-pro).

Opening the Avid Title Tool

Before you can start creating title magic, you need to open the Avid Title Tool application.

To open the Title Tool:

1. Select **CLIP > NEW TITLE**. Alternatively, select **TOOLS > TITLE TOOL APPLICATION.**

   As shown in Figure 10.1, a New Title dialog box opens, asking you to select a titling application.

2. To prevent Media Composer from asking you to make this selection every time you want to create a title, select the **PERSIST?** check box.

Figure 10.1 The New Title dialog box.

3. Click **TITLE TOOL**.

   When you select any of the title tools, you are actually launching a separate application. You will see the application icon for it in the Windows OS taskbar or the Macintosh OS Dock.

Quick View: The Avid Title Tool

The Avid Title Tool offers the following controls (see Figure 10.2):

- Toolbar
- Styles and templates
- Border controls
- Video Background toggle
- Font and Paragraph format controls
- Text Color and Fill controls
- Drop Shadow controls
- Crawl/Roll buttons
- Title Tool menus

 The green highlight indicates an active tool.

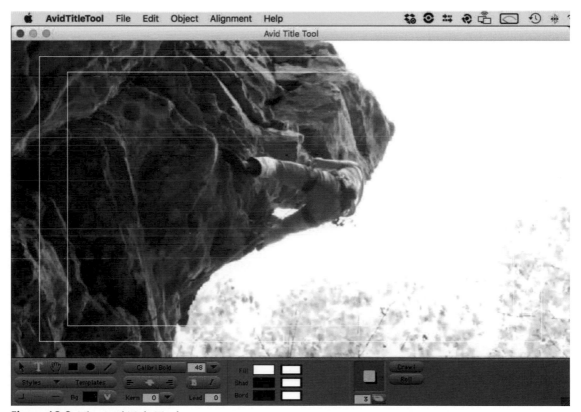

Figure 10.2 The Avid Title Tool

In addition to the interface controls, there are a number of very useful commands in the menus at the top of the screen. Here are a few of the most useful ones.

Edit Menu:

- **Cut/Copy/Paste:** Standard functions

- **Undo:** Reverts the last action

- **Select All:** Selects all title elements or text within a text box

- **Duplicate:** Creates a copy of the selected element

Object Menu:

- **Bring Forward/To Front:** Moves the object in front of others

- **Send Backward/To Back:** Moves the object behind others

- **Safe Title Area:** Displays an overlay guide for safe action/safe title

- **Soften Shadow:** Opens a dialog box to soften the edge of drop shadows

Alignment Menu:

- **Center in Frame Horiz:** Centers the object horizontally in the frame

- **Center in Frame Vert:** Centers the object vertically in the frame

- **Show Alignment Grid:** Displays a grid of alignment dots

- **Align to Grid:** Enables snapping of objects to the alignment grid

 Did you see the Roll and Crawl buttons? That's right, you can use these to create a credit roll or crawling title. For more information, go to Help > Contents > Creating Rolling and Crawling Titles.

Creating a Basic Title

The Title Tool uses tools and concepts that are common to many drawing or graphics applications. As a result, working in the Title Tool is intuitive and easy.

To create a basic title:

1. With the **TEXT** tool active (default) click on the image where you want text to appear and begin typing.

2. Click the **ARROW** tool.

3. Position the **TEXT** by doing one of the following:

   - Drag the text to the desired location within the frame

   - Choose auto-alignment commands from the Alignment menu

   - Drag the control points at the corners of the text box to resize the text box, and then use the **PARAGRAPH** controls to modify the alignment within the text box.

4. Optionally, use the **FONT** controls to modify the look of the text.

5. Optionally, change the color of the FILL, SHADOW, and BORDER.

6. Optionally, adjust the DROP SHADOW controls.

7. Close the TITLE TOOL window.

8. Click the SAVE button in the pop-up dialog box that appears.

9. In the Save Title dialog box, type a NAME, and then select a BIN, DRIVE, and RESOLUTION for the title, as shown in Figure 10.3.

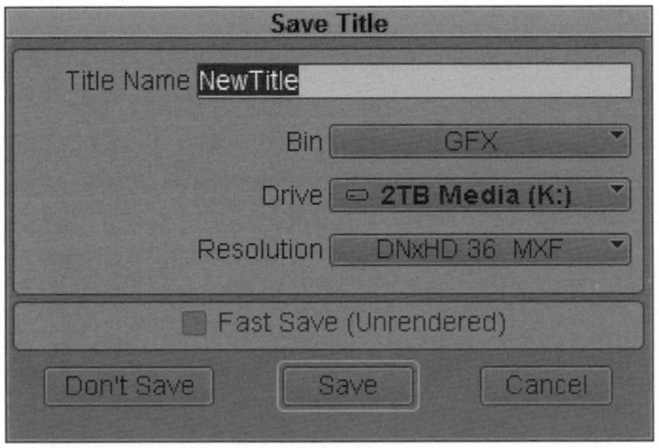

Figure 10.3 The Save Title dialog box.

The title is saved to the bin and a Title Clip icon appears, as shown in Figure 10.4.

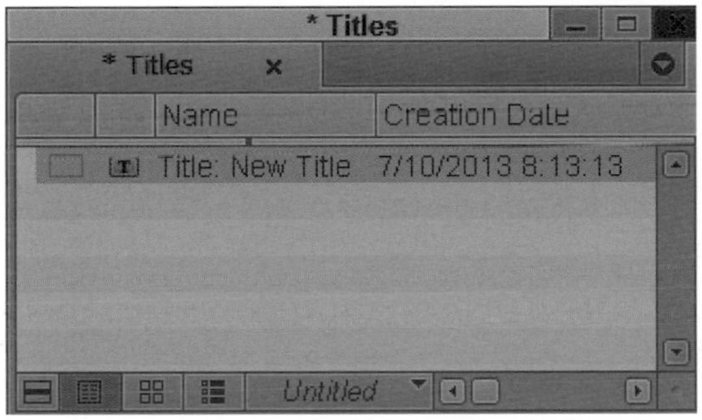

Figure 10.4 The title is saved.

Editing the Title to the Sequence

Once the title is created, the process of editing it to the Timeline is really no different from cutting in any other master clip. You load, mark, and overwrite it in the same way that you do other clips. Perhaps the only difference is that titles very frequently go onto an upper track of video. Typically, this track is created in the sequence just for the titles as a way to keep the sequence organized. If you already have an empty top track, such as V2, use that one. If not, you need to add one.

To edit a title into the sequence:

1. Load the TITLE into the Source monitor (if it's not already there).

2. Set an IN mark partway into the title.

    This leaves some useful handle material at the beginning, just in case you need to trim it longer from the Head at some time in the future.

3. Watching the Center Duration display at the top of the Composer window, drag the POSITION INDICATOR the approximate duration desired for the title. Then click MARK OUT.

4. Add a **VIDEO TRACK** to the sequence by doing one of the following:

   • Select Clip > New Video Track.

   • Right-click in the Timeline and select New Video Track.

5. Patch the Source V1 Track Selector to the V2 Record Track Selector. Make sure that on the record side, only V2 Track selector is enabled. Determine a location for the title in the sequence, then place a Mark IN.

6. Overwrite the Title into the sequence.

7. Using **LIFT/OVERWRITE** and **OVERWRITE TRIM**, reposition and/or trim the title to the desired location and length.

   The final step to adding a title to the sequence is to adjust how it appears and disappears. With straight cuts, the title would abruptly appear and disappear. But what if you want the title to nicely fade up and fade down?

   You can use a dissolve for the fade in and fade out, or you can use a handy feature called "Fade Effect." Let's give that a try.

To fade a title up and down:

1. Park the **POSITION INDICATOR** over the title segment.

2. Verify that the track which contains the title (in this case V2) is enabled. If not, select it.

3. Click the **FAST** menu in the Composer window to open the Tool Palette.

4. Click the **FADE EFFECT** button, shown in Figure 10.5.

Figure 10.5 The Fade Effect button.

5. In the Fade Effect dialog box, type the number of **FRAMES** you want the title to fade up and fade down. (See Figure 10.6.)

Figure 10.6 The Fade Effect dialog box.

6. Click **OK**.

   The title will fade up and down automatically. If you want to adjust the timing, simply click Fade Effect again and enter different values.

Exercise Break: Exercise 10.1
Pause here to practice what you've learned.

Modifying a Title

The creative process is an evolution, not a singular moment. Whether you are the one driving the creative vision or it is the producer, director, or client, it is inevitable that you will need to change a title even after it has been designed, approved, created, and cut to the Timeline.

To modify an existing title in the sequence:

1. Right-click on the **TITLE SEGMENT** in the Timeline and select **ADD/EDIT TITLE**, as shown in Figure 10.7.

Figure 10.7
To update a title, choose Add/Edit Title from the right-click menu.

An Edit Title dialog box will ask if you want to promote the title into a Marquee application title.

2. Select the **PERSIST?** check box; then click **NO**.

The Title Tool opens, and the current title from the Timeline is loaded.

3. Make any changes you want; then close the **TITLE TOOL**.

4. A dialog box opens, asking if you want to save the existing title. Click **SAVE**.

The changes are saved, the title is updated in the Timeline, and the title is automatically loaded again in the Source window.

 Exercise Break: Exercise 10.2
Pause here to practice what you've learned.

Review/Discussion Questions

1. How do you add a video track to the Timeline? Why is this frequently necessary when adding titles?

2. How do you open the Avid Title Tool?

3. Which tool in the Title Tool allows you to add or select text and draw text boxes?

4. How do you create a drop shadow on your text?

5. List the steps to revise a title.

Lesson 10 Keyboard Shortcuts	
Key	**Shortcut**
I or E	Mark IN
O or R	Mark OUT
6	Play IN to OUT
B	Overwrite
Ctrl-click/Command-click	Places the position indicator on the first frame (head) of a segment
Ctrl+Y (Windows)/Command+Y (Mac)	Create a new video track

Creating Titles

Before we export our finished sequence we are going to put a title on it. Avid Media Composer has its own Title Tool and also comes with Marquee, an Avid product, and New Blue Titler, a third party product. Only the New Blue Titler can be used in projects greater than HD's 1920 x 1080 frame size (which are known as UHD projects). You will learn to use it in the MC110 course. For this project the Title Tool will do everything we want.

Media Used: Rock Climber

Duration: 20 minutes

GOALS

■ Create a Simple Title

■ Edit it into the sequence

■ Revise the Title

Exercise 10.1: Create a Title

In this exercise, you will create a simple title and add it to the opening sequence, then revise the title.

The process of creating a title sequence for a video is as much about the images over which the title plays as it is about the text on screen. The first part of the exercise presents a real-world scenario in which you need to make changes to the sequence before creating the title.

Currently, the sequence starts with a sync interview shot so the director would like some action to put the title over. He also has an idea for a little soundbite to go with it.

1. Find **R9_07 BOULDERING WALL CONTINUATION** and take four seconds of it. Starting around 00:02:34:00 is good,

2. Click on **MARK IN** in the Toolbar under the Source monitor or press the I or E key on the keyboard to mark an IN point at the beginning of the shot.

3. Click on **MARK OUT** in the Toolbar under the Source monitor or press O or R key on the keyboard to mark an OUT point after the four seconds.

    The highlighted section between the IN and OUT points shows the selected section.

4. Click on the **PLAY IN TO OUT** button in the Toolbar under the Source monitor or press 6 on the keyboard to review the section.

    If it is correct cut it in.

5. Check that the blue Position Indicator is at the beginning of the sequence. If it is not drag it there, click at the beginning of the sequence or press the Home key.

6. Make sure all your tracks are enabled on the record side.

7. Click the **SPLICE IN** button or press V on the keyboard.

    Now we will add the soundbite.

8. Find **R02_03(A) INTERVIEW**. Find the words "I'm Matt Rogers and I'm a Rock Climber." To save time I'll provide the timecodes - Mark IN at 00:26:44:12 and Mark OUT at 46:17.

9. Click on **MARK IN** in the Toolbar under the Source monitor or press the I or E key on the keyboard to mark an IN point at the beginning of the statement.

10. Click on **MARK OUT** in the Toolbar or press O or R key on the keyboard to mark an OUT point after the statement.

    The highlighted section between the IN and OUT points shows the selected section.

11. Click on the **PLAY IN TO OUT** button in the Toolbar or press 6 on the keyboard to listen to the section.

    The end has to be quite clipped as the director speaks. If it is correct, cut it in.

12. **PATCH A1 TO A2** and leave only this enabled.

13. Place the position indicator about 1 second into **R9_07 BOULDERING WALL CONTINUATION.** Click **OVERWRITE** or press B.

    Where the position indicator is placed determines the image you will see as background (see image) in the Title Tool.

14. **CTRL**-click (Windows) or **COMMAND**-click (Mac) to place the position indicator on the first frame of **R02_03(A).**

    In order for a title to be visible at the same time while over a video segment, it has to sit in the track above it. So, we need to create a new video track.

15. Select **TIMELINE>NEW>VIDEO TRACK** or press Ctrl+Y (Windows) or Command+Y (Mac) Y.

16. Patch Source **V1** to Record **V2**.

17. Deselect all tracks except **A2**. Click **MARK CLIP** or press T to mark the shot.

    We want the title to coincide with this soundbite.

18. **RESELECT V2.**

19. Select **CLIP > NEW TITLE** or **TOOLS>TITLE TOOL APPLICATION**. The application selection window opens, select the checkmark next to Persist, and click the button labeled **TITLE TOOL.**

    The Title Tool opens.

20. Type "**ROCK CLIMBER.**"

21. Select the **ARROW** tool, and then click the words of the title. You have now selected what is called the Text Box.

    The boundaries of the text box will become visible, and they include small, gray handles for resizing the text box.

22. Select the Font **CALIBRI BOLD** and the point size **48**.

    If your title has changed from one line to two or more, it's because the Text Box is too small for the larger text. Grab one of the handles on the right side to resize the box larger.

23. Making sure the Text Box is selected; center the text by clicking on the **CENTER** button.

    This has only centered the text in the box, which is not necessarily in the center of the screen.

24. Choose **ALIGNMENT > CENTER IN FRAME HORIZ.**

25. Choose **ALIGNMENT > CENTER IN FRAME VERT.**

    To add some depth and readability, you will next add a drop shadow.

26. In the **DROP SHADOW** controls, click and drag the **ROUNDED RECTANGLE** slightly down and to the right.

    A shadow box will appear behind the rounded rectangle that represents the drop shadow on the text. We want something very subtle here.

27. Click in the text field under the Drop Shadow controls and type "**3**". Then press **ENTER**.

 Figure 10.8 Drop Shadow controls.

28. Finally, soften the shadow: **SELECT OBJECT > SOFTEN SHADOW**.

29. Type **8**, and then press **ENTER**.

    We could do a lot more. Add color, even a gradation between two colors but the director is happy with this classic white title.

30. Click the **X** button in the top corner to close the Title Tool.

    A dialog box will ask if you want to save the title.

31. Click **SAVE**.

    The Save Title dialog box opens.

32. Choose a **BIN**.

33. Choose a **DRIVE** (your Instructor will advise you).

34. Choose a **RESOLUTION** (codec) from the "Resolution" menu, select Avid's high quality codec DNxHD175.

35. Because you have a Mark IN and a Mark OUT already in the Timeline you are also given the option to "**PLACE IN THE TIMELINE IN>OUT**." Select this option.

36. Click **SAVE**.

    Media Composer will save the title to the bin and render the media to the drive. When finished, the title will automatically be loaded in the Source monitor, ready for you to edit. In this case, because you selected the "Place in Timeline" option, the title is also edited into the sequence.

37. Play through the title.

    Notice that it pops on and pops off. We could add a dissolve at each end but there is a more efficient way to fade it up and down.

38. Click the **FAST menu** in the Composer window to open the **TOOL PALETTE**.

39. Click the **FADE EFFECT** button.

40. Enter **12** for the **FADE UP** and **FADE DOWN** values.

41. Click **OK**.

42. Play the sequence. Figure 10.9 shows the final sequence with the title in place.

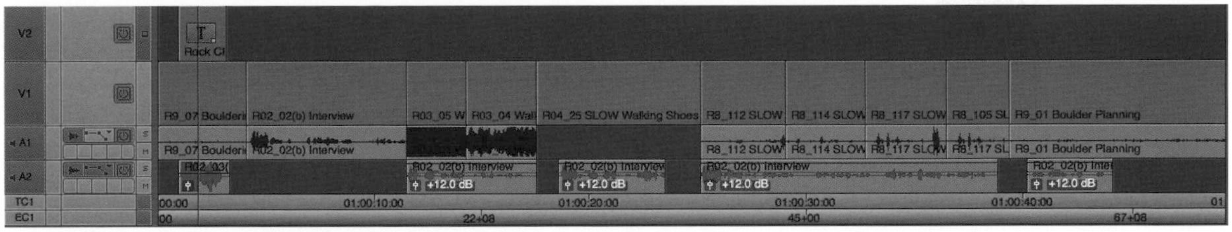

Figure 10.9 Final sequence with the Title in place.

Exercise 10.2: Revise a Title

Mark's soundbite has given the director the idea that he would prefer that the title was "Matt Rogers – Rock Climber."

1. Move the position indicator to the title segment.

2. Right-click on the title segment, and choose **ADD/EDIT TITLE** from the contextual menu.

3. If the dialog window opens asking to promote the title for use in the Marquee titling app, click the check mark next to **PERSIST**, and then click **NO**.

    The Title Tool opens with the title from the sequence loaded for editing.

4. Click in front of the R of Rock and type in **MATT ROGERS** and press the **ENTER** key.

5. Click the **CENTER TEXT** button.

6. Choose **ALIGNMENT > CENTER IN FRAME HORIZ**.

7. Choose **ALIGNMENT > CENTER IN FRAME VERT**.

8. Once you have something you are happy with, close the **TITLE TOOL**.

    The system automatically updates the title in the sequence and in the bin.

9. Play the opening of the sequence to see if you are happy with the new title.

Exporting Your Video

Ready to show your video to the world? Great! Then it's time to export it.

In this lesson, you will learn to set the Export settings to post your video to YouTube.

Media Used: The Rock Climber

Duration: 20 minutes

GOALS

- Configure export settings for YouTube or Vimeo
- Save an Export Template
- Export the sequence for YouTube

Exporting Your Video

Congratulations! You've finished your video. Now you are ready to post it for the world to see! It is time to export your sequence.

Outside of broadcast and feature film production, exporting a file for posting to the Web is one of the most common types of delivery today. Whether you are posting to YouTube, Vimeo, your company's Web site, or that of your client's, you will need to export the finished program as a file out of Media Composer.

In this section, you will learn the steps to follow and the settings to use to get your video ready for viewing on the World Wide Web.

Exporting a File

Media Composer includes a number of export templates that are useful for a variety of common workflows. These make the export process very simple and straightforward.

To export a sequence using an export template:

1. Load the finished **SEQUENCE** into the Timeline.

2. Select **FILE > OUTPUT>EXPORT TO FILE**. Alternatively, right-click on the **RECORD MONITOR** and choose **EXPORT**.

    The Export As dialog box opens.

3. Navigate to the **FOLDER DIRECTORY** in which you wish to save the exported file.

4. If necessary, rename the **FILE**.

5. Click the **EXPORT SETTING** menu and select the desired setting from the list, as shown in Figure 11.1.

6. Click the **SAVE** button to begin the export.

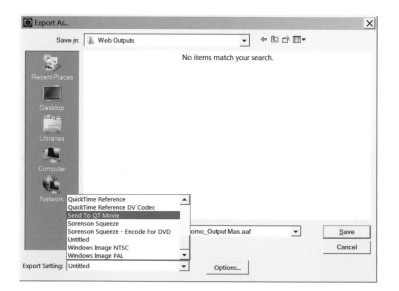

Figure 11.1 The Export As dialog box.

 While Media Composer is exporting, you will not be able to use the application.

Changing the Export Options

Although Media Composer includes prebuilt settings for many common workflows, there will be times when you want to customize the export settings. For example, Media Composer does not include a prebuilt setting for exporting to YouTube, but exporting to YouTube is something you may want to do frequently. Let's go through the basic steps to customize the export settings. Then you will build one for YouTube.

To export using custom settings:

1. Load the sequence into the Timeline, if it's not already there.

2. Right-click on the Record monitor and select Export.

3. Navigate to the **FOLDER DIRECTORY** in which you want to save the exported file.

4. If necessary, rename the **FILE**.

5. Click **OPTIONS** button (see Figure 11.2) to open the Export Settings dialog box where you can customize your Export Setting.

Figure 11.2 The Options button in the Export As dialog box gives you access to the Export Settings.

 You can also open and modify the Export Settings directly from the Settings pane of the Project Window.

The Export Settings dialog box, shown in Figure 11.3 has numerous options, all of which will change based on what is selected in the Export As drop-down menu at the top of the window. The settings and controls shown in Figure 11.3 appear because the Export As menu is set to QuickTime Movie. If a different setting were selected, the options would be different.

When exporting for Web delivery, QuickTime Movie is still the most common delivery format, but not all QuickTime movies are the same. The QuickTime format is nothing more than a container file, a wrapper that can hold many types of media. To use a metaphor, telling someone that you will give them a QuickTime is no more descriptive than telling them you will give them a sandwich. Sure, they know it's not pizza, but there are still many questions you haven't answered. What kind of bread? What's inside? Is it hot or cold?

The Export Settings dialog box gives you full access to all the settings you need to correctly deliver your QuickTime movie file. It is better to spend a little time researching the best settings for your distribution format than to waste hours going through the trial-and-error route. Even if posting to your own Web site, ask your webmaster or the company hosting the site for the recommended settings to ensure that your export will work on the site.

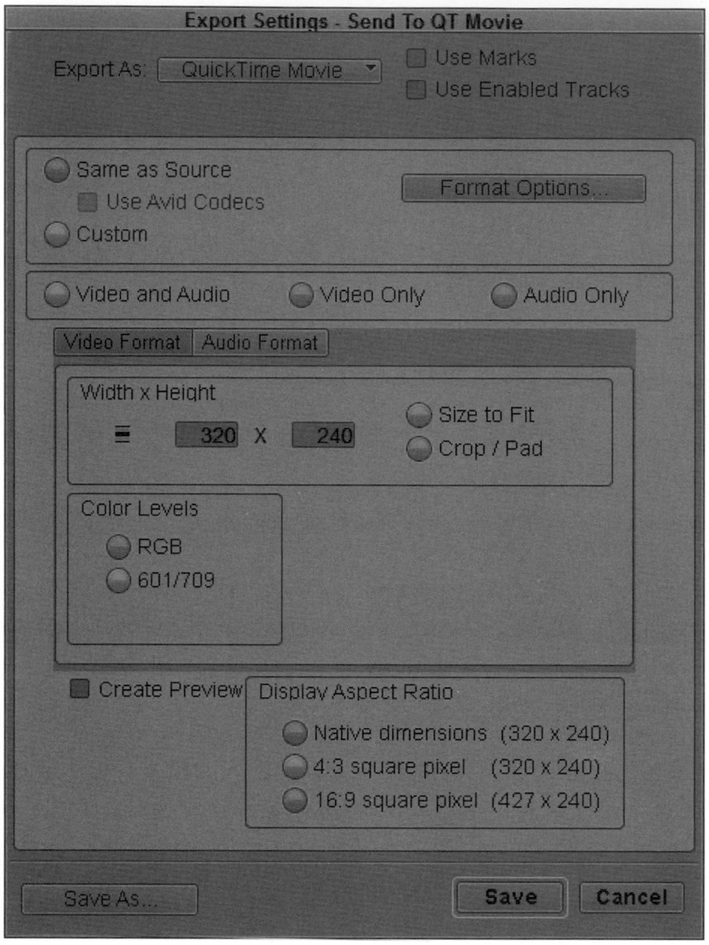

Figure 11.3

The Export Settings dialog box offers a wide range of controls over the export format.

Before you start using them, take a moment to familiarize yourself with the following controls:

- **Export As menu: Use this drop-down menu** to change the type of file to be exported —i.e., AAF, QuickTime Reference, Graphic, etc.

- **Use Marks/Use Enabled Tracks check boxes:** When enabled, these check boxes limit the exported file to the area within edit marks placed on the sequence and to active tracks, respectively. When these are disabled, the entire sequence is exported.

- **Same as Source/Custom option buttons:** Same as Source encodes the exported file in the current media format. If set to Custom, the Format Options button becomes accessible – and this is where the real power lies!

  Format Options allows you direct access to the format settings of QuickTime, shown in Figure 11.4, to change the codec, frame rate, data rate, etc.

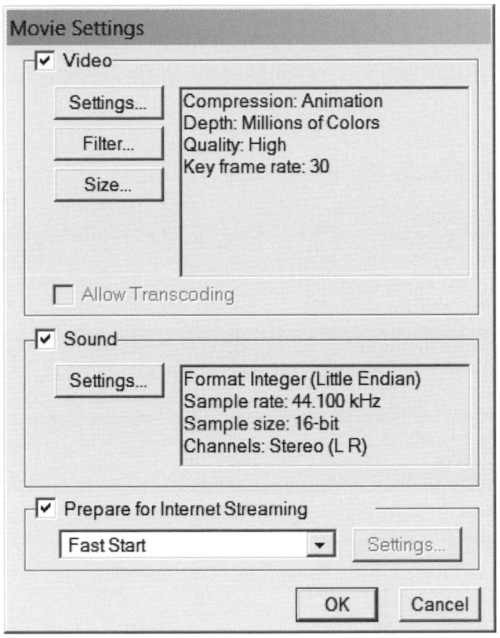

Movie Settings

☑ Video
- Settings...
- Filter...
- Size...

Compression: Animation
Depth: Millions of Colors
Quality: High
Key frame rate: 30

☐ Allow Transcoding

☑ Sound
- Settings...

Format: Integer (Little Endian)
Sample rate: 44.100 kHz
Sample size: 16-bit
Channels: Stereo (L R)

☑ Prepare for Internet Streaming
Fast Start   ▼   Settings...

OK   Cancel

Figure 11.4

The Movie Settings dialog box gives you direct access to the QuickTime encode settings.

- **Video and Audio/Video Only/Audio Only radio buttons:** Use these to control whether audio and/or video is exported.

- **Video Format/Audio Format tabs:** These tabs contain additional settings for the frame size and audio track configuration.

- **Frame Size Presets menu:** This Fast Menu opens a list of common frame sizes.

- **Color Levels area:** Select "Scale from Legal to Full Range" for viewing on computers and mobile devices or "Keep as Legal Range" for television broadcast.

- **Save As button:** This button allows you to save the current settings as a new preset.

 Heads up! The default setting for QuickTime Movie has the radio button set to Video Only. If you want audio included, be sure to move the radio button to "Video and Audio," as shown in Figure 11.3

Understanding QuickTime Reference Files

QuickTime Reference is an option in the Export As menu. Unlike a standard QuickTime movie, a QuickTime Reference file is an empty container file that holds no media of its own. Instead, as the name implies, it references the original media files used by Media Composer. QuickTime reference files are useful for passing the video information between applications, but because QuickTime Reference files contain no media, they must be used on the same system. If you send this file to someone on a different computer, they will not be able to see the video.

Export a Movie File for YouTube

YouTube accepts a wide array of video and audio files. To ensure your video looks its best, Google has published detailed settings information. We will use those and, in the exercise, walk you through step-by-step how to create a template for exporting to YouTube.

Figure 11.5 shows an excerpt; you can view the full document online at:

http://support.google.com/youtube/bin/answer.py?hl=en&answer=1722171&topic=2888648&ctx=topic

---

YouTube Help   🔍

YOUTUBE ⇥   GET SUPPORT

Recommended upload encoding settings

Container: MP4   ^

   • No Edit Lists (or the video might not get processed correctly)
   • moov atom at the front of the file (Fast Start)

Audio codec: AAC-LC   ^

   • Channels: Stereo or Stereo + 5.1
   • Sample rate 96khz or 48khz

Video codec: H.264   ^

   • Progressive scan (no interlacing)
   • High Profile
   • 2 consecutive B frames
   • Closed GOP. GOP of half the frame rate

Figure 11.5 An excerpt of the advanced encoding settings for YouTube.

Would you rather post your videos to Vimeo? If so, check out Vimeo's "Compression Guidelines" (https://vimeo.com/help/compression) and its "Media Composer Export-for-Vimeo Tutorial" (https://vimeo.com/24064111).

Exercise Break: Exercise 11.1
Pause here to practice what you've learned.

Review/Discussion Questions

1. In which menu can you find the Export command?

2. In which window can you change the codec used to export the video?

3. Which option in the Export Settings window must be selected before you can access the Format Options?

4. Which Color Levels option should be used when exporting a video for playback on a computer?

5. Your sequence contains audio, but the QuickTime movie you just exported does not. Which two Export Settings could have caused this?

    a. Use Enabled Tracks setting

    b. Video Compression setting

    c. Audio Bit Depth setting

    d. Frame Size setting

    e. Video and Audio radio buttons

6. What is the difference between a QuickTime movie and a QuickTime Reference file?

7. Describe the process to create a new export template.

Exporting your Sequence

Export the finished sequence for posting on YouTube.

Media Used: The Climber

Duration: 15 minutes

GOALS

- Create an Export template for YouTube

- Export your sequence to QuickTime for YouTube

Exercise 11.1: Exporting your Sequence

Follow the steps below to output your final sequence with formatting and encoding as recommended by Google for posting to YouTube. (See "Exporting a Movie File for YouTube" in this lesson.) This will serve as your "delivery specification". Now, let's get your masterpiece out to the world!

Exporting your sequence:

1. Load **MATT ROGERS ROCK CLIMBER** if it is not in the Record monitor already.

2. Right-click in the Record monitor and choose **DUPLICATE**.

3. Rename the duplicate sequence, "Matt Rogers Rock Climber for YouTube".

4. Right-click the Record monitor and choose Export (or select **FILE MENU > EXPORT**).

    The Export As dialog opens.

5. Navigate to the Desktop, and then click the **NEW FOLDER** button.

6. Name the folder, **WEB OUTPUTS**, and then open it.

7. Choose **SEND TO QT MOVIE** from the **EXPORT SETTING** menu, as shown in Figure 11.6.

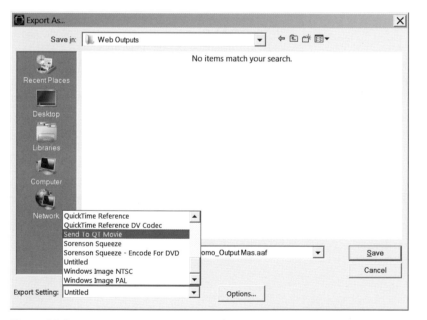

Figure 11.6 Choose Send To QT Movie.

8. Click **OPTIONS** to open the Export Settings dialog box.

9. Verify that **USE MARKS** and **USE SELECTED TRACKS** are deselected.

10. Click the **Custom** option button. Then click the **Format Options** button to the right.

The Movie Settings dialog box opens with default settings, as shown in Figure 11.7. You will use the settings detailed below to specify the compression settings.

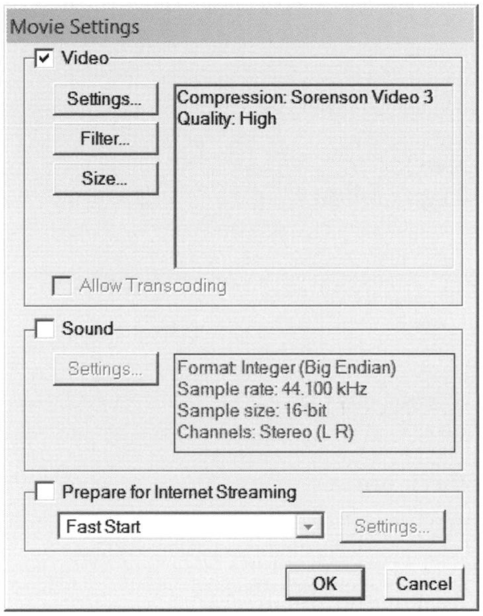

Movie Settings

☑ Video
Settings...   Compression: Sorenson Video 3
Filter...   Quality: High
Size...

☐ Allow Transcoding

☐ Sound
Settings...   Format Integer (Big Endian)
               Sample rate: 44.100 kHz
               Sample size: 16-bit
               Channels: Stereo (L R)

☐ Prepare for Internet Streaming
Fast Start   Settings...

OK   Cancel

Figure 11.7 The Movie Settings dialog box.

11. In the Video section, click **Settings**.

The Standard Video Compression Settings dialog box opens.

12. Open the **Compression Type** drop-down menu and choose **H.264**, as shown in Figure 11.8.

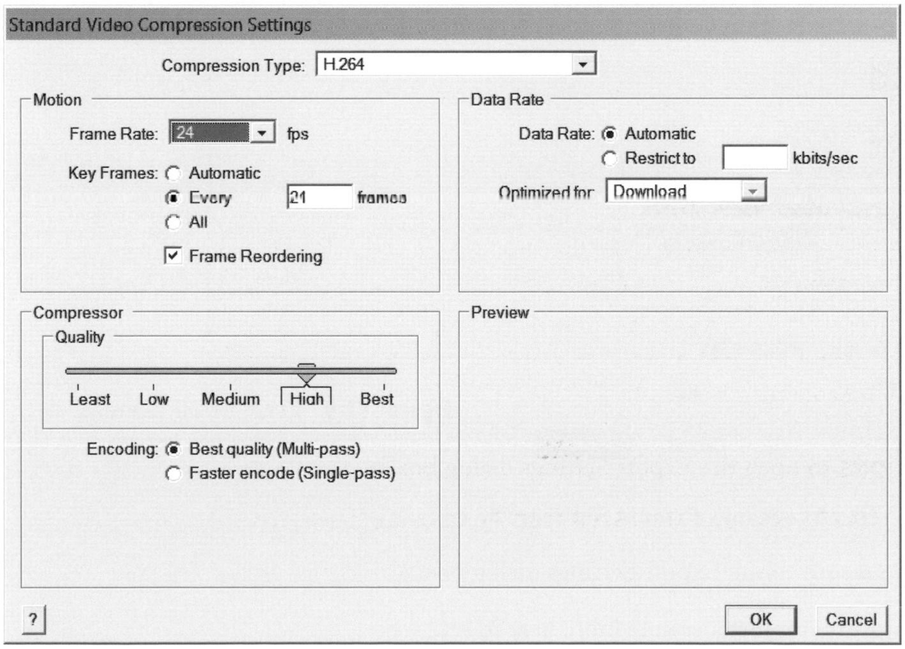

Standard Video Compression Settings

Compression Type: H.264

Motion
Frame Rate: 24 ▼ fps
Key Frames: ○ Automatic
            ● Every 21 frames
            ○ All
            ☑ Frame Reordering

Data Rate
Data Rate: ● Automatic
           ○ Restrict to ___ kbits/sec
Optimized for: Download ▼

Compressor
Quality

Least Low Medium High Best

Encoding: ● Best quality (Multi-pass)
          ○ Faster encode (Single-pass)

Preview

OK   Cancel

Figure 11.8 Use the Standard Video Compression Settings dialog box to set the compression to H.264.

13. Click **OK**.

You are returned to the Movie Settings dialog box.

14. In the Video section, click the **SIZE** button.

15. Use the drop-down menu to set the dimensions to **1920×1080 HD**.

16. Select the **DEINTERLACE SOURCE VIDEO** check box.

17. Click **OK** to return to the Movie Settings dialog box.

18. Select the **SOUND** check box.

19. Click the **SETTINGS** button in the Sound section.

20. Use the drop-down menus to set the audio encoding as follows:

   • **Format:** AAC

   • **Channels:** Stereo (L R)

   • **Rate:** 44.1 kHz

21. Click **OK** to return to the Movie Settings dialog box.

22. Select the **PREPARE FOR INTERNET STREAMING** check box.

   The default setting, **FAST START**, is correct.

23. Double-check your settings. They should appear as shown in Figure 11.9.

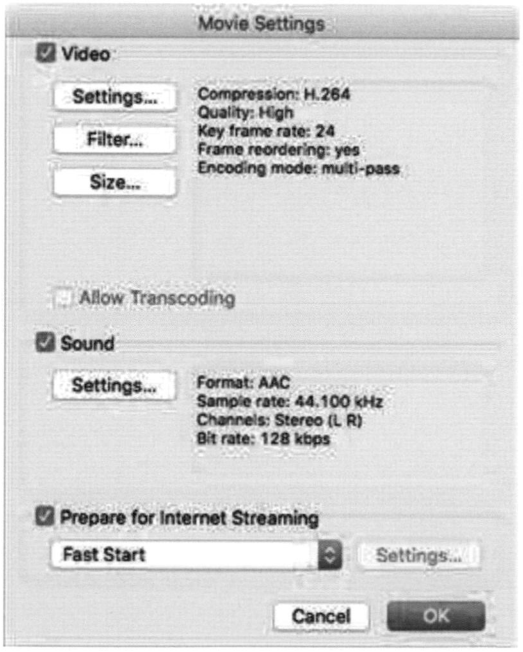

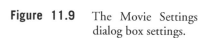

Figure 11.9   The Movie Settings dialog box settings.

24. If necessary, fix any settings that are not correct.

25. Click **OK** to return to the Export Settings dialog box.

   You are almost there. Just a couple more here to set.

26. Click the **VIDEO AND AUDIO** option button.

27. On the Video sub-tab, click the **FAST** menu and choose **1920×1080**.

28. Under Color Levels, click the **BUTTON** labeled "Scale from Legal to Full Range."

29. Finally, under Display Aspect Ratio, click the **NATIVE DIMENSIONS** option.

   Whew! Well done. But let's not have to do all that setup again, shall we? Instead, let's save this as a preset.

30. In the bottom-left corner of the dialog box, click the **SAVE AS** button.

31. Name the preset **YOUTUBE H.264 1080_24P**. Then click **OK.**

32. Click **SAVE** to return to the Export As dialog box.

   You will notice that your new template is listed in the Export Setting menu. In the future, you won't need to enter the settings again. Instead, you can just pick the setting from the list.

 You can use this setting as a starting point. If you want additional YouTube settings for other frame sizes or frame rates, start with this one and then modify only those settings that need to be changed.

33. Click **SAVE** to export the file.

34. When the export is finished, minimize or hide Media Composer and navigate to the **WEB OUTPUTS** folder to play your file in QuickTime.

   It's always a good idea to verify that it plays properly after exporting.

Congratulations! You have completed a video project, carrying it from input to output.

Technical Fundamentals

Working effectively on any editing system requires familiarity with certain technical concepts. These concepts form the foundation of everything that happens in an editing system. In this lesson, we will focus on those related to solving common technical problems and basic media management.

Media Used: Running the Sahara

Duration: 60 minutes

GOALS

- Troubleshoot offline media
- Relink offline master clips to online media
- Locate media files associated with a clip
- Restore a saved bin from the Avid Attic
- Use the Media Tool to identify and delete project media

Fixing Technical Problems

Two of the most worrisome problems for an editor is to have media go missing, or to lose work. This section will arm you with skills to address both of these problems, while minimizing the impact on the project.

The broader topic of troubleshooting in general is, quite literally, a course unto itself. If you have an interest or aptitude for the technical side of things, you may consider taking the Avid course CS400 Editing Systems to become an Avid Certified Support Representative (ACSR). ACSR is a respected certification in the industry, required by many large broadcasters and post-production facilities of their technical support staff.

 Find out more about ACSR certification online at
www://www.avid.com/US/support/training/certification/editing-support-representative.

Troubleshooting Missing Media Files

The master clip in your bin is not the same thing as your actual video file. One represents the other. They are separate items with a linked relationship.

All clip types (master clips, titles, motion effect clips, etc.) in your bins are bundles of text information ("Metadata") that point to/refer to the actual media files. The term used to describe this is "Linking." When Media Composer creates media files (capturing from tape, importing, etc.) it place the files in a specific location, the "Avid MediaFiles" folder. At the same time, it creates the clip which refers to the media. We say that the clip is "linked" to the media file(s). Similarly, when we AMA link to camera files, Media Composer also creates clips that link to those file(s).

If Media Composer can't find the corresponding media file on any drive, it flags the clip in the bin as "Media Offline." This is displayed in several places. If the clip is loaded into the Source monitor, Media Composer shows you the "Media Offline" slide in the monitor. In the bin, an "Offline" column shows which tracks are not linked to a media file. The Timeline will also, by default, highlight offline clips in bright red. (This is a Clip Color setting, enabled by default, and available in the Timeline Fast menu.) All are shown in Figure 12.1.

Figure 12.1 The "Media Offline" slide in the monitor, the Offline column in the bin and the red color in the Timeline.

Media can go offline for a few reasons:

■ The files were moved or renamed.

■ The files were deleted, either intentionally or accidentally.

■ The drive can be turned off or disconnected.

■ Worst of all, the drive could crash.

For these reasons and more, you should always have a backup (or duplicate copy) of the media files.

> **Some things in life are inevitable: taxes and hardware crashes! It is critical to back up your media files, especially if you are working with file-based cameras that record to a disk or card instead of tape. After recording the footage, back up the card, then back it up again. After capturing or transferring the footage to your media drive, back up the drive. This will save your project, your sanity, and your reputation.**

Follow the steps to troubleshoot offline media. Each individual step may succeed in restoring the media.

To troubleshoot offline media:

1. Make sure all drives or camera cards containing linked or Avid Native media are connected to the system and are visible to the OS.

   On Windows computers, choose **START > MY COMPUTER**. The drives should appear next to the boot drive.

   On Macintosh computers, the drives should appear on the desktop.

2. If a drive does not show up (referred to as "being mounted"), follow the procedures for reconnecting your drive to the system as specified by the computer and drive manufacturers. Be sure to double-check the physical connections. A loose cable can prevent the drive from mounting properly.

3. Within Avid, select FILE > MEDIA > REFRESH MEDIA DATABASES.

    This re-examines all the system's media databases. (This can take some time to execute if you have large amounts of media.)

4. If you moved the media drive or media files between two systems, the links may have been lost between the media files and the Avid application. To troubleshoot this issue, you would use the Relink feature.

5. If none of these procedures work, you may have to take more drastic measures and delete the media database files themselves.

    This forces the Avid application to rescan all media files and re-establish a link with the Avid Native media files on your media drive. (This does nothing to help reconnect AMA Linked files, e.g. camera native media.) Deleting the media databases should only be done after trying all other troubleshooting methods. This is because if you have a lot of media files, the rescan/rebuild can take a very long time. Additionally, it is best to consult with a system administrator before using this method.

To delete and rebuild media databases:

1. Exit MEDIA COMPOSER.

2. Open an OS WINDOW and double-click your media drive.

3. Navigate to the numbered folder AVID MEDIAFILES\MXF\1.

4. Delete the MSMMMOB and MSMFMID files.

5. Repeat for each numbered FOLDER and on each media DRIVE.

6. Relaunch MEDIA COMPOSER.

    Upon launch, Media Composer will scan each of the directories from which you deleted the databases. Be advised, this may take some time.

Relinking Avid Native Media Files

You can restore the pointers between the clip or sequence and Avid Native media files using the Relink commands. When you select subclips or sequences and choose the Relink command, the system searches for master clips that contain the material included in the selection. When you relink master clips, the system compares information such as source tape name, timecode information, and channels captured. If the search is successful, the system establishes new links to the available media files.

To relink offline items in a bin:

1.   Click the **BIN** with the offline items to activate it.

2.   Click the bin **FAST** menu and choose **SELECT OFFLINE ITEMS**.

     All items with offline media files are selected automatically.

3.   If there are offline items in other bins that you also wish to relink, repeat steps 1–3 in those bins, without deselecting the items in the current bin.

4.   Right-click a **SELECTED ITEM** in the bin and choose **RELINK**.

     The Relink window opens, as shown in Figure 12.2. Use the settings in this window to relink media in a wide range of workflow situations. You can relink to very specific resolutions or to any available media (as you will do now).

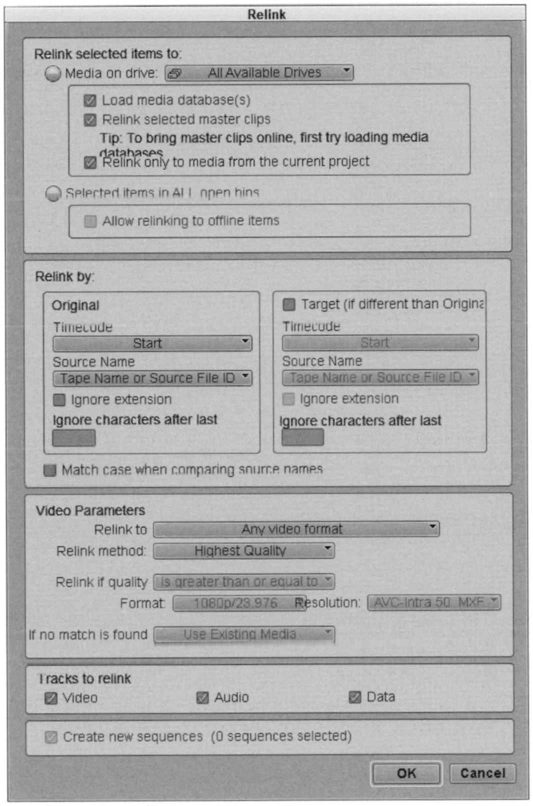

Figure 12.2
The Relink options give you precise control over which files are linked.

5.   In the top section (Relink Selected Items To); ensure that the **MASTER CLIPS** check box is checked. If subclips or sequences are highlighted in the bin, also select the **ALL OTHER ITEMS** check box. For **MEDIA ON DRIVE**, choose **ALL AVAILABLE DRIVES**.

6.   Uncheck the **RELINK MEDIA FROM THE CURRENT PROJECT** option.

     If you have media in the sequence borrowed from another project, this will allow Media Composer to relink to that file as well.

7.   In the **RELINK BY** section, deselect **MATCH CASE WHEN COMPARING TAPE AND SOURCE FILE NAMES**.

     Matching case is usually unnecessary; deselecting this ensures the widest range of possibilities when relinking, especially if media has been recaptured.

8. If you're working with AMA linked media, select the **ALLOW RELINKING OF IMPORTED/AMA MEDIA BY SOURCE FILE NAME** check box.

9. In the **VIDEO PARAMETERS** section, choose **ANY VIDEO FORMAT** for **RELINK TO**; also choose **HIGHEST QUALITY** for **RELINK METHOD**.

10. If you are relinking a sequence, deselect **CREATE NEW SEQUENCES**. When finished, your settings should reflect those shown in Figure 12.3.

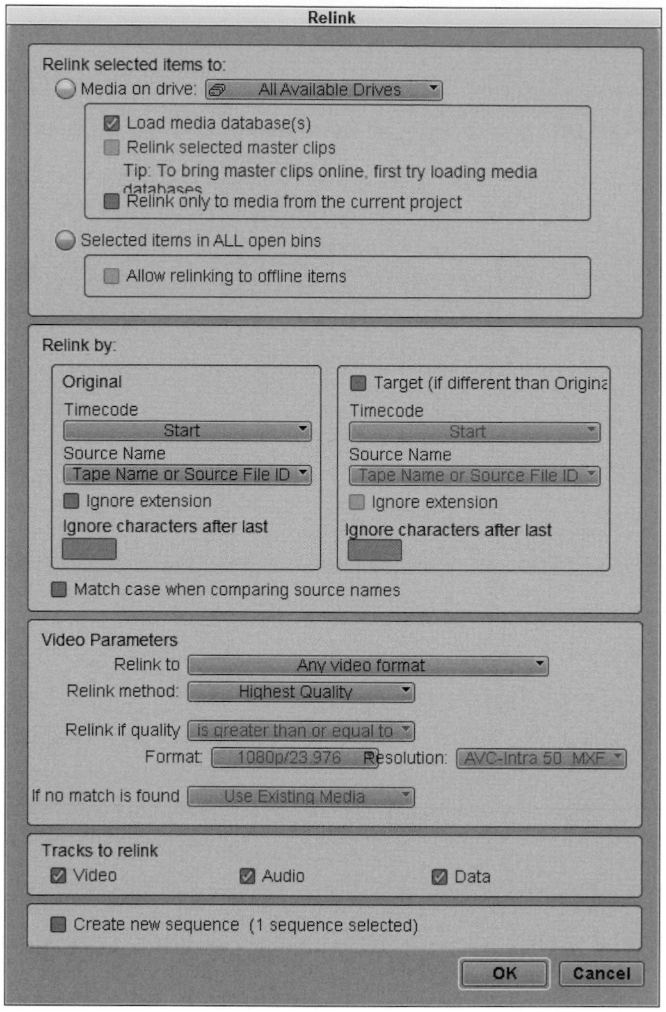

Figure 12.3 Use these settings to relink all possible media

11. Click **OK**.

Media Composer reloads the database files and relinks your clips to any matching media files it finds.

Relink to Linked Files

Relinking to linked media files, e.g. camera native files, is not done using the same Relink command. Instead, you will use the command "Relink to File(s)."

As you learned in Lesson 2, one disadvantage of working with linked media files is that you are solely responsible for keeping track of those files. To relink the files, you need to know where they are. If you are unsure, it may be helpful to locate the media files for other linked media that are still online. See the next topic, "Identifying a Media File."

To relink linked files:

1. Select the offline master clips in the bin.

2. Right-click on one of the selected clips and choose **RELINK TO FILE(S)**.

   A standard browser window opens. Displayed at the top is the name of the first selected clip to be relinked.

3. Navigate to the folder containing the clip and select it.

4. Click **OPEN**.

   Media Composer will relink the selected file, plus all other selected files it can match to files in the same directory.

Identifying a Media File

It's important to note that you can have multiple copies of the clips (metadata pointers) pointing to the same media file. When you clone a clip from one bin to another or duplicate a sequence, you're just creating another copy of that metadata. No new media is created; another set of pointers is created. See for yourself.

To see the media files linked to a clip:

1. Open the bin and select the master clip for which you want to find the media, such as **CU LITTLE GIRLS FEET AND HANDS**.

2. Right-click the master clip and choose **REVEAL FILE**, as shown in Figure 12.4.

   Media Composer opens an operating system (OS) window to show you the MXF file(s) on the drive. On Macs, this is called the Finder; on Windows, the Explorer.

 On Windows, you can see only one media file at a time. After viewing the first, a pop-up dialog box in Media Composer will ask "Reveal Next?" This will happen for as many files as are associated with that master clip.

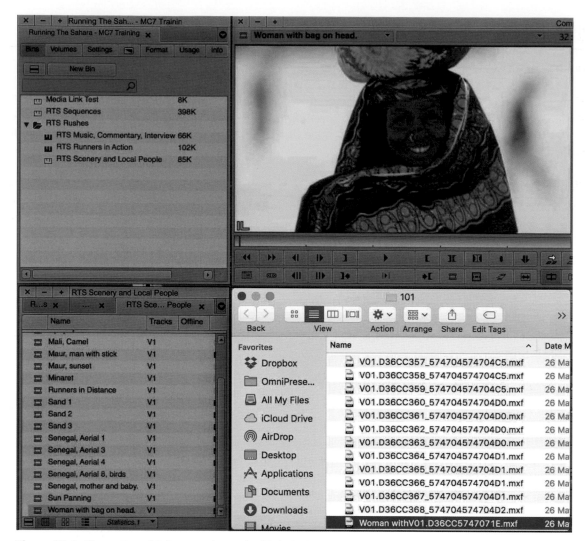

Figure 12.4 Choose Reveal File to see the media file linked to a master clip.

Master clips that are created by cloning or duplicating all share the same media file. Want proof? Duplicate or clone the master clip and Reveal File on the new master clip. You will find the same media file as the original.

Exercise Break: Exercise 12.1
Pause here to practice what you've learned.

Recovering Lost Work

It's a scary thing to lose work you've done on a sequence.

Bins, like any computer file, can become corrupted. Technical problems can also cause a computer to crash. More frequently, you can lose work because you simply forgot to save at opportune times—like right before you tried that really great idea for the scene that doesn't look so good in the morning. If you forgot to duplicate the sequence before trying the new idea, you may have no way to return to the previous version.

Media Composer has an automatic backup feature to protect your work in situations like these. The backup feature saves copies of all open bins at regular intervals and stores them in a special folder called the Avid Attic. The Auto-Save setting is part of the Bin settings, and is described in detail in Lesson 1, "Personalizing the Application."

Here, you'll learn how to use the copies in the Attic to restore lost work.

To retrieve a bin from the Attic folder:

1. From within the Avid application, move any **SEQUENCES** you might replace to another bin and delete the **BIN** you will replace.

    This places the bin in the Trash folder, which is adequate for this procedure.

2. Minimize or hide Media Composer. (If you are experiencing technical difficulties, you may wish to quit and restart the system, but this is not required.)

3. Navigate to the **\USERS\PUBLIC\PUBLIC DOCUMENTS\AVID MEDIA COMPOSER\AVID ATTIC** (Windows) or **MACHD/USERS/SHARED/AVID MEDIA COMPOSER/AVID ATTIC** (Mac) folder.

4. Find and open the **FOLDER** for the current project and open the **BINS** folder within it.

    Inside the Bins folder, you will see a folder for every bin that was created in the project.

5. Open the **FOLDER** for the bin you are restoring.

    The files are numbered sequentially. The number of bin copies will vary. There may be several or hundreds.

6. Use the OS display settings to display the file details, as shown in Figure 12.5. You need to see **DATE MODIFIED**.

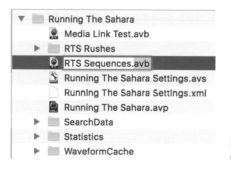

Figure 12.5 Use Date Modified as a guide to which version of the bin to restore.

7. Using the file information as a guide, select the **FILE** that roughly corresponds to the version of the sequence you want to restore. ("It was right after we went for coffee, so maybe 10:30?") Press **CTRL+C** (Windows) or **COMMAND+C** (Mac) to copy the file. For purposes of added protection, do not remove the file.

8. In the same OS window, navigate to the actual project **FOLDER**.

    Remember, private projects are located in the Documents folder for your OS User. Shared projects are located in the Shared Documents folder.

9. Paste the **FILE** into your project folder.

10. Change the file extension from the number to **.AVB**, as shown in Figure 12.6.

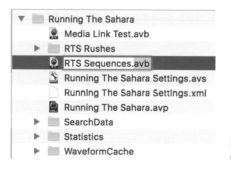

Figure 12.6

Change the file extension to .avb before reactivating Media Composer.

11. Reactivate **MEDIA COMPOSER**.

    The bin file appears in the Project window. If the bin does not appear automatically, save the project and the updating should cause it to appear.

12. Open the **BIN** you copied from the Attic and check the sequence to see if you restored the correct one. If not, simply repeat the process, choosing another version of the bin.

 Exercise Break: Exercise 12.2
Pause here to practice what you've learned.

Deleting Media

Media Composer is famous for its robust media management. It is designed to keep the user from having to directly interact with the media files. Instead, you are given simple, powerful tools to manage your media through the software (using the Media Tool). If you are accustomed to directly interacting with your media files, this can feel restrictive. You will soon come to appreciate the freedom you have to focus on the creative process of editing.

All media files created by Media Composer through capture, import, render, and so on go to the same place, shown in Figure 12.7: *media drive*\Avid MediaFiles\MXF\1.

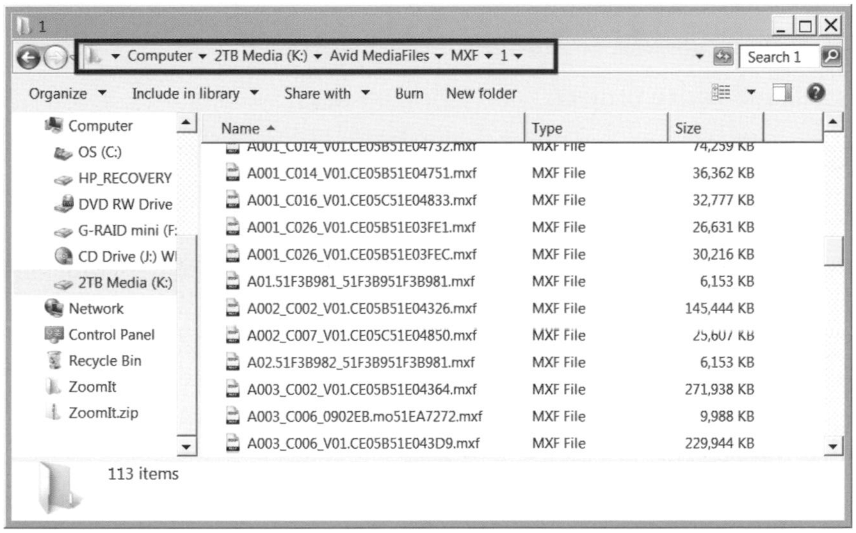

Figure 12.7 All Avid media files are organized together in the same location.

Media Composer puts all the files it creates from all projects into the same folder (indicated with a 1) until it reaches the limit: 5,000 files. Then it creates a folder named with a 2, and so on. Besides the MXF media files, each folder has two database files: msmFMID.pmr and msmMMOB.mdb. See Figure 12.8. Media Composer uses the database files to track each file's metadata and all the metadata links that relate to those media files.

MATT VO 1.A01.D36CC5747071C.mxf
MATT VO 2.A01.D36CC5747071D.mxf
Maur, man V01.D36CC5747071E.mxf
Maur, runnV01.D36CC5747072A.mxf
msmFMID.pmr
msmMMOB.mdb
Niger, SanV01.D36CC5747071A.mxf
Niger, SanV01.D36CC5747071B.mxf
Niger, SanV01.D36CC5747071C.mxf

Figure 12.8 The two Avid database files catalog the media in the folder.

You have no direct control over which file goes into which folder, nor can you separate the files by project. Again, this may be frustrating at first. You may want to double-click a media file to see which clip it is. Or, you may want to grab all the clips from one project and organize them into a folder. Instead of going to the files, you use the tools provided in Media Composer to manage your media more efficiently.

Using the Media Tool

You manage your media using the Media Tool. It allows you to see the media files in all mounted hard drives in a display that looks like, and has the same display features, as your bin. You can use the Media Tool to view or delete the available media files or even media files for specific tracks in the media file. The Media Tool also allows you to track down all media files used in a particular project or sequence.

Right now, use the Media Tool to see all the media files on your drive for the project "Running the Sahara."

To identify all the media associated with a project:

1. Open the **PROJECT** whose media you want to see.

2. Choose **TOOLS > MEDIA TOOL**.

    The Media Tool Display dialog box opens, as shown in Figure 12.9. Here you can select the drives, projects, and media file types you want to see. Precomputes are rendered files.

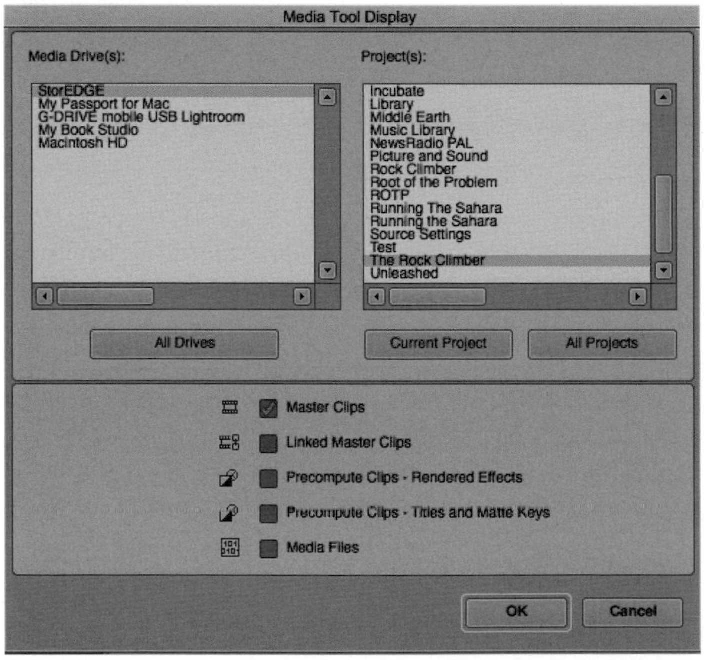

Figure 12.9 Select the drives and project for which you want to see media.

 Media files are associated with the project in which they are created. Master clips borrowed from another project will only show up in the original project in which they were created.

3. Click the **ALL DRIVES** button; then click the **CURRENT PROJECT** button.

4. Ensure that the **MASTER CLIPS** check box is checked, and then click **OK**.

    The Media Tool opens, displaying the online master clips associated with this project, as shown in Figure 12.10.

When you choose to view the master clips, Media Composer presents associated V1, A1, and A2 files together as a master clip for convenient viewing. You should not need to select media files for display in the Media Tool. Displaying the actual media files is equivalent to looking at the files at the OS level and is typically used only to troubleshoot a problem with the assistance of the Avid Technical Support staff.

Name	Tracks	Offline	Start	End	Duration	N
Injury on the road.	V1		11:31:14:18	11:31:18:05	3:17	
Drums, night	V1		19:19:29:12	19:19:32:00	2:18	
RTS Trailer Audio.wav	A1-2		01:01:56:11	01:02:54:06	57:25	
Runners in Distance	V1		16:36:01:14	16:36:04:24	3:10	
Minaret	V1		00:12:42:28	00:12:48:25	5:27	
Injury in tent, detail.	V1		18:53:38:26	18:53:41:24	2:28	
Injury in tent	V1		18:53:22:09	18:53:25:22	3:13	
Break cam 1	V1		13:42:04:26	13:42:08:12	3:16	
Agadez, runners, reunion	V1		12:03:08:08	12:03:12:22	4:14	
Maur, runners planning	V1		09:14:38:24	09:14:43:20	4:26	
Break cam 1A	V1		13:41:34:15	13:41:37:23	3:08	
Runner 2 Greeting at car	V1		09:35:59:24	09:36:05:09	5:15	
Break cam 2	V1		13:39:09:14	13:39:12:12	2:28	
Break cam 3	V1		13:45:21:05	13:45:24:04	2:29	
Runner 1 Night INT	V1		19:17:26:28	19:17:32:07	5:09	

Figure 12.10 The Media Tool looks and functions much like a bin.

The Media Tool looks and functions very much like a bin, making it immediately familiar. It provides the same database functionality as a bin, including the ability to sort, sift, display column headings, and view clips in Frame, Text, or Script view.

Deleting Project Media

One of the primary uses of the Media Tool is for deletion. Unlike when you delete from a bin, deleting from the Media Tool will only delete media from the drive, not master clips or other bin-level metadata. For example, if you were to copy media to the incorrect drive, or were to import, capture, or render media to the wrong resolution, you could delete those files most easily from the Media Tool.

A reminder: Media Composer will not delete linked media, e.g. camera native media. Linked media does appear in the Media Tool, but if you attempt to delete it, you will only be deleting Media Composer's record of it as part of the project. The media file itself will not be deleted.

To delete media using the Media Tool:

1. Open the **MEDIA TOOL**.

2. In the Set Media Display window, select the **DRIVE(S)** from which to view media, and the **PROJECT(S)**, and the **FILE TYPES** you wish to view. (The most common are master clips and precomputes, which are renders.)

3. Click **OK**.

    The Media Tool opens, displaying the clips.

4. Optionally, you can change the information displayed to make a more informed decision.

    a. Right-click on the **COLUMN HEADER** for any column and select **CHOOSE COLUMNS**.

       The Bin Column Selection window opens.

    b. Select the **COLUMNS** you wish to display (e.g. "Drive" to display what drive the media resides) and deselect the others.

       Using the information in the bin columns, you will determine which clips to delete.

5. Select the **CLIPS** you wish to delete.

6. Press **BACKSPACE** or **DELETE**.

    The deletion dialog box opens, as shown in Figure 12.11.

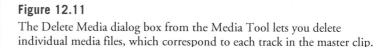

Figure 12.11

The Delete Media dialog box from the Media Tool lets you delete individual media files, which correspond to each track in the master clip.

7. If necessary, deselect any **FILES** you wish to preserve.

8. Click **OK** to delete the media.

On larger projects, the Media Tool is sometimes used to delete media that will not be used in the sequence, although it was initially input. For example, a one-hour documentary film could easily have more than 20 hours of footage captured. Your initial rough cut may be 2.5 hours long, and after screening it with the director, it is decided that you got all the best stuff in. The final film will be drawn only from what is in that 2.5-hour sequence so you could safely delete the unused (17.5) hours of footage from your drives. The Media Tool gives you the ability to identify the unused media files, so you can remove them from your drive. As you progress to the next course, MC110: Media Composer Fundamentals II, you will learn how to do some more complex media management tasks such as this.

At the completion of your project, you can use the Media Tool to very quickly and easily delete all the project's media from your drives when the project is complete.

Technique: Concluding a Project

Knowing how to properly wrap up a project is important to your long-term success. One of the tasks is to delete all project media from the media drives regularly used for editing. If not done properly, "orphaned" files—media from old projects for which you no longer have master clips in bins—are left behind, collecting on the drives.

Deleting media, though, is just the final step. Prior to deleting the media, all project assets need to be archived in some way. Typically, this means preserving the original media sources, saving a copy of the project folder, and copying all sequence media to another drive that can be stored long-term. (Copying the sequence media to another drive would be done using Consolidate.) Once those tasks are complete, you can safely delete all project media, confident that you could restore the project at a later date if needed.

To delete all project media:

1. Verify that all archive tasks have been completed.

2. Disconnect the archive drive, if still attached (this is an important safety measure).

3. Open the Media Tool.

4. Click the All Drives and Current Project buttons.

5. Select Master Clips and Precomputes. Then click OK. The Media Tool opens, displaying the project media.

6. Press Ctrl+A (Windows) or Command+A (Mac) to select all items.

7. Press Backspace or Delete.

8. Select all available tracks in the Delete Media dialog box and click OK.

9. Click OK again to confirm the deletion.

 Exercise Break: Exercise 12.3, 12.4, and 12.5
Pause here to practice what you've learned.

Review/Discussion Questions

1.   What does "media offline" mean?

2.   Name three reasons media can be offline.

3.   Which function can be used to find the media for a clip?

   a.   Match Frame

   b.   Find Bin

   c.   Find

   d.   Reveal File

4.   True or False. The master clip in your bin contains the actual video and audio media.

5.   True or False. If you delete a master clip from the Media Tool, you will delete the media file.

6.   Some of your media is offline. Which is a good troubleshooting step?

   a.   Delete the master clips.

   b.   Delete the MXF folder.

   c.   Delete the database files.

   d.   Delete the sequence.

7.   Name the function that is used to reconnect to linked media files, and where it is found in the interface.

8.   Name the media database files (the first three letters).

9.   In which folder ("directory") are the media database files found? (Name the full directory path.)

10. Discussion: Which is more valuable in a project—the media or the metadata (clips or sequences)?

Lesson 12 Keyboard Shortcuts

Key	Shortcut
Ctrl+C (Windows)/Command+C (Mac)	Copy
Alt-drag (Windows)/Option-drag (Mac) a clip to a bin	Makes a copy of the clip (not the media)
Ctrl+D (Windows)/Command+D (Mac)	Duplicates a clip or sequence

Technical Fundamentals

Understanding the relationship between your media and your project (metadata) and being able to maintain that relationship is critical to starting your project, completing it and cleaning up at the end of it.

Media Used: Running The Sahara and The Rock Climber

Duration: 30 minutes

GOALS

- Locate media files associated with a clip
- Relink linked media files
- Delete Avid media database files
- Restore a saved bin from the Avid Attic

Exercise 12.1: Identify Avid Native Media Files

On occasion, you may want to find the media associated with a particular clip. In this exercise, you will use Reveal File to identify the media files associated with a master clip.

Media Used: Running the Sahara

Duration: 5 minutes

1. Open the RUNNING THE SAHARA project.

2. Create a new BIN and name it MEDIA LINK TEST.

3. Open the RTS SCENERY AND LOCAL PEOPLE bin and select the master clip WOMAN WITH BAG ON HEAD.

4. Alt-drag (Windows) or Option-drag (Mac) the clip to the MEDIA LINK TEST bin.

    A clone is created with the same name as the original.

5. Right-click the first master clip WOMAN ON WALL in the CULTURE bin and choose REVEAL FILE.

    Media Composer opens an operating system (OS) window to show you the MXF file on the drive. On Macs, this is the Finder; on Windows, it is the Explorer.

6. Without closing the OS window, activate MEDIA COMPOSER again.

7. Right-click the master clip WOMAN WITH BAG ON HEAD in the MEDIA LINK TEST bin and choose REVEAL FILE.

    Media Composer opens an OS window to reveal the same file as it did in step 5, illustrating how cloned clips share the same media file as the original master clip.

Exercise 12.2: Hide and Restore Avid Native Media File

Media Composer will only see the Avid MediaFiles folder if both the location and name are correct. In this exercise you will see what happens if one or other is changed.

1. Find your AVID MEDIAFILES FOLDER in whatever drive or partition it resides.

2. Edit the name by putting an X in front to change the name to XAVID MEDIAFILES.

3. Look at the result in Media Composer.

    If you have a sequence in the Timeline it is colored red and the frame where the position indicator is sitting shows "Media Offline." Any video clip you load into the Source monitor will show "Media Offline" and in the bin if you have an Offline column all tracks will be listed there.

4. Now go back and remove the "x."

5. Again, look at the result in Media Composer. Everything should be back online.

6. If it is not, make sure that the media folder is correctly names as "Avid MediaFiles" with no added spaces or additional characters. If that is not the issue, then highlight all the clips and select CLIP>RELINK.

7. Deselect "RELINK ONLY TO MEDIA FROM THE CURRENT PROJECT."

8.   Deselect "MATCH CASE WHEN COMPARING SOURCE NAMES."

9.   In Relink to: select ANY VIDEO FORMAT.

10. Click OK.

     This should bring the media online.

Exercise 12.3: Delete Media Databases

Very occasionally, clips will not relink even though we are sure the media is available. In this case, there is a possibility that the media databases have become corrupted. We can test whether this is the case by deleting the databases and letting Media Composer recreate them.

1.   Find your AVID MEDIAFILES FOLDER in whatever drive or partition it resides.

2.   Open it.

     There will be a folder called MXF.

3.   Open the MXF FOLDER to find a folder called 101.

4.   Open this and find the media databases, MSMFMID.PMR and MSMMMOB.MDB.

5.   Delete these files and go back into Media Composer.

     Media Composer will scan the folders from which you have deleted the databases and create brand new ones.

Exercise 12.4: Identify, Hide and Restore Linked Camera Native Media File

Media Composer does not restrict where we put linked camera media, but if we move it, it goes offline. It is up to us to know where it has gone and to redirect Media Composer to look for it.

1.   Open THE ROCK CLIMBER project.

2.   Open THE ROCK CLIMBER RAW FOOTAGE bin.

3.   Select R02_02(b) INTERVIEW.

4.   Right-click and choose REVEAL FILE.

     Media Composer opens an operating system (OS) window to show you the MXF file on the drive. On Macs, this is the Finder; on Windows, it is the Explorer. This shows us that the linked QuickTime file is in a folder called Rock climber QTs which is wherever we first placed it.

5.   Create a new folder called RC and drag the ROCK CLIMBER QTS FOLDER into it.

     Within Media Composer, you will see that all the clips are offline.

6.   Select the OFFLINE MASTER CLIPS in the bin.

7. Right-click on one of the selected clips and choose **RELINK TO FILE(S)**. (It is further down below in the menu underneath the selection named "relink.")

    A standard browser window opens. Displayed at the top is the name of the first selected clip to be relinked.

8. Navigate to the folder containing the clip and select it.

9. Click **OPEN**.

    Media Composer will relink the selected file, plus all other selected files it can match to files in the same directory.

Exercise 12.5: Restoring a Bin from the Attic

Despite your careful efforts to avoid it, there will likely come a time when you will lose work either due to a mistake or because of a technical problem with the system. In this exercise, you will practice the skills to minimize your loss.

Media Used: The Rock Climber

Duration: 10 minutes

1. Open the **THE ROCK CLIMBER** project and **THE ROCK CLIMBER SEQUENCES** bin.

2. Load the **MONTAGE** sequence.

3. Using the editing functions of your choice, make dramatic, destructive changes to the sequence. This might include rearranging segments, removing large sections of the sequence, deleting tracks, breaking sync, etc.

4. **SAVE** your changes.

5. Create a new **BIN**, titled **ATTIC TEST**.

6. While pressing the **ALT** key (Windows) or the **OPTION** key (Mac), drag the **OUTPUT SEQUENCE** to the new bin to duplicate it.

7. Close the The Rock Climber **RTS SEQUENCES** bin.

8. Select the **THE ROCK CLIMBER SEQUENCES** bin in the Project window and then press **BACKSPACE** or **DELETE**.

    The bin is move to the Trash.

9. Minimize **MEDIA COMPOSER**.

10. Open an OS window and navigate to the **ATTIC** directory:

    • **Windows:** C:\Users\Public\Public Documents\Avid Media Composer\Avid Attic folder

    • **Mac:** MacHD/Users/Shared/Avid editing application/Avid Attic folder

11. Navigate through the Attic's subfolders to find the folder for your HR sequences bin: **\BINS** The Rock Climber **** The Rock Climber **SEQUENCES**.

12. If necessary, change the OS window to **LIST VIEW** to see the **MODIFIED DATE** column.

13. Find the newest copy of the **BIN** that was last modified more than 20 minutes ago and select it.

14. Right-click the selected bin and choose **COPY**.

15. Navigate to the location of your project. Assuming it's the location identified in the preface, go to:

    - **Windows:** C:\Users\Public\Public Documents\Avid Media Composer\Shared Avid Projects\ The Rock Climber

    - **Mac:** MacHD/Users/Shared/Avid Media Composer/Shared Avid Projects/ The Rock Climber

16. Right-click in the **WINDOW** and choose **PASTE**.

    The bin copy from the Attic is pasted into the project folder with the other bins.

17. If using a Windows system, change the extension of the bin copy from the number to .avb.

18. Maximize **MEDIA COMPOSER**.

    The new The Rock Climber Sequences bin appears in the Project window. If it has not appeared, save the project. The refresh that happens during the Save process should cause the bin to appear.

19. Open the **THE ROCK CLIMBER SEQUENCES** bin from the Attic, and load the **MONTAGE**.

20. Verify that the sequence has been restored to its former glory.

Index